The Soviet Revolution

Perestroika and the Remaking of Socialism

edited by
Jon Bloomfield

LAWRENCE & WISHART
LONDON

Lawrence & Wishart Limited
144A Old South Lambeth Road
London SWB 1XX

First published 1989

© Lawrence & Wishart, 1989

Each essay © the author

Photoset in North Wales by
Derek Doyle & Associates, Mold, Clwyd
Printed in Great Britain by
Billings and Sons Ltd

Contents

Jon Bloomfield

Introduction

'The only absolute is change' is a classic Marxist maxim. Yet during the Brezhnevite decades the Soviet Union appeared to defy this maxim with impunity. Politically the country appeared frozen, immobile, set in concrete. Yet suddenly and unexpectedly it's a society in movement, full of life, energy and dynamism. There's a real cultural revolution underway.

This has certainly caught the imagination of public opinion in the West. There is a tangible curiosity and at times fascination with the startling developments in the Soviet Union. A stream of TV series, feature and magazine articles and cultural exchanges as at the Edinburgh Festival are signs of this newly-awakened interest. They are indicative of a profound change in popular perception and mood, which finds more direct political expression in opinion poll surveys. These consistently record both a very sharp drop in the number of people who believe that the Soviet Union poses a serious military danger to Western Europe and a high approval rating for the Gorbachev leadership.

The new flow of informative reporting, detailed analysis and frequent personal interviews of both major personalities and ordinary Soviet citizens is all the more dramatic because of the contrast with what preceeded it. The closed character of Soviet society and the Cold War predilections of Western governments and most media served to complement each other. The outcome was a widespread public ignorance about the Soviet Union, to which the Thatcher government added its own distinctive contribution with its cavalier cuts in Russian studies courses at British universities in the mid-1980s. This book is intended as a modest contribution to the overcoming of that ignorance, to increasing knowledge about the Soviet Union and to a greater understanding of the terrain on which the future of perestroika will be decided. It is written to be accessible to the general reader, the political activist and the college student so that each can gain a sense of the dynamics of change within Soviet society and where they might lead.

That dynamism appeared non-existent in the Brezhnev 'era of stagnation'. This period from the mid 1960s effectively thwarted and killed off the destalinisation process begun under Nikita Khrushchev at the 20th Congress of the Communist Party of the Soviet Union (CPSU) in 1956. However, it could not halt the deeper social processes and economic developments which ultimately necessitated a wholesale re-examination of existing socialism and the political and economic system inherited from Stalin. That system, however its initial record is judged, had clearly exhausted all its potential. The driving into internal exile of its most articulate nuclear scientist, Andrei Sakharov, symbolised its political bankruptcy; and reliance on raw materials such as oil, gas and timber for the bulk of its export income highlighted its economic backwardness. As the practical applications of the scientific and technological revolution accelerated in the advanced capitalist countries the contrast with the inertia of the Soviet economy became more stark. This combination of the internal failures of the neo-Stalinist system and external economic developments propelled a coalition for change to come together, composed of disparate elements within both the Communist Party and the government apparatus. This development was at first tentative, under Andropov, and then, after the setback of the brief Chernenko interlude, it resumed with Gorbachev's election as General Secretary in March 1985. By then the need to change the old order had become urgent.

Initially, the qualitative and dramatic character of the necessary changes was not acknowledged; however as the process unfolded, and as glasnost helped to reveal the true extent and depth of the system's crisis, so the Gorbachev leadership recognised the limits of a technocratic drive for economic efficiency and an end to corruption. Just as the Czechoslovaks under Alexander Dubcek had found 20 years earlier, initial economic reform accompanied by moves towards destalinisation led inexorably to far-reaching democratisation. The Gorbachev leadership began to realise that it was impossible to break with just one part of the 'command-administrative system' which Stalin had bequeathed and which in its essentials still remained in operation. In such a tightly centralised system any significant economic reform had to be accompanied by political change. Stalin's monolithic conception of the role of the party meant that any alterations in economic methods and management inevitably disrupted the existing centralised means of party operation and control. The Stalinist system bound the state, the party and the people into one enforced unity; but the objective needs for economic decentralisation, for the use of market mechanisms to gauge consumer needs, for increased initiative by technically skilled labour and for a much more active involvement by people in their enterprise and work were major factors pressing for a more diverse, pluralistic political system in which ordinary citizens were no longer afraid to voice their concerns. Alongside these economic imperatives powerful philosophical, historical and moral arguments have been presented for political reform. The historical debate over Stalin which has gripped the country has been crucial in this respect. It has been about coming to terms honestly with a traumatic past, while also ensuring that the political mechanisms are in place which avoid any possible repetition.

Not surprisingly in such a fast-moving and novel situation tensions have arisen within the CPSU leadership. While there is agreement about the failures of the Brezhnev era and the need to modernise the economy, the more cautious, conservative elements within the leadership such as Ligachev and Chebrikov are clearly uneasy about a wider, more broadly-conceived democratisation. In contrast, a more whole-hearted democratic tendency of whom the most prominent are Gorbachev, Alexander Yakovlev and Eduard Shevardnadze, are well aware of the limitations of technical reform and are anxious to stimulate and encourage popular initiative and individual commitment in support of the process of reconstruction, 'perestroika'. This is a theme which is explored by several essays in this volume.

The Gorbachev forces are engaged in a dual strategy,

seeking to mobilise progressive forces in support of 'perestroika', from above and from below, relying on this combination to overcome resistance in the party and among the bureaucracy. They recognise that the process needs a dual cutting edge to continue to drive forward, with a combination of political and economic reforms: hence the importance placed on glasnost; on judicial reforms guaranteeing individual legal rights; on giving land to the peasants on long leases; on granting new rights to works councils and the right to elect factory directors; and on making party officials accountable through contested elections. These are all measures designed to foster and create an active civil society, to stimulate individual and collective involvement in the transformation of the country, to overcome the legacy of fear and keeping one's head down and to create 'a culture of democracy' as Gorbachev terms it.

The emphasis of this approach is on consent rather than coercion, on the creation of an active bloc of social forces to generate the momentum necessary to overcome institutional inertia and bureaucratic resistance (an approach which clearly owes a debt to the Italian marxist Antonio Gramsci). Painfully aware of the very real objective difficulties, and the political and cultural resistance which they face, the Gorbachev leadership knows that it has to avoid theatrical flourishes and gestures. Simple denunciations of bureaucrats and backsliders will not suffice to turn the situation round. This partially explains the political opposition to Boris Yeltsin, the Gorbachev protege sacked as Moscow party leader in autumn 1987. His commandist style and approach smacked too much of the Khrushchev era – while the methods used to remove him showed that not all Stalinist practices were consigned to the dustbin of history. Yet, if the Yeltsin affair was – and continues to be – drastically mishandled, the Gorbachev forces seem very conscious of the failures of Khrushchev's first attempt at reconstruction. They know that any re-emergence of adventurist tactics, of going for short-cuts because of the inadequate pace of reform, will threaten their overall strategy. At the same time in his election campaign Yeltsin was able to arouse and generate the vocal and active support for perestroika among ordinary people which is crucial to the overall success of the project. Thus there is a very fine line to tread to drive the process of perestroika forward while sustaining rather than fracturing its popular base. This has already required astute political judgement by the Gorbachev leadership and will continue to do so. Pursuing the strategy for a long haul, they are ultimately dependent on their ability to arouse extensive public support for their project. In today's conditions they are aware that perestroika will not succeed if it is imposed. The conduct and results of the special party conference in summer 1988, and the subsequent consolidation of the firmest advocates of perestroika within the Politburo in September, helped to carry the process forward politically, as did the tremendous interest in, and relatively smooth conduct of, the first elections to the Congress of People's Deputies. However, the ultimate success of the Gorbachev project, especially given the severe shortcomings in the economy and in agriculture, and the tumultuous national questions, remains uncertain: any collapse would not result in a return to the Brezhnev era but would herald a much harsher militarist regime.

During the Brezhnev era by and large the West European Left kept its distance from the Soviet Union. The main impact of the dwindling band of Soviet apologists was restricted to the bitter battles fought out within Communist Parties over issues such as Czechoslovakia, Afghanistan and Poland. So despairing of the situation had most of the Left become that few dissented when the Italian Communist leader Enrico Berlinguer declared after the imposition of martial law in Poland in winter 1980/1981 that the reform impetus of the 1917 revolution was exhausted. The truth is that few foresaw the political dynamism, energy and commitment that would emerge from within this stagnant, sclerotic society. The Gorbachev revolution has taken politicians, commentators and intellectuals of all shades of opinion by complete surprise.

As its momentum has accelerated Western opinion has become more perplexed and intrigued by the phenomenon. At its root, this bewilderment arises from a basic theoretical flaw, namely the view that the Soviet Union is a monolithic/totalitarian society, which can't *really* change while the Communist Party is in charge. Thus after an initial welcome and burst of curiosity the intellectual guardians of the New Right, particularly in Britain and the United States, have begun to warn us about the danger of dropping our guard, of fostering illusions about Gorbachev, about the wolf in sheep's clothing. These sentiments are more frequently voiced when defence issues are at stake but they reflect a more general assessment about the fundamental impossibility of the system to change. From this flows the endless stream of pessimistic assessments and warnings of Gorbachev's imminent demise, but also and more importantly, a failure to grasp the underlying dynamic of the whole process. Hence the constant surprise from Western governments and commentators at the radical nature of perestroika. This is most obvious in the arena where they are most directly affected, namely international relations, where they have been repeatedly wrong-footed and placed on the defensive. Here, a theoretical block, an inability to recognise the potential within Soviet policy for fundamental change, has profound political consequences.

Ironically, the same trend of thought is to be found in parts of the Left. Various strands within the socialist movement, which accurately criticised the deformations of the Stalin era, refuse to acknowledge any prospect for change arising from within the existing ruling parties in the socialist countries. Parts of the Trotskyite Left, but more significantly sections of the liberal Left and the peace movement, simply do not believe that change can come from within the system. This position has three significant flaws.

Firstly, basing its outlook on the totalitarian model of Soviet society, its monolithic categories cannot conceive or recognise divergent political trends of substance arising from within the Communist Party. Thus one author wrote in the *New Statesman* 'the official ideology – whether of the Brezhnev or Gorbachev variety', as if they were essentially the same. As with the Prague Spring, a radical reform current has emerged from within the Communist Party, seeking to transform the character of existing socialism. Gorbachev is engaged in a real struggle: jobs and futures are on the line – and the shadow of Dubček serves to remind all reformers of the high price of failure. This is hardly a matter of minor differences between members sharing a common ideology.

Secondly, this 'totalitarian' line of thought seeks to separate the official from the unofficial, the party from the people, the state from civil society, indeed, in a simple political dichotomy, the bad from the good. Yet the reform process itself arises from, and is partly driven by, objective social trends. The Gorbachev revolution gives and creates space for the emergence of civil society. A key aspect of his programme is to break the Stalinist model which fused party, state and people into one homogeneous bloc. The reform programme can only succeed with the emergence of powerful, autonomous social organisations, with a flourishing of individual and co-operative initiative and with genuine political debate. There are scores of contradictions and confrontations in this process, but only those with set theoretical predispositions can fail to recognise that the development of Soviet civil society connects directly and intimately with the Gorbachev agenda.

Thirdly, the 'totalitarian' view allows for no sense of historical process, of how these societies and indeed their ruling parties change. On the Left this leads to ahistorical judgements and moral purism: because the USSR has not done certain things it does not merit support. However, the experience of perestroika confirms that there are powerful, if not yet hegemonic, reforming currents within the Soviet Union. In their turn these are also encouraging echoing responses within Eastern Europe. All these societies have commenced or are on the brink of momentous change. In all instances the crucial issues are the trajectory of their political leaderships, the directions in which they are heading, the dynamic of the process.

The essays in this volume seek to answer some of those questions. They do not hide the enormity of the task at hand. Those reprinted from *Marxism Today* illustrate how the crisis of Soviet socialism unfolded and the manner in which the Gorbachev leadership has sought to tackle them to date. The new essays focus on the major issues now facing perestroika and the dilemmas and difficulties the whole process faces. There is no facile optimism here, although the spark of hope and excitement is present. While the authors come from diverse traditions, their writing is informed by one common standpoint: that the USSR has the capacity to transform itself. The theme running through the book is that the structural transformation of Soviet society encouraged and initiated by the CPSU leadership is a feasible option both theoretically and practically. Indeed, the drama and tension arises precisely from the uncertainty as to whether this capacity will be fulfilled.

The outcome will have repercussions not just on the way Soviet people live as they enter the 21st century but also on the general condition of socialism. The old system has failed and the old totems have fallen with it – the all-embracing state plan, centralised allocation of goods, the disdain for markets. In the different conditions of the West the 1970s saw the exhaustion of traditional social-democratic policies and programmes. While sections of the Left called for a Third Way between Stalinism and social democracy none seemed able to find the route. Instead it has been the neo-liberal philosophies of the New Right which have held sway and been able to speak the language of the computer, robotic and communications revolution. The rapid onset of the scientific and technological revolution, the transform-ation of modern production and consumption and the accompanying shifts in social structure have left socialism on the defensive. To date the Gorbachev revolution represents its most authentic response. In its way, and in its own backward conditions, it is seeking to address the issue that faces the Left everywhere: can socialism modernise itself? Can it solve the key questions posed by the present age or is it irrevocably stuck with the ideology and culture of the mass industrial age from which it came?

To these questions there are no pre-ordained answers. In breaking from Stalinism, Communist Parties have to forego any belief in a divine right to rule. In discarding mechanistic Marxism they have to acknowledge that there is no certainty that socialism is the society of the future. But if it is to have a future, it will be as Fedor Burlatsky describes it – a 'public, self-managing socialism', a 'qualitatively new model of a more effective, democratic and humanistic socialism'. In these definitions we can see a convergence with other socialist traditions which are also seeking to break free from their previous statist and bureaucratic limitations. Here we

see a new socialism taking shape, which retains the
traditional values of co-operation, emancipation and social
solidarity but places them in a pluralist setting. This new
model seeks social cohesion through diversity not uniformity. While free from utopianism, it corresponds to the
socialist traditions which herald the 'withering away of the
state' rather than to those which exalt its endless expansion.
It will be on this terrain, and on no other, that the socialism
of a new type will be built.

In different ways and with distinctive emphases a common
ideological evolution is discernible here within both
Communist and Social Democratic traditions. They are
moving towards a new consensus in their conception of
socialism, which in turn facilitates and forms a firm
foundation for closer political liaison and co-operation. The
treatment of all progressive parties as equals, and the ending
of the privileged status of Communist Parties within an
'international communist movement' flows logically from
this new ideological synthesis. Here the CPSU is treading
the path pioneered by the Italian Communist Party. The
close and positive relations of both parties with the German
SPD expresses most clearly this evolving common identity.

The 'New Times' in which we live, and the new thinking
about socialism which they demand, means that not only are
the old leftist debates between Stalin and Trotsky
superseded, but, more importantly, the cleavage between
Lenin and Kautsky, which split the working class movement
into social democratic and communist parties at the end of
the first world war, becomes obsolete. During his address to
the United Nations (December 1988), Gorbachev touched
obliquely on this theme. Having paid tribute to the 'huge
impulse to human progress' made by the French and Russian
revolutions he went on to say that:

> A new world is emerging today ... We should certainly rely on
> the experience we have accumulated but at the same time we
> should see the fundamental difference between what existed
> yesterday and what is taking place now.

The achievement of a synthesis which draws on the best
elements of both bourgeois democratic and socialist
revolutions, and combines them with new thinking on

contemporary problems, is the task at hand. To date no part
of the West European Left has successfully achieved such a
synthesis. This is not surprising: it is no simple matter, for
instance, to break the patriarchal nature of existing
socialism, or to transform its traditional productivist
commitment, or to decentralise to stimulate popular
initiative and national and regional autonomy within a stable
constitutional framework. These are just a few of the issues
which the Soviet people will have to resolve if the USSR is to
shift from the backward primitive socialism of the
command-administrative model to a self-managed socialism
of a new type.

Four years of perestroika have already brought startling
changes to the USSR, which previously were inconceivable.
Sustaining the pace and extending the impact of perestroika
will prove harder and, while the primary responsibility lies
within the Soviet Union, the governments and peoples of the
West have a role to play here too. To negotiate seriously and
quickly on both conventional and nuclear weapons would
give a major boost to the reform movement. Firstly, it would
enhance the prestige and standing of the Gorbachev
leadership. Secondly, it would significantly demilitarise the
European continent, reduce the levels of public fear and,
within the Soviet context, lessen the appeal of those wanting
to sustain high military spending. Thirdly, it would create
the conditions in which the Soviet government could
accelerate the reduction in size of the Soviet Army,
transferring much-needed labour and financial resources to
the civilian sector of the economy.

Even with a favourable international settlement the
outcome of the Gorbachev revolution will remain uncertain.
It is moving into uncharted territory and has formidable
objective difficulties and historic legacies to overcome. So
far those leaders committed to perestroika, and above all
Gorbachev himself, have shown a remarkable determination, dynamism and strategic sense of purpose. However,
further innovative thinking and the generation of new
dynamics within civil society will be necessary to sustain the
momentum. Whatever the outcome, the forward march of
perestroika will be neither speedy nor straightforward. Yet,
in a harsh climate for the Left, here at least are real grounds
for some optimism of both the will and the intellect.

1. Problems and Prospects 1982–85

Brezhnev, Andropov and Chernenko

Roy Medvedev

The USSR After Brezhnev

Roy Medvedev wrote this wideranging analysis of Soviet society shortly before the death of Brezhnev. His characterisation of the Brezhnevite era as one of 'stagnation' is now widely accepted. At this point Medvedev was clear on the need for change, but not overly optimistic about the possibilities.

The Soviet communist system, it is often asserted, has never undergone any *real* change; it came into being, and continues to exist and function to this day, changing only some of its external features. Stalinism is thus seen as the direct and logical continuation of Leninism, while 'Khrushchevism' and 'Brezhnevism' are seen as no more than mutations of an improved and modernised Stalinism. This view is mistaken. Soviet society has passed through many stages in its development; not only its external forms, but also substantive elements relating to its very nature have undergone change.

Singling out the most important shifts, four main eras associated with the names of Lenin, Stalin, Khrushchev and Brezhnev can be identified. Each was in many important respects a repudiation of its predecessor, while in other, no less important respects preserving continuity with the past, basing itself upon its achievements and the social structures and mechanisms created by it. Each successive new era solved many of the acute problems and tensions bequeathed by its predecessor, while at the same time accumulating a burden of new problems and tensions.

Transitions from one era to the next were usually painful

First published in *Marxism Today*, September 1982

and difficult, rather than smooth and even. There were
periods of transition from one era to the next, and different
phases – those of consolidation, maturity and decline –
within each. The first main era began in autumn 1917 and
ended ten years later. The second continued for almost 25
years until 1953. The third lasted a further ten years. The
fourth, which began in 1965, continues to the present time.

It is important to appreciate that these were genuine
historical eras, differentiated by something more than the
personal qualities of those whose names they bear. They
differed as regards class and economic structure, the level of
public well-being, the methods of political and economic
administration, the character and distinctive features of the
ruling elite, the international position of the Soviet Union
and the principles governing its foreign and domestic policy,
the technical level of its armed forces and its military and
strategic concepts. The role of social and political
institutions, the prevailing moods and outlook, the general
culture, style of behaviour and habits of ordinary citizens
and leaders also differed. So, too, did art, architecture,
literature and many other values and manifestations of
public life.

On the threshold of a new era

Clearly, these eras were differentiated not only by particular
historical events or objective cycles of economic and social
development, but also by the groups or even individual
leaders who stood at the head of party and state. The Soviet
Union has no strictly defined mechanism for the change or
re-election of the head of state and party. Politbureau
members can serve on that supreme organ of party authority
for 10, 20 or 30 years. A new leadership usually begins with
reform and a solution to the problems and tensions which
have accumulated by the close of the preceding era. But with
time it too acquires a burden of mistakes and problems, the
responsibility for which it cannot place at the door of its
predecessors and which therefore become very difficult to
eradicate. People simply grow old and lose the capacity for
radical reform and self-criticism. The objective logic of
society's historical development proves to be too dependent

upon the subjective logic of the ascendancy of a political leader.

But there is a view that in the Soviet Union it is the *apparat* – the system of administration and authority – or the ruling elite itself which chooses and puts forward its leaders. Men like Stalin, Khrushchev or Brezhnev came to the fore, it is argued, because they conformed to the system's requirements and demands. The *apparat* needed such leaders at the time in question, and they did what was necessary in the light of the character and objectives of their era and the requirements of the leading element in party and state. There is undoubtedly much truth in this. The emergence of a 'leader' completely hostile to the established apparatus of power, to the system and character of administration and the administrative stratum, to the aspirations and needs of the ruling elite, is impossible in the Soviet Union. But it should not therefore be concluded that the individual has only minimal capabilities and an insignificant role in the Soviet administrative system. Once having achieved power, a political leader can step-by-step transform not only the style and methods of administration and the composition of his own personal staff, but also that of the entire main body of the ruling elite. He can create new administrative bodies and exert an influence over every aspect of social and cultural life, the tempo and forms of economic development and the character and specific features of foreign and domestic policy. It is this which enables historians and political scientists to 'personify' the eras traversed by the Soviet Union.

Even the not-too-perceptive observer who is familiar with the present situation in the Soviet Union can see that it now stands on the theshold of great changes. The era which began with the October 1964 plenary meeting of the Central Committee of the Communist Party of the Soviet Union (CPSU)[1] has come to an end in terms of logic, politics and economics. It has also come to an end in terms of the subjective capabilities of those who have led party and state during the past 15 years. This does not mean that life has come to a halt, or that new decisions and initiatives are impossible. But their implementation and development will be a matter for the new era at whose threshold the Soviet Union and Soviet society now stand.

It may well be that the Soviet Union will have to pass through some sort of transitional period during the next few years; indeed, it may well be that this period has already begun in the winter and spring of 1982 and that it will continue for at least two or three years. The new era will probably last till the end of the century. In this situation the desire on the one hand to review the past and on the other to predict some of the characteristics and features of the approaching new era – that is, the changes which may take place in the Soviet Union during the next 15–20 years – is natural.

The general features of the departing era

'Stability' was one of the chief characteristics and watchwords of the Brezhnev era. This does not mean that there were no major events or reforms, no internal political struggles or international difficulties. But these usually came about not on the initiative of the Soviet leadership, but rather contrary to its desires and inclinations. Certainly there were more political events and changes in other parts of the world – in the Middle East, Africa, Latin America, Western and Eastern Europe, China or the United States – between 1965 and 1980 than there were in the Soviet Union. For the Soviet Union, the 70s were the most tranquil decade of our century.

This relative stability did not mean that the Soviet Union marked time. It has changed during the last 17-18 years, and in many respects the changes have been of very great importance.

In the West it is often stressed that the USSR was unable to fulfil by 1980 the over-ambitious economic programme discussed at the beginning of the 60s. Nor were most of the targets of the more modest 8th, 9th and 10th Five-Year Plans achieved. Nevertheless the overall economic potential of the Soviet Union increased very substantially between 1965 and 1980. Its gross social product increased 2.4-fold over the last 15 years. Industrial output went up 2.7-fold. The situation in agriculture was less satisfactory. Gross output in 1980 was only 35 per cent up on 1965, and still less in 1981. There has been a good harvest only once in the last five years – in 1978. It should be added that the population of the Soviet Union went up by about 15 per cent between 1965 and 1980, while the urban population increased by more than 30 per cent.

Although many state plan targets were not achieved, centralised planning remains the main regulator of Soviet economic development, matching national priorities with economic resources. The Soviet economy thus consists of a number of autonomous sectors or 'tiers' which work not only at different tempos, but also at different technical and technological levels. The defence and aerospace industries, for instance, still enjoy undoubted priority. So, for the first time since the war, the Soviet Union has attained approximate parity in strategic weapons with the United States. 'Heavy' industrial capacity grew relatively quickly. In 1980 the Soviet Union overtook the United States and became world leader in the production of steel and iron, oil, cement, mineral fertilisers, diesel and electric locomotives, metal-cutting machine tools, the export of timber and the production of sawn timber, tractors, steel pipes, many rare metals and a number of other important items. But it still lags a long way behind the main capitalist countries as regards the technology of basic forms of production, instrument engineering, chemicals, radio-electronics, electricity production and the quality of machine tools and other machines.

The construction industry, especially housing, has made great strides. Consumer goods output has increased considerably, and there has also been a significant improvement in their variety. Many items hitherto considered to be in extremely short supply are now almost always available. But although retail trade turnover went up more than 2.5-fold between 1965 and 1980, the list of items in short or extremely short supply is still very long.

Though total industrial output has grown steadily, annual rates of growth have declined – to 5 per cent by the mid-70s and to 3.5 per cent by the end of the decade. Rates of growth in agriculture were still lower – only about 1.5 per cent per year. Nevertheless the gross social product continues to grow.

The Soviet economy was already facing great difficulties at

the end of the 60s. The 1965 economic reform, which was intended to stimulate growth, was not carried through and was abandoned. The end of the 60s was also the time of the Soviet Union's greatest international isolation. The conflict with China was widening. Many predicted an extremely difficult decade for the Soviet Union. But such predictions proved correct only in part.

In the 70s new factors emerged in world politics and economics which, while making things more difficult for the West, by contrast made it easier for the Soviet Union to overcome its own difficulties. The increase in the world prices of many raw materials and the almost ten-fold increase in those for oil and gas enabled the Soviet Union not only to develop rich new fields beyond the Urals with comparative rapidity, but also to increase its foreign trade, thus making good many of the deficiencies of its own production. Its total foreign trade grew 7.5-fold between 1965 and 1980. Oil, petroleum products and gas made up 44 per cent of Soviet exports in 1980. Machinery, plant and transport equipment on the other hand accounted for 40 per cent of Soviet imports. The more-than-ten fold increase in gold prices during the 70s was also very advantageous to the Soviet Union, which is the world's second largest producer after South Africa. Despite the increase in world cereal prices, the Soviet Union was able substantially to increase its purchases of grain, meat and other foodstuffs, thus making good shortfalls in its own production. Arms sales to Third World countries also accounted for a not inconsiderable share of Soviet exports.

Detente, which was also supported by very influential circles in the West, formed the keystone of Soviet foreign policy from the early 70s. The Soviet Union was as a result able to emerge from its international isolation. Relations not only with Western Europe, but also with the United States underwent a gradual improvement. A number of agreements on the limitations of strategic and other weapons and on cultural and economic co-operation were concluded. The convening of the Helsinki Conference of the European, US and Canadian heads of government and the signing of its far-reaching Final Act became possible. But this was the high point of detente, which was not developed further in subsequent years. On the contrary, relations between the Soviet Union and the West again began to deteriorate. On the one hand the US Senate's refusal to ratify SALT II, the NATO decision to install new 'Eurostrategic' missiles in Western Europe and the West's attempts to play the 'China card' against the Soviet Union, and on the other the Soviet intervention in Afghanistan, the internal crisis in Poland and the introduction of martial law are just a few of the events which have soured relations. Soviet-US relations have undergone a marked deterioration, though a number of West European countries retained many elements of detente in their policies. Commercial and economic relations between the Soviet Union and Western Europe in any event remain stable and continue to expand.

Soviet-Chinese relations are still far from friendly, or even normal. But the bitter hostility of the years of the so-called 'Cultural Revolution' has gone.

The Soviet Union greatly strengthened and extended its influence in the Third World in the 70s. The improvement of relations with Egypt and the Camp David agreements were perhaps the only major US successes in the Third World. The US suffered a major defeat in Vietnam, while the downfall of the Shah and the establishment of popular rule in Nicaragua were serious setbacks. Vietnam joined the Council for Mutual Economic Assistance and strengthened her ties with the Soviet Union, which also gained new allies in Africa: Ethiopia, Angola and Mozambique. Friendly relations were established in Nicaragua. Relations between the US and the Western countries on the one hand and the Latin American countries on the other have become more difficult in the wake of the Anglo-Argentine conflict.

At home, the dissident movement and its campaign for change were undoubtedly of fundamental significance. Though small in number, it signalled the genesis of political struggle and of an independent public opinion. It began in 1965 as a protest by a section of the intelligentsia and young people against attempts to rehabilitate Stalin, but as it developed it divided into many currents voicing varied forms of discontent among various sections of the population. Many currents had a national coloration. Others opposed restrictions on religious life and encroachments upon

freedom of conscience. Diverse socialist currents voiced
criticisms of the shortcomings and defects of 'real' socialism.
The liberal-democratic human rights movement opposed all
infringements of the rights of Soviet citizens, from the right
of free access to information and freedom of the press to the
right to emigrate.

These currents evolved in difficult conditions of misinfor-
mation, pressure and repression. They passed through many
phases of suppression and renewal. But systematic
administrative and legal harrassment, the emigration of
substantial numbers both of some national groups and of
dissidents, disenchantment and the withdrawal of a section
of the intelligentsia had manifestly weakened the movement
by the end of the 70s. Neither events in Poland nor those in
Afghanistan had any significant influence upon the various
dissident currents. This in no way implies that the
authorities' campaign against them has succeeded in
reducing public dissatisfaction with the state of affairs in the
country. By the beginning of the 80s this dissatisfaction had
grown significantly compared with the beginning of the 70s,
and it is one of the most serious problems which will have to
be reckoned with in the next few years.

A growing number of problems

The Soviet Union approached the threshold of the new era
with a heavy burden of acute economic, political and also
foreign policy problems. But those whose analysis of the
present crisis leads them to make too sombre predictions are
mistaken. The Soviet Union has faced many crises in the
past, and the current one is not the worst. But mistaken too
are those who underestimate the complexity of the growing
number of problems and who hope to solve them with the
aid of the old methods and stereotypes.

Food is one of the most acute present-day problems.
Supplies have deteriorated sharply. This can be seen even in
Moscow, but the situation is especially serious elsewhere.
Rationing has been introduced in most industrial centres,
and many items in short supply can be bought only with
special coupons and in insufficient quantities. The shortage
of meat and dairy products is particularly acute; potatoes

and some other vegetables, fruit and fruit juices, eggs and jams – the list can be extended – are in short supply. Food shortages, indeed, are the main cause of the growing public discontent.

The present shortages are in no way comparable to those during the 1930–35 famine period, or to the hardships of the first postwar years. Neither total nor *per capita* food production is less than it was, for example, 20 years ago. Average annual cereal production in 1976–80 was almost 70 per cent higher than in 1956–60; the production of vegetables was likewise up by more than 70 per cent, that of meat by more than 90 per cent, milk production went up by more than 80 per cent, and that of eggs by more than 160 per cent. The population increased by about 25 per cent. Potatoes were the only basic agricultural product whose production failed to increase over the last 25 years. How, then, are we to explain the present problems with the supply of food? The reasons are many.

Agricultural production was manifestly inadequate even 20 years ago. But so, too, were the earnings of collective farmers and state farm workers and the real wages of factory and office workers. People had to economise on everything, including food. Between 1960 and 1980 the production of consumer goods and foodstuffs grew more slowly than earnings. A very large unsatisfied demand emerged, which was only partly reflected in the 15-fold increase in savings bank deposits. In a capitalist state, this would have led to a substantial increase in food prices. In the Soviet Union, although there is modest inflation, the state maintains prices for staple foodstuffs at constant and low levels by means of massive subsidies.

It must in fairness be said that great efforts have been made to boost farm output during the last 15 years. During the 15 years 1950–65, investment in agriculture amounted to about 75,000 million rubles; between 1966 and 1980 it totalled 288,000 million rubles. It went up from 12,000 million roubles a year during the 8th Five-Year Plan to 26,000 million a year during the 10th. But at the same time the average annual increase in gross agricultural output dropped from 18,000 million rubles in the 8th Five-Year Plan to 13,000 million in the 9th and 10,000 million in the

10th. During the last 20 years crop yields and livestock productivity have grown much more slowly than the costs of production of the main agricultural products. Grain yields went up from 11 centners per hectare in 1960 to 15 centners per hectare in 1980. Over the same period costs of production went up from 38 to 76 rubles per ton. Potato yields fell over the last 20 years, while costs increased almost fourfold[2]. Many more similar examples could be cited.

According to the statistics, real incomes have grown twice as fast as agricultural output over the past ten years, while the prices of staple foodstuffs have remained stable and very low. It is this which gives rise to the present acute imbalance between supply and demand. The main problem for the next ten years will be that of bringing about a substantial increase in farm output and a substantial decrease, if not in the costs of production of foodstuffs, then at least in the rate of growth of such costs. Some increases in food prices cannot be excluded. This will encourage the more economic use of some commodities and the reduction of waste without reducing consumption.

Farm output is a particularly weak link in the Soviet economy. But there are also big problems in other sectors. Growth in the electricity and other energy industries has been slack in recent years, while the introduction of more efficient machines and technology has been slow. Many large power stations in the eastern parts of the country are operating below capacity though plants and urban areas are not getting enough electricity. The coal industry faces particular difficulties; output has decreased rather than increased over the last four years. But the gas industry is expanding more rapidly than other sectors.

The relocation of the main enterprises of the energy industry and of a significant number of energy-intensive plants in other branches in the eastern parts of the Soviet Union has greatly increased the strain on transport, which lagged behind the needs of the economy during the 70s.

As we have already noted, rates of growth in industry and agriculture have declined from plan to plan. This in itself need cause no concern. In developed countries a moderate industrial growth rate is often preferable; progress should be in the direction of the manufacture of better, more durable products and multi-purpose machines. The wealth of society can continue to increase even given zero growth. The manufacture of 1,000 tons of pipe which will last 100 years without any need for repairs is infinitely preferable to the manufacture of 2,000 tons which will become scrap metal within 10 or 15 years. But the decline in growth rates was not accompanied by an adequate improvement in quality and durability. Waste, irrational use of raw and other materials, poor quality products, bad maintenance – all are constant themes in the Soviet press. Extensive factors have been largely exhausted as a means of securing growth. But the potentialities of intensification are being utilised very slowly; labour productivity is increasing too slowly; so is the quality of output; we still lag behind the West as regards machinery and technology. While the West suffers from unemployment, the Soviet Union suffers from an acute shortage of labour because of insufficiently high productivity and restrictions on freedom and also because of regional variations in living standards.

But the main cause of the difficulties of the Soviet economy continues to be the contradiction between the steadily growing complexity of the modern economic mechanism, the increasing interdependence of its component parts and the steadily increasing involvement of the Soviet Union in the international division of labour on the one hand, and on the other the excessive centralisation of economic management. This in turn is caused by bureaucratism, the monopolisation of decision-making by a single centre, the insufficient flexibility of planning and management, the under-estimation of medium-sized and small undertakings, the restriction of initiative at almost every workplace from factory floor to manager's office, the lack of adequate incentives for change, innovation and higher productivity, the absence of reasonable elements of competition and market influences, the insufficient participation of workers' collectives in a great deal of decision-making, the inadequate encouragement for enterprise and initiative, over-rigid economic linkages and insufficient democracy. Freedom of speech and information are as necessary in economics as in politics. Without them there can be no genuine freedom for the discussion of economic problems and no genuine debate on economic,

technical and scientific issues. Without democracy the
promotion of more competent, skilled and enterprising
managers is impossible. The inadequacy of democracy
affects both the trade unions and their leadership, as well as
the work of party branches, local party organisations and the
central party leadership. In Soviet conditions this has a
negative effect upon the solution of many economic
problems at the level of the factory, the industry and the
economy as a whole.

The Soviet Union and its economy are the central link in
the system of the Council for Mutual Economic Assistance
(CMEA). Gradual economic integration is a natural process
of world economic development in the second half of the
20th century. It is taking place in Western Europe and in
many parts of Africa, Asia and Latin America. Socialist
integration within the framework of CMEA should facilitate
and accelerate the economic growth of member-countries.
But it is encountering many obstacles, political as well as
economic, of which we will note just a few.

Integration normally occurs between neighbouring countries, based on historically-evolved ties and traditions. But
the CMEA today includes countries like Vietnam and Cuba
which are many thousands of kilometres away from the
Soviet Union. Economic co-operation is in this case
prompted mainly by political considerations, and brings in
its train the payment of large 'overheads', above all by the
Soviet Union. CMEA also faces many problems in Central
and Eastern Europe. Many of the countries of the region
were before the war among the poorest in Europe. They
took the capitalist road later than other countries, and their
development was hindered by shortages of natural
resources, dependence upon the larger European countries
and the fragmentation and mutual antagonisms of the area.
Their economic integration with the Soviet Union was
natural and beneficial to all parties. But it has so far
developed even more slowly in many respects than that
between the West European capitalist countries.

Obstacles to further progress are emerging on both sides.
Far reaching economic integration will clearly eventually
lead to a measure of political integration. But so far, thanks
to Soviet objections, the frontiers between the Soviet Union

and the European socialist countries remain closed. Not only is there no free movement of labour or goods; there is not even free movement for tourists. The manager of a Soviet factory which has bought machinery from Poland or Czechoslovakia cannot speedily send an expert to those countries should it become necessary to get spare parts urgently and pay the costs out of factory funds, by-passing the Ministries of Foreign Trade and Finance. Foreign trips take months to organise and require decisions by Moscow.

CMEA, also faces difficulties arising from centrifugal forces which are a consequence of nationalism. This, in turn, is the consequence of the centuries of subjection and political dependence endured by the peoples of Eastern Europe and the Balkan peninsula. In the 70s a number of CMEA countries tried not only to counterbalance their economic relations with the Soviet Union with economic ties with the West, but also to make a 'dash for growth' with the aid mainly of credits and loans running into many thousands of millions from Western governments and banks. These attempts ended in failure – in the case of Poland, in real economic and political catastrophe. The situation in Poland continues to be extremely difficult, although the Soviet Union is giving a great deal of economic assistance. But there is as yet no certainty that Soviet and Polish leaders will find the most sensible way out of the situation. Poland will remain one of the most difficult problems facing the Soviet leaders during the next few years.

The difficult situation in Poland and in Soviet-Polish relations, the worsening of relations with the West and especially with the United States, the partial re-birth of the cold war atmosphere, the threat of a new round or costly new spiral in the arms race, the military and political problems in Afghanistan, the continuing confrontation with China and the economic problems at home all suggest that the 80s are unlikely to be as 'tranquil' for the Soviet Union as the 70s. Mention must also be made of the extremely slow development of all aspects of culture, the poverty of the spiritual life of the Soviet people, and the dogmatisation of the social sciences and all aspects of socialist ideology. Reference must be made to the moral crisis of society, which finds expression in the spread of corruption, alcoholism,

criminality, mass pilfering and the abuse of power at many
levels. The Soviet Union set up a system of universal free
education a long time ago. But the position of the school
teacher is still difficult. The teacher still does not enjoy
sufficient esteem and authority in our society, while the
material status of teachers remains low, as does that of
ordinary doctors, engineers and many other members of the
intelligentsia. The solution of all these problems is similarly
hindered by the absence of genuine socialist democracy.
Young people are as a rule apolitical and indifferent to acute
social problems, to the problems which should become the
main subjects of concern for the new leadership.

Reforms, well prepared and well considered, must
become the main focus of attention for this new leadership.
The slogans of 'stability' and 'tranquility' are no longer
adequate for the 80s. The economic stimuli for industrial
and agricultural growth must be improved, and management
re-organised in a rational manner, extending the rights of
republics, regions, economic areas and individual plants.
There must be more scope for personal and private initiative
in service and small-scale production. The pressure of the
bureaucratic pyramid on the economy and society as a whole
must be eased, and a more resolute campaign waged against
corruption and abuses.

Abroad, the Soviet Union must exert every effort to halt
the new round in the arms race and seek out new paths for
detente and economic co-operation in both West and East.
The achievement of these objectives does not, of course,
depend solely upon the Soviet Union. Optimal solutions for
the problems of Polish-Soviet and Soviet-Afghan relations
must be persistently sought. The problems of Polish-Soviet
relations cannot be solved by the introduction of Soviet
troops into Poland, nor can those of Soviet-Afghan relations
now be solved merely by the withdrawal of Soviet divisions.

The democratic rights and freedoms of Soviet citizens,
especially freedom of speech and press, freedom of access to
information and ideas, and also freedom to circulate
information and ideas, must be consistently extended. Only
in this way is it possible to ensure the rapid development and
extension of the creation of the spiritual values which the
Soviet people need no less than they need more and better

material benefits. A truly socialist culture cannot develop within the rigid framework of restrictions imposed by censorship and bureaucracy.

Will the new leadership be able to solve these and many other problems? That question will in part be answered during the next few years.

The forthcoming change of leadership

Persistent questions about radical changes in the Soviet leadership were first posed in reports by Moscow correspondents and articles by Sovietologists and 'Kremlinologists' as long ago as the beginning of 1975. All kinds of points of view were expressed about a new leadership for the CPSU. Since then the US presidency has changed hands three times, Italian and Japanese prime ministers have come and gone several times over, there have been fundamental changes in Britain and France, and the Chinese leadership has undergone a complete transformation. But the Soviet leadership has meanwhile remained largely unchanged.

But it can today with confidence be stated that both the Soviet Union and its Communist Party are now face to face with the problem of the renewal of leadership. The deaths of Kosygin and Suslov demonstrated that even Politbureau members cannot stay in power for ever.

When Lenin withdrew from the leadership of the Soviet state in 1923 for health reasons the average age of the leading group in the Central Committee of the RCP(b) and the Council of People's Commissars of the USSR was only a little over 40. When Stalin died, it was about 55. By the time of the removal of Khrushchev, the average age of members of the Presidium of the Central Committee of the CPSU was getting on for 60. Lenin, Stalin and Khrushchev all frequently spoke of the need to combine young and old in the leadership. Only the concept 'young' as applied to a leader has changed. In Lenin's day it was a party official elected to the Central Committee at 30. In Stalin's time, it was a 40-year-old Central Committee member or a 35-year-old People's Commissar. In Khrushchev's day, senior officials of 45 or 50 were considered 'young'.

Today the average age of Politbureau members is over 70;

not only those between 55 and 60, but even those long past 60 are considered 'young'. This is not a normal state of affairs. We are certainly not opposed to old and experienced leaders. But a too-obvious violation of the principle of combining young and old in the higher ranks of party and state is difficult to justify. It makes the forthcoming change more difficult and painful. Furthermore, in Soviet conditions major reforms and important new initiatives are usually undertaken by those who can expect at least eight to ten more years of active political life.

It is not difficult to foresee that new people will assume the leadership of state and party within the next few years. They will have to solve some old problems, or some completely new problems, in a new way. But this will in all probability be a period of transition rather than a new era, for one of the main problems of the next few years will be the promotion to leading posts of a substantial group of party and government officials who are today no more than 45 or 55, and who will have to acquire the experience and practical knowledge needed by those who lead a country as large and important as the Soviet Union. It will in all probability be this generation which will have to lead the Soviet Union and its Communist Party in the 90s and the first decade of the 21st century. It is natural to ask how the generation which is today 50 differs from that which is 70.

The generation which is today about 50 not only did not take part in the revolution or the Civil War; it did not participate in the Second World War either. It did not suffer the losses from wars, repression and famine suffered by previous generations. Nor do people of this generation have the record of service in revolution or war of which their predecessors were so proud and which constituted the basis for a diversity of legends and cults. It may well be that political leaders who lack a record of service in the past will strive the harder to acquire such a record by new initiatives in the future. The new generation of Soviet politicians is unlikely to maintain the atmosphere of routine and stagnation which characterised Soviet political life in the 70s.

The new generation of Soviet leaders will on the whole be better educated, more flexible and more inclined to innovation. There can be little hope that it will also be more democratic or more tolerant of criticism or dissent, although even this possibility cannot be wholly excluded. It will promote technocrats rather than bureaucrats; knowledge and ability will be no less important than personal and political ties as criteria for advancement.

The new leaders at all levels of party and government will certainly be vigorous supporters of socialist and Marxist ideology. But they will have neither the fanaticism nor the dogmaticism of previous generations. They will be pragmatists rather than ideologues. Stalin was already dead when the generation which is today about 50 entered active political life. They have risen slowly, if only because the more senior posts in the Soviet hierarchy did not become vacant in the 50s, 60s and 70s with the same rapidity as in the years of Stalin's despotism. They have insufficient experience of work at the top, but they know the situation and moods at the bottom better.

The political consciousness and outlook of the present generation of Soviet leaders was shaped mainly between 1930 and 1950; that of the new generation, and of future generations, was shaped between 1950 and 1970. They could not but experience the impact of the 20th and 22nd Congresses; the era of Khrushchev means more to them than that of Stalin. So it may be expected that they will in some respects carry forward some of Khrushchev's initiatives and restore his name to the history of the Soviet state and party. It is unlikely that they will try to extol Stalin or take the road of Stalinism. They will be better equipped to solve the difficult problems of foreign and domestic policy than were their predecessors, while these problems will themselves be more difficult in ten years' time. But all this is no more than mere speculation, not scientific prediction; the peaks of power are frequently scaled by those who are far from being the best representatives of their generation.

Political prediction is a very uncertain business. It is crystal-gazing rather than an exact science, even though the whole of Soviet life is seemingly permeated with planning for the future.

When the theoreticians of 1920–25 tried to look a mere 10 to 15 years into the future, they sketched for their readers and listeners a society very different from that which in fact emerged under the 'leadership' of Stalin and his associates. The theoreticians of the 40s were similarly mistaken in all their predictions about Soviet society 10 or 15 years later. The theoreticians of the Khrushchev era left us a document – the Programme of the CPSU – in which they described Soviet society as it would be in 1980 in considerable detail. It is not difficult to see that a very great gulf exists between their predictions and present-day reality. What guarantee can there be that our own predictions for 2000 or even 1990 will be any more accurate?

The problems of society can be discussed and the best means of solving them debated. But it is difficult to predict how in fact they will be solved, or whether indeed they will be solved at all. It is difficult to predict how society and its leaders will resolve new and still more difficult problems ten years hence. We can but express the hope that they will be solved in a better and more rational manner than has been the case in past eras. But we cannot but also voice a great many fears. It can even be said, viewing the world as a whole and the increasingly difficult position of the Soviet Union in it, that our fears are today greater than our hopes. I shall be happy if the majority of my fears prove mistaken.

Translated by Dennis Ogden

Notes

[1]This was the meeting at which Khrushchev was replaced by Brezhnev as First Secretary of the Communist Party – *ed*.

[2] Figures on yields and productivity relate to the USSR as a whole, those on costs to collective farms only. State farm production costs are as a rule 7-15 per cent higher than those of collective farms. All figures are quoted from the official statistical yearbooks of the central office of statistics. The main economic indicators of Soviet agriculture still of course, lag far behind those of W European and US agriculture.

Julian Cooper

The Andropov Interlude

Julian Cooper wrote this short piece, on a short leadership, immediately after the death of Andropov, before Chernenko's succession was decided. It's interesting that in April 1984 Andropov's limited and technocratically orientated polices were welcomed as a considerable advance.

Yuri Vladimirovich Andropov's occupancy of the post of general secretary of the Communist Party of the Soviet Union was the shortest by far of any Soviet leader. While his death at the age of 69 after several months of illness is too recent for a full assessment of his contribution, it cannot be disputed that there have been important developments in the Soviet Union since the death of Brezhnev.

What, specifically, changed under Andropov? First, there was the turn to greater realism. Of great significance here were his major political statements, 'The teaching of Karl Marx and some questions of building socialism in the USSR', and his speech at the June 1983 plenary meeting of the central committee on the new party programme. There are parallels with previous changes of leadership. After Stalin, the party frankly acknowledged the existence of many problems and energetically, if not always wisely, set about their solution. Later, exaggerated estimates of the progress achieved began to gather strength and found their expression in the new party programme adopted in 1961.

After Khrushchev, the concept of developed socialism as a relatively prolonged stage on the road to communism reflected, initially at least, a more realistic assessment of the position reached and the magnitude of the tasks ahead. In

First published in *Marxism Today*, April 1984

the course of time, however, this concept began to undergo gradual redefinition and interpretations became increasingly complacent and triumphalist. Andropov made clear his conviction that the USSR is still in the early stages of developed socialism and faces a long period during which it must be gradually improved. Communism has been deferred yet again. This theoretical issue has great practical significance: it makes possible a more frank acknowledgment of existing shortcomings and contradictions, and opens the way to their solution by means which otherwise could be considered retreats on the forward march to communism.

In the late 1970s and early 1980s the economic situation in the Soviet Union deteriorated. The decline in the rate of growth of national income experienced over many years became more marked, accentuated by a series of poor harvests. The labour supply situation worsened, in part for demographic reasons, but also as a consequence of the maintenance of an investment policy orientated towards the building of new enterprises, requiring additional labour, rather than the re-equipping of existing capacity. The output:capital ratio of the economy was showing an increasingly unfavourable downward trend, worsened by the poor return on the large-scale investment in the agricultural sector, and the need to develop the inhospitable northern and eastern regions in order to secure supplies of raw materials and fuel.

In these circumstances, inflationary pressures mounted. Experiencing difficulties in attracting and keeping workers, factory managers were increasingly lax in their interpretation of the rules for wage and bonus payments, with the result that in some industries pay grew faster than labour productivity. With earnings outstripping the growth of output of consumer goods, savings accumulated and conditions were created fostering the expansion of the 'second economy' – the acquisition of goods and services 'on the side', 'under the counter' and through resort to bribery and corruption. The position was made worse by the apparent lack of energy and resolution on the part of the Brezhnev leadership, which was reluctant to acknowledge the extent to which all was not well.

On the economic front, the party under Andropov

appears to have been pursuing a two-stage strategy. With the aim of improving short term economic performance and the general moral climate in the country, there has been a concerted drive for greater discipline at all levels and the rooting out of corruption and second economy activities. The necessity for a 'business-like' approach is now constantly stressed. Meanwhile, discussion on ways of improving the planning and management of the economy intensified with much more frank recognition of the seriousness of the problems to be tackled. Some practical measures were adopted, including an economic experiment in several industrial ministries, which began in January this year. With the aim of promoting 'socialist entrepreneurship' in the pursuit of higher productivity and greater efficiency, the obligatory planning indicators for the enterprise have been simplified and reduced in number, and the rewards for good performance (and penalties for failure) enhanced.

If successful, the main features of the experimental system will be generalised for the next five-year plan beginning in 1986. In 1983 the economy showed signs of real improvement: national income grew by just over 3 per cent and industrial output by 4 per cent. The consumer supply situation improved and the harvest was the best for a number of years. This positive trend has been maintained into 1984. In January industry grew by 5.2 per cent and 94 per cent of the growth was achieved through higher productivity; for the latter, one of the best results ever achieved.

In his last political statement in December 1983, Andropov indicated that wide-ranging discussion of measures to improve the performance of the economy should continue. While all economists seem to agree that more changes are needed if the economy is truly to shift to an intensive growth path, there is no consensus on what should be done. Ideas being promoted include the need for still greater enterprise autonomy, the dismantling of much of the traditional administered supply system, changes in the organisational structure of the economy to reduce the power of the industrial ministries and promote greater horizontal co-operation, and some extension of private activities, notably in the service sector.

But it is clear that the essential features of the system of central planning are not in question. The term 'economic reform', implying the need for a radical transformation of the entire system of economic management, with potential political implications, has not been used. Despite speculation in the Western press, there is no evidence that the Soviet Union is considering the adoption of a Hungarian-type economic reform. (Indeed, it is highly debatable whether such a reform is at all appropriate to the very different circumstances of the Soviet economy.) Meanwhile, there have been signs of the party leadership's growing impatience with the economists for their apparent inability to come up with practical solutions and, significantly, one of the first post-Andropov measures has been the adoption of a central committee resolution sharply critical of the Academy of Science's Institute of Economics.

Another development of potential importance has been the process of renewal of personnel at all levels following an unprecedentedly long period of cadre stability. Not only have new faces appeared in the politburo and secretariat, but quite a substantial number of ministers and regional party heads have been replaced, in the main by men (no new women in leading posts) in their fifties. Restaffing has also affected the central committee apparatus: significant changes include the formation of a strengthened economic department under Ryzhkov(54), an experienced former enterprise director and planning official, and the replacement as head of the Science and Education Department of S P Trapeznikov(72), a long time associate of Brezhnev, by V A Medvedev(55), an economist and previously rector of the party's Academy of Social Sciences. The process is likely to continue in so far as there are still many leading party and government officials in their seventies; one minister of a strategically important industry is now 85. Other positive changes included the regular publication of summary accounts of the weekly politburo deliberations, the initiation of moves towards the clearer demarcation of the spheres of competence of party and state bodies, the enhancement of the role and rights of work brigades and collectives, representing some extension of shopfloor involvement in management, and the non-appearance of a cult of personality of Andropov himself, in significant contrast to the late Brezhnev period.

The appointment of Andropov offered real opportunities for improving the international climate. Reagan, Thatcher and other NATO leaders blew them away in a gale of vituperative rhetoric. The spiralling arms race has taken another turn, the hands of the clock have edged closer to midnight and the Soviet leadership may now believe that it has no choice but to further strengthen the country's military might. The CIA and NATO now acknowledge that since 1976 the rate of expansion of Soviet defence expenditure has been half that originally estimated; it declined more or less in step with the falling rate of growth of national income.

To the extent that defence expenditure is now increased, the task of improving the performance of the economy and raising living standards will be made more difficult. But despite its current problems, the Soviet economy still has substantial underlying strengths and reserves, and any calculation that it can be pushed into crisis through external pressure is profoundly mistaken. On the contrary, historical experience suggests that such pressure will serve to intensify the resolve and energy with which internal problems are tackled.

Soviet leaders now refer guardedly to the 'difficulties' of the late 1970s and early 1980s. It is to Andropov's credit that in his brief period of office the drift of Soviet society was halted and a sense of forward movement restored. The Soviet people will expect his successor to continue on the same path.

Monty Johnstone

The Case for Democracy

This article, written one month before Chernenko's death, and published in March 1985, looks at the problems of democraticisation facing the Soviet Union at that time. Monty Johnstone's analysis of the background to the main problems, and his pinpointing of Gorbachev as the new leader most likely to take on the task of solving them, shows some perspicacity. However even Monty Johnstone was not optimistic enough, at that stage, to see how far Gorbachev could go in reforming the political system.

A quarter of a century ago the socialist countries were making an impact on the world with their impressive rates of economic and social progress. Extrapolating from them, the 22nd Congress of the Soviet Communist Party in 1961 adopted a new programme which stated that by 1970 the USSR would surpass the USA in production per head of population. By 1980 Soviet labour productivity would exceed that of the USA in 1961 by roughly 100%, there would be 'an abundance of material and cultural values for the whole population' and '*a communist society will in the main be built in the USSR*'.[1]

Since then, the socialist countries, in most cases preserving full employment in contrast to the capitalist countries, have continued, on the whole, to advance more rapidly than the latter and to expand rather than cut their social services and education. However there has been a pronounced decline in rates of growth in the European socialist countries from 10 per cent in the 1950s to 7 per cent in the 1960s, 5 per cent in the 1970s, down to a planned rate

---

First published in *Marxism Today*, March 1985

for 1981–85 of around 3.5 per cent annually. The share of the socialist countries in world industrial production, which rose from 20 per cent in 1950 to 23 per cent in 1960, has since then only risen to its present level of 40 per cent. Soviet industrial production has only risen since 1970 from 65 per cent to 67 per cent of the US level. Labour productivity in Soviet industry has since 1976 been officially listed each year as 'more than 55 per cent' and in agriculture as 'about 20-25 per cent' of the US level. The heady targets of the 60s have long since been consigned to oblivion.

The Soviet Communist Party has now indicated that the most important feature of its next congress in 1986 will be the adoption of a new edition of the party programme. Avoiding reference to the present programme's concluding words of 24 years ago – 'The party solemnly proclaims: the present generation of Soviet people shall live in communism'[2] – General Secretary Chernenko now says that 'experience shows that before tackling the tasks directly connected with the building of communism, it is necessary to pass through a historically long stage of developed socialism, a stage which our country is now beginning.' This formulation of the issue, he claims, 'enjoys unconditional support' from the Soviet public. To the question whether this is not postponing the communist perspective, he says somewhat confusingly: 'The answer is a simple and unequivocal: of course not.[3] However his perspective now appears blurred and distant. Whilst Chernenko speaks in general terms about the importance of developing a 20-year economic-technical programme for the USSR for 1986–2005 and looks forward to 'ultimate' success in 'peaceful economic competition' with capitalism, he does not give any dates for this, remarking that 'it is not desirable to overburden it (the re-edited programme) with details.'[4] No self-critical analysis is made of the previous perspective unanimously adopted by a party congress – as the new draft will no doubt be at the next – and for many years proclaimed by its leaders past and present to be the 'blueprint of communism'.

Unfulfilled expectations and the contrast between promise and performance in the USSR and other socialist countries have led, internally, to growing signs of apathy, malaise and dissatisfaction, which have from time to time in different countries assumed critical proportions. Externally, they have invalidated the conception of the socialist countries exerting 'an ever-increasing influence on the struggles of the peoples in the capitalist countries' and 'by the force of example ... revolutionising (their) thinking'.[5] Paradoxically, after a decade of world capitalism's worst economic crisis for half a century, the attractive power of the socialist countries has diminished. Every socialist in Britain who is not completely isolated or blinkered knows this from his or her own experience. In the case of France statistical confirmation has come in a survey which shows that in the last decade the proportion of the population holding a negative opinion about the functioning of the socialist system in the Soviet Union and Eastern Europe has risen from 43 per cent to 69 per cent whilst those expressing a positive one has declined from 28 to 11 per cent. Among young people the negative view is even higher.[6]

A variety of factors have contributed to this worsened image. They include the detention of dissidents in prisons and psychiatric hospitals, the invasions of Czechoslovakia and Afghanistan, the Sino-Soviet conflict, and martial law and the suppression of trade union freedoms in Poland, along with growing economic problems. These things were not created by anti-communist propagandists, although they certainly play into their hands. They are structural rather than conjunctural and arise from an authoritarian and bureaucratic form of socialism, whose roots lie in the Stalin period.

Stalinism

The Russian Revolution of October 1917 blazed the trail that has led to the overthrow of capitalism and the building of socialism in 15 countries. But the character of that socialism has been deeply marked by the condition of backwardness in which it had to be built first of all in the Soviet Union and later in most of the other socialist countries. This backwardness contrasted strikingly with the high levels of economic, social and cultural development which Marx considered the prerequisites for socialism and which he saw in his time only in the advanced Western capitalist countries. For the USSR the conditions were particularly unfavourable. Firstly, it was isolated and forced to carry through an industrial and cultural revolution with its own limited resources and with enormous material shortages, conditions in which, as Marx and Engels wrote, want is generalised and 'all the old crap' is restored.[7] Secondly, until three years after the revolution it was forced to wage war against counter-revolutionary forces and invading armies from 14 capitalist states, and after that to prepare itself for another invasion, which inflicted the most enormous losses on it from 1941 to 1945. Thirdly, under conditions of Tsarist absolutism, which existed until 1917, Russia had only developed a 'primordial and gelatinous' civil society (Gramsci), in contrast to Western countries where voluntary organisations can play an autonomous role and give expression to a diversity of democratic and social aspirations.

Despite everything, the Soviet Union performed the tremendous task of carrying through its plans of socialist industrialisation, becoming the world's second industrial power and driving back the invading armies. But the conditions under which this had to be undertaken favoured the development of an extremely centralised political and economic state system with a high degree of bureacratisation and militarisation. Effective power at a national level came to be concentrated more and more, after Lenin's death in 1924, in the hands of Stalin, whose mass terror caused the deaths of many millions of Soviet citizens, including a very high proportion of the communists who had built up the Soviet state in its early years. Repressive methods of a similar character were also used after the Second World War in the new socialist states of Eastern Europe under the influence of Stalinist ideology and sometimes under the direction of 'instructors' from the Soviet secret police. Dissent, real or suspected, was equated with treason and links with hostile foreign powers, and was dealt with by prison or execution, sometimes after confessions extracted by torture.

Stalin's death in 1953 opened up a new period in the history of the Soviet Union and most other socialist countries. As Isaac Deutscher, the most perceptive Marxist analyst of Soviet development, showed already at that time, Stalinism had been undermined by its very success in carrying through a major industrial and cultural revolution. The needs and aspirations of a great industrial state with an expanding planned economy, an increasingly educated population and an avowed commitment to Marxism conflicted with despotism, arbitrary mass terror and the 'primitive magic' of Stalinist ideology.[8]

Deutscher's prediction that this would set in motion a process of de-Stalinisation was amply borne out in the period from 1953 with the restoration of socialist legality, the dismantling of the apparatus of terror and the return of vast numbers of political prisoners from Stalin's labour camps. It also involved the replacement of Stalin's one-man rule by a collective leadership, which showed itself more responsive to the needs of the people. A more realistic appraisal was publicly made of the lag in Soviet industry and particularly agriculture in comparison with the West, steps were taken to stimulate more initiative from below, a much greater emphasis was placed on the production of consumer goods, and very important material concessions were made to the peasantry. Three years after Stalin's death, at a closed session of the 20th Congress of the Party in 1956, Khrushchev was to reveal some of the most shocking aspects of the last 20 years of Stalin's rule. However his explanation of what went wrong, in terms of the cult of Stalin's personality, diverted attention from the structure of power and social relationships, of which the Stalin cult was only one expression. It also encouraged the illusion that, with Stalin gone and collective leadership restored, the whole problem belonged to the past.

The process of de-Stalinisation proceeded fitfully and unevenly. This partly reflected the style and limitations of Khrushchev, who as party first secretary from 1953 to 1964 was more responsible than anyone else for pushing it through. Partly it resulted from resistances at all levels in the party and state apparatus, which were checked but not eliminated with the ousting in 1957 of the 'anti-Party group' of Molotov, Kaganovich and Malenkov, who had sought to remove Khrushchev as first secretary.

Although calling for democratic initiative, Khrushchevite

de-Stalinisation cannot be seen as proper socialist democratisation, since the working people remained excluded from the decision-making process. (Nor indeed, as we shall see, was it a full de-Stalinisation.) From being effectively exercised by one man who could not be removed even by the Political Bureau or Central Committee of the Party,[9] central political power now came to be exercised collectively by the Political Bureau answerable to the larger Central Committee. However the unanimity, which had been the hallmark of congresses of the Party, the Soviets and the trade unions under Stalin, continued as before. This precluded the open debate which had characterised congresses in Lenin's time, even when the young Soviet state's internal and external position had been extremely precarious, and without which it is not possible to speak of genuine democratisation. Thus no dissenting voice was heard at the 20th Congress and the Party was not informed until after the defeat of the 'anti-Party group' that its members had since 1953 been arguing against many of the Party's new policies.

Although in this period there was wider involvement at most levels of the Party and state apparatus, the mass of the people were never brought out of the passive support role, which had been allotted to them under Stalin. They were given neither the encouragement nor the opportunity really to exercise independent political initiative. By the summer of 1964 political apathy was replacing the interest stimulated by the 20th and 22nd Congresses, partly encouraged by the contrast between the spectacular targets proclaimed in the new party programme mentioned earlier and the big increases in food prices in 1962, followed by the bad grain harvest the next year which necessitated the import (not for the last time) of a large amount of grain from capitalist countries.

At a Central Committee meeting in October 1964 Khrushchev was replaced as first secretary by Brezhnev. It was officially announced that he had resigned because of his 'advanced age' (he was 70) and 'poor health'. Subsequently he was publicly criticised for 'subjectivism' and 'voluntarism'. He was removed by a combination in the party leadership of political hardliners worried at the possibility of further de-Stalinisation and administrators concerned at the unsettling effect of his unpredictability and continual reorganisations.

Khrushchev's departure brought to a close the period of de-Stalinisation and, with a few exceptions, of the rehabilitation of Stalin's victims. It ushered in the 18-year Brezhnev period of stabilisation, in which conservative forces and habits increasingly asserted themselves. If under Khrushchev there had been a high turnover of party officials at all levels, under Brezhnev exactly the opposite was the case and higher officials were able to enjoy a secure privileged life.

There was no return to the Stalinist terror, but from 1966 repressive action was initiated against a developing dissident movement and new legislation was introduced for this purpose.

From 1977, when he added the post of President of the USSR to that of General Secretary of the Party, more and more of a Brezhnev cult was built up, and along with an unrivalled number of medals he was even awarded a prize for literature. However collective leadership continued to be exercised by the Politbureau (or a central group within it), in which septuagenarians representing the major Soviet institutions were increasingly to predominate. In the absence of any provision for leadership reselection, Brezhnev retained his leading positions right up to his death in 1982, even though during his last years his failing health made his leadership increasingly nominal and led him, even in interviews on Soviet television, to read from a prepared script. In such a situation stability turned into immobility accompanied by an alarming growth of official corruption and nepotism (particularly pronounced in the Caucasian and Central Asian republics), shielded from exposure by the absence of any possibility of independent investigative journalism into the misconduct of senior state and party officials. In conditions of boredom and frustration, alcoholism is recognised to have assumed alarming proportions with serious effects on both productivity and personal relationships.

Andropov, who succeeded to Brezhnev's Party and state posts, lost no time in initiating measures against corruption, into which his earlier years as head of the KGB had given him considerable insight. In addition he undertook a shake-up in the Party and state, securing the replacement of about a fifth of the regional party secretaries and a not inconsiderable number of ministers on grounds of age, inefficiency, corruption or opposition to reforms. He applied his acute intelligence to the problems of the economy, emphasising the need to 'overcome the accumulated inertia' that he saw there.[10] He was anxious to study the experience of other socialist countries like Hungary to find ways of overhauling hidebound Soviet methods of economic management.

Andropov stood for a more dynamic approach, authoritarian and technocratic rather than democratic, as opposed to the bureaucratic nudge, fudge and inertia of the Brezhnev period. However for half of his 15 months as General Secretary he was seriously ill and he died in February 1984 at the age of 69, having had time to see his initial efforts rewarded by a limited improvement in economic performance in 1983.

His successor Chernenko, aged 73, a close associate of Brezhnev and apparently also a sick man, seems to represent a stop-gap. He shows neither the originality of mind nor the dynamism needed to give the kind of leadership required for tackling the deep-rooted problems now confronting the Soviet model of socialism, some of whose characteristics will now be examined.

The Soviet model of socialism involves a great concentration of political and economic power in the hands of the leadership of a constitutionally unchallengeable and irremovable Communist Party. Article 6 of the Soviet Constitution, adopted under Brezhnev in 1977, defines the Party as 'the leading and guiding force of Soviet society and the nucleus of its political system, of all state organisations and public organisations.' This sanctions the exercise of party control not only over a highly centralised state apparatus, incorporating the great bulk of the economy and disposing of a strong military and police apparatus, but also over all public organisations, such as trade unions, youth and sports organisations, the press and academic and cultural institutions.

Such control is operated through the *nomenklatura* system, under which appointments to all the key posts from local to national level in party, state and social organisations like trade unions can only be filled by people whose 'candidatures are previously examined, recommended and approved' by the party committee at the appropriate level.[11] Within the party itself the system requires that candidates for election or appointment to committees and positions regarded as important have first to be approved by members of higher committees.

The party, with its 18½ million members, is in practice subordinated to a small Political Bureau, which meets at least once a week and reports every six months or so to the very much larger Central Committee. Party Congresses are held every five years and at none of them since 1927 has there been any controversy or divided vote on any major political issue. This does not of course mean that by some metaphysical process unanimity reigns on all the enormously complex problems of home and foreign policy. Very strong differences do naturally exist but the nominally highest body of the Party – the Congress – does not hear of or decide on them. They are debated in private by the Secretariat and the Politbureau – after consultation with relevant specialists – and, exceptionally, by the Central Committee.

Such structures in fact nullify the stipulation of Article 2 of the constitution that 'all power in the USSR belongs to the people', just as actual power relations 50 years ago made a mockery of the provision of the 'Stalin Constitution' of 1936 that 'all power in the USSR belongs to the working people of town and country.' We must distinguish between *real* power and formal, legal power which may be fictitious. Claims that power is in the hands of 'the people', 'the working people' or 'the working class' (the latter having been asserted in the Soviet Union up to 1961 when a 'state of the whole people' was officially declared to have taken the place of the 'dictatorship of the working class') need to be based on empirical evidence, not on constitutional or programmatic formulations ritualistically repeated.

It is contended that since the working people of the USSR showed their confidence in the Communist Party by following its leadership in the October Revolutions, the civil

war and the Second World War, their power today is
expressed in and through its position as the governing party.
This would, however, only be true if, *de jure* and *de facto*,
the working people were in a position, if they wanted, to
change the government. Such a possibility does not exist
today in any of the socialist countries, since in none of them
are the working people given the chance to choose between
alternative parties and/or programmes.[12] This would appear
to be excluded by the provisions in almost all their
constitutions laying down the leading role of the Communist
(or other Marxist-Leninist) Party in the state, even where
(as in Bulgaria, Czechoslovakia, the German Democratic
Republic and Poland) there is more than one legal party. It
thereby becomes unconstitutional to envisage what Lenin
described as the great advantage of the Soviet system in
1918: 'if the working people are dissatisfied with their party
they can elect other delegates, hand power to another party
and change the government without any revolution at all.'[23]

The fact that for historical reasons the Communist Party
finds itself as the only party functioning in the Soviet Union
today should not in itself preclude the possibility of elections
being contested by other candidates, sponsored by different
groups of citizens, presenting alternative polices, although
this might logically lead to other parties being formed.
Stalin, discussing his new constitution with an American
journalist in 1936, told him: 'You think there will be no
election contests. But there will be, and I foresee very lively
election campaigns.'[14] Unfortunately, however, from that
day to this no such contests have ever taken place.

Unlike some other socialist countries, where in some
constituencies there are more candidates than seats[15]
(though it is not at present possible to stand on alternative
platforms), in all elections in the USSR there is only one
candidate. Whilst initially there are a number of nominations from public organisations and work collectives, the
invariable practice is for only one name to be selected from
among them to go on the ballot paper. Although this
candidate is not necessarily a member of the Communist
Party, it is the representatives of the appropriate committee
of the Party who, at a closed meeting, will have the decisive
say in determining the one name to go before the electors,

from whom they thereby remove the possibility of choice. An attempt in 1979 by a group of citizens in the Sverdlovsk District of Moscow to put up the Marxist critic Roy Medvedev as a candidate was ruled out of order. Under such circumstances elections become a kind of plebiscite with a predetermined result.

The Supreme Soviet, whose composition is designed formally to reflect the social composition of the country, meets only for a few days every year to approve the budget and give unanimous support to governmental policies, although in recent years more deputies have been involved in the work of its commissions concerned with specific spheres of responsibility.

The essential hallmark of socialist democracy, as Marx and Lenin never tired of emphasising, is its involvement of the working people in running the state at all levels. The Soviet press cites figures of millions of citizens involved as deputies and 'activists' and taking part in nationwide discussions. But if *quantitative* indices were the measure of Soviet democracy, we would have to accept that it was operating at a very high level in 1936, in the midst of Stalin's mass repressions, when it was claimed that 51.1 per cent of the adult population took part in discussing the draft of the 'Stalin Constitution'. However it is necessary to probe behind superficial appearances and apply *qualitative* criteria to ascertain the extent to which participation is effective in *deciding* the main lines of national and foreign policy, as opposed to taking part in approving and implementing policies worked out in their essentials at the top behind closed doors.

In its controversy with *Pravda* in 1982, the Italian Communist Party leadership appositely asked: 'In what party meeting, in what trade union and production assembly, in what Soviet can the communist who dissents and the citizen who objects to general political questions (apart from discussion on particular aspects of a practical or organisational nature) express their disapproval, and how is this reported in public?[16]

The Soviet media exclude all information paternalistically deemed 'unsuitable' for the general public, although there is a special restricted service of information and translations which makes it available to the trusted few. There has of late been an increase in the number of letters and reports in the press pinpointing particular local and workshop grievances. Yet a basic distrust for the working people is shown by the fact that in recent years Soviet newspapers and statistical handbooks have stopped publishing annual grain production or infant mortality figures. In 1982 no Soviet papers published the Italian Communist Party's reply to *Pravda*'s attack on its policies, any more than they carried the Czechoslovak Communist Party's reply to the Warsaw Pact parties' letter of criticism in July 1968, although the *Pravda* article and the 'Warsaw Letter' were published in full in the press of the parties criticised. In 1980, with the development of Solidarity in Poland, the Soviet authorities resumed the jamming of foreign broadcasts on a large scale.

Already early in the Brezhnev period objective information about 'sensitive' periods of Soviet history began to dry up. Access to archive material has become far more difficult. This has gone along with an increased watering down of the criticisms of Stalin. Thus the 1982 edition of the one-volume *Encylopaedia of the Soviet Union* deletes all mention of the 'serious violations of socialist legality and mass repressions' under Stalin, quoted in the 1979 edition from a 1956 Central Committee resolution.

Whilst the number of 'prisoners of conscience' held in Soviet prisons and psychiatric hospitals – which Amnesty International has estimated at about 10,000 – is tiny compared with the millions herded into labour camps under Stalin, it is deeply disturbing that after nearly 70 years of Soviet power it should be felt necessary to meet dissenting views with repression rather than reasoned argument. Nor is it a justification to say that people are nowadays only put in prison after due process of law if the laws under which they are sentenced involve restriction or deprivation of fundamental liberties. Some are of a catch-all political character such as Article 190 (1) added to the Criminal Code of the RSFSR in 1966, under which many dissidents have been jailed for 'slandering the Soviet state and social system.' Article 72 of the Soviet Constitution stipulates, 'Each Union Republic shall retain the right freely to secede from the USSR'. However, any attempts publicly to advocate or organise for this, or to satisfy legitimate national grievances and aspirations within the framework of the USSR, are treated as nationalistic anti-soviet activity and dealt with under the criminal codes of the national republics which make this illegal.

Soviet economy

The economic advance of the Soviet Union continued at an impressively high rate up till the 1960s. It could claim that, taking 1913 as 100, its national income stood in 1960 at 2,674, whereas that of the USA stood at 348 and of Britain at 204. From this, and similar rates of growth in other socialist states, the conclusion was drawn that 'high growth rates are a law of socialism'.[17] The targets that were formulated on this assumption have not been realised, as Tables A and B illustrate (particularly strikingly in the more modern branches of production). These show the falling off of the impressive earlier rates of progress of key industrial and agricultural items targeted by the 22nd Party Congress, as well as comparing targets and attainment. Although the statistics, all taken from Soviet publications, are obviously of considerable relevance for an informed Soviet participation in the revision of the Party programme now underway, no such comparison has ever appeared in the Soviet press.

The type of highly centralised command economy, which was so successful in securing the extensive development required in the period of industrialisation, has proved quite unsuited to the intensive development required for a more advanced consumer-oriented economy. There has for years been a need to combine the advantages of socialist economic planning with far more flexibility, autonomy and market-oriented enterprises, and democratic control over decisions taken at both factory, farm, regional and national levels. Such radical economic reform, though under discussion since the 1960s, has been blocked through concern as to where it might lead. What we are dealing with here is not only well-established economic administrators with a strong vested interest in preserving the existing structures and a distrust of innovation. It is also a question of fear at top levels in the party and state of the pluralistic *political*

Table A   USSR Industrial Production

Product	1950	1960	CPSU 1961 Estimate for 1970	1970	CPSU 1961 Estimate for 1980	1980	1984
Electric power (thousand million Kwh)	91.2	292.3	900-1000	741	2,700-3,000	1,294	1,493
Steel (million tons)	27.3	65	195	116	250	148	154
Oil (million tons)	37.9	148	390	349	690-710	603	613
Gas (million tons)	5.8	47	310-325	198	680-720	435	587
Coal (million tons)	261	513	685-700	624	1,180-1,200	716	712
Mineral fertilisers, in conventional units (million tons)	5.5	13.9	77	55.4	125-135	104	n/a
Synthetic resins & plastics (thousand tons)	67.1	332†	5,300	1,673	19,000-21,000	3,637	4,800
Artificial synthetic fibres (thousand tons)	24.2	211	1,350	623	3,100-3,300	1,176	1,400
Cement (million tons)	10.2	45.5	122	45.5	233-235	124	130
Textiles (thousand million square metres)	3.4	6.6	13.6	8.9	20-22	10.7	11.8
Leather footwear (million pairs)	203	419	825	678	900-1,000	743	764

† As given at 1961 Congress. Subsequently revised to 312 thousand tons.

Table B   USSR Agricultural Produce

Product (in million tons)	1950	1960	CPSU 1961 Estimate for 1970	1970	CPSU 1961 Estimate for 1970	1980	1984	Target for 1990
Grain	81.2	134†	230	186.8	290-310	189.1	*	250-255
Sugar beet	20.8	57.7	86	78.9	98-108	81.0	85.3	102-103
Meat (Slaughter weight)	4.9	8.7	25	12.3	30-32	15.1	16.7	20-20.5
Milk	35.3	61.7	135	83.0	170-180	92.7	97.6	104-106
Eggs (thousand million)	11.7	27.4	68	40.7	110-116	63.1	76.0	78-79

* Individual year's grain production not given. Average annual production for 1976-80: 205.0 million tons.
† As given at 1961 Congress. Subsequently revised to 125.5 million tons.
Sources: USSR in Figures (Moscow) – various years; N S Khrushchev, *Report on the Programme of the CPSU* (October 18, 1961); L I Brezhnev, *The Soviet Food Programme* (24 May, 1982); *Pravda*, 25 January 1985.

consequences of giving greater autonomy to enterprises. It conjures up to them the spectre of economic self-management organs like the workers' councils which constituted a pivotal part of the Czechoslovak economic reform of 1968. This was bitterly denounced as 'anti-socialist' by the Soviet leaders, who ensured that it was scrapped after the invasion. Resistance to economic reform is undoubtedly reinforced by conditions of international tension. To the extent that Western imperialism pushes the USSR – against Soviet wishes and interests – into an accelerated arms race, this increases arms-related production at the expense of consumer industries and strengthens conservative attitudes and pressure groups committed to a highly centralised economy with priority given to heavy industry. A relaxation of international tension would greatly improve the prospects for Soviet economic reform.

The Soviet Union today stands at the crossroads. Its needs, and those of other countries which have adopted the Soviet model, have for many years come increasingly into conflict with deeply entrenched authoritiarian power structures holding back its political, economic, social and cultural development. A freer rein is needed for genuinely independent initiative both inside and outside the existing structures, including for the development of an autonomous women's movement, without which – despite important advances – women will not achieve in practice the equality which is officially proclaimed.

Soviet leaders face a dilemma. On the one hand they recognise and proclaim the need to stimulate political interest and social involvement, which is a necessary condition for reversing the decline in economic growth rates. On the other hand they do not want to carry through reforms which are so radical as to allow independent popular initiatives which they cannot control. Yet Soviet experience in recent years has been demonstrating again and again that you cannot have one without the other. Limited reforms in the political and economic spheres are periodically introduced with great fanfares, but then run out of steam in the face of bureaucratic inertia. Critical remarks made last year in a Central Committee resolution calling for improvements in the democratic functioning of the Soviets were being made in the second half of the 1930s, and again in 1957 when similar decisions were taken. Criticisms of overcentralisation and the need for a reorganisation of the economy to encourage initiative on a regional, local and enterprise level were voiced at the time of the economic reforms of 1957, 1965 and 1979, none of which have brought the desired results. It is by no means sure that further limited reforms of this type are likely to be more successful – perhaps less so, having lost credibility over time having all been 'tried before'.

In selecting Chernenko as Andropov's successor, the party leadership has plumped for playing safe rather than for innovation. The disconcerting memory of Khrushchev could not have been far from their minds, and will no doubt weigh with them when the time comes – perhaps not so far ahead – to choose the next General Secretary. It does not seem very likely that this crucial office will once again be given to a septuagenarian. But what is certain is that the greatest care will be taken by the Politbureau to exclude anyone who might turn out to have the makings of a Khrushchev, not to speak of a Dubček.

The best that realistically can be hoped for is that a younger person – and Gorbachev seems by far the most likely candidate in that category – is appointed with the resolve, as well as sufficient health, strength and time ahead of him, to mobilise wide popular support to carry through a dynamic and sustained reform of the economy and overcome the deep-seated bureaucratic forces that will try to block it. If he (no 'she' has for over twenty years been on the Politbureau, from among whose members general secretaries are chosen) is to succeed in this he will need to accompany it with steps towards loosening paternalistic control over political, social and cultural life, and particularly over the media, access to information and foreign contacts and travel. This would represent a turn towards modernisation and efficiency – no doubt with technocratic features – rather than socialist democratisation. But, unless one resorts to hope rather than analysis, it is not possible to see what forces in the Soviet Union today we could expect to be in a position to take the initiative in carrying through genuine socialist democratisation like that being undertaken by Dubček and the Czechoslovak communists between January and August 1968, which was so tragically ended by predominantly Soviet military intervention.

After the October Revolution of 1917 the Soviet Union became and remained for many decades the main revolutionary force in the world. Despite its important peace initiatives and assistance to peoples struggling against imperialism,[18] the attractive power of its form of socialism has diminished, especially for the West where it is seen as denying some of the essential freedoms won many years ago in bourgeois democratic countries. Today the socialist forces in the West need to provide the world with a more attractive conception of socialism, which draws on all that is best in a long democratic tradition and in more recent democratic movements like feminism, and which is clearly distinguished from the monolithic Soviet model. In this way we could also contribute to the development in the Soviet Union and other socialist countries of a process of renewal based on freedom which, in Marx's words, 'consists in converting the state from an organ superimposed upon society into one completely subordinate to it.'[19]

Notes

[1] *Programme of the Communist Party of the Soviet Union*, Moscow 1961, pp 61–64. Emphasis in original.

[2] *Ibid*, p 128. By communism the programme understands a society of abundance implementing the principle 'From each according to his ability, to each according to his needs.'

[3] K Chernenko, 'Assert Life's Truth and Socialism's Lofty Ideals', *Information Bulletin*, Prague 22/1984, p 34.

[4] *Pravda*, 26 April 1984.

[5] *36 Million Communists say* ... (Statement of the World's Communist Parties, November 1960), p 4.

[6] *Révolution*, Paris 23 November 1984, p 12.

[7] K Marx/F Engels, *Werke*, Berlin 1958, vol 3 pp 34-35.

[8] I Deutscher, *Russia after Stalin*, London 1953.

[9] Khrushchev, in the closed session of the 20th Congress, quoted another member of the Politbureau who said that when party leaders were invited to see Stalin they did not know where they would be sent to next, home or to jail.

[10] Speech by Y Andropov, *Soviet News* London, 17 August 1983.

[11] *Partiinoe Stroitel'stvo*, Moscow 1971, p 283.

[12] Such a chance was given to the people of Nicaragua last year despite the extreme threat the country was under from US imperialism and the 'contras' which it backs, but Nicaragua's economic system does not allow it (yet) to be classified as socialist.

[13] V I Lenin, *Collected Works*, Lawrence and Wishart 1964, vol 26, p 498.

[14] *Interview between J Stalin and Roy Howard*, Moscow 1936, p 15.

[15] This practice is being extended in Hungary despite the fact that, like the Soviet Union, there is only one political party.

[16] E Berlinguer, *After Poland*, London 1982, p 101.

[17] Resolution of 21st Congress of Communist Party of the Soviet Union Moscow 1961.

[18] The vital sphere of Soviet foreign policy, which deserves extended treatment, falls outside the scope of this article.

[19] K Marx, 'Critique of Gotha Programme', in Marx/Engels, *Selected Works*, Moscow/London 1950 vol 2 p 29.

2. The Perestroika Offensive
Political debate 1986–87

Archie Brown

Gorbachev and Reform of the Soviet System

This assessment of Gorbachev's intentions, and the problems he faced at the beginning of 1987, was written in March 1987. The text published here is identical with the version which appeared in Marxism Today, *but the footnotes from the original article in* The Political Quarterly *have all been restored. Archie Brown has provided an updating of this piece to April 1989 at the end of the chapter.*

Western publics were not very well prepared by their mass media for the changes which began to take place in the Soviet Union under the General Secretaryship of Yuri Andropov and which – following the Chernenko interregnum – are being carried much further under the leadership of Mikhail Gorbachev. Disproportionate attention was focused on the health and person of the top leader. While the subject of the succession to Leonid Brezhnev was a very important one, Brezhnev merely had to disappear from public view for a week or more (as he often did in his later years) for massive attention to be concentrated on his life expectancy and the possible identity of the next General Secretary of the Soviet Communist Party.

That even under the conservative Brezhnev there were different political tendencies within the Soviet Communist Party – in broad terms (though many further distinctions can be made) reformist, conservative and neo-stalinist – went largely unnoticed. A vast amount of attention was, of

First published in *The Political Quarterly*, Vol 58, No 2, April–June 1987; this somewhat abbreviated version published in *Marxism Today*, June 1987.

course, paid in the mass media to overt dissent, and the average Western newspaper reader or television viewer could have been forgiven for picking up an exaggerated idea of the dissidents' salience within Soviet political life and for coming to the conclusion that apart from them the Soviet Union consisted entirely of like-minded conformists.

Yet those Brezhnev years also saw debate, much of it esoteric, conducted in Soviet specialist journals and books. Many of the people who stayed within the boundaries of the system were far from satisfied with the status quo. Some criticised it from a neo-stalinist or a Russian nationalist standpoint; others (and it is they who are coming to the fore today) as advocates of economic and political reform. Those who wished to exercise influence and avoid the marginalisation which became the fate of most Soviet dissidents (for the political context in the Soviet Union was very different from that of Poland where a great part of the nation were 'dissidents') abided by certain rules.

Thus, for many economic reformers this meant praising the Hungarian economic reform rather than directly advocating a significant role for markets within the Soviet economy (especially after Kosygin's attempted reform, which was launched in 1965 and which made some nods in the direction of the market, petered out in the face of conservative opposition, of which Brezhnev was a part). Similarly, the rules of the game involved (and still involve) emphasising the need for development of the 'democratic' component of 'democratic centralism' rather than making a frontal attack on that latter concept. They likewise entailed – and accommodated – advocating the recognition of the existence of different interests in Soviet society and the idea of 'diversity within monism' rather than embracing the notion of political pluralism which (especially following the 'Prague Spring') remained firmly taboo.

Without such efforts by within-system reformers, people who tried to push further the limits of the possible and broaden the political space within them (rather than attempt to destroy such boundaries totally and destroy themselves politically in the process), there would be no changes of the kind which are under way in the Soviet Union today. The reform-minded wings of the party apparatus and of the party intelligentsia were an important part of the coalition which supported Gorbachev when he overcame considerable conservative opposition to attain the General Secretaryship. Today they are the most enthusiastic element in the coalition which bolsters his power.

There were also, of course, 'objective factors' which led to the policy innovation which we are now seeing. These included a secular decline in the rate of economic growth from the 1950s to the early 1980s, a growing technological gap in many sectors of the economy between the Soviet Union and the most successful capitalist countries and growing international tension (with the associated burden and insecurity imposed by the spiralling military competition between the Soviet Union and the United States). But though Gorbachev appeared to some Western observers (myself included) to be both a reformer and a very likely future General Secretary some years before he got that job, it would be a mistake to think that there was an inevitability about his coming to office and to the acceptance of the policies which are now being pursued.[1] When I asked a Soviet jurist in Moscow in October 1984 whether the very seriousness of the economic and political problems would not lead to the adoption of many of the policies which we see now (and with Gorbachev implementing them as the most likely successor to the already physically failing Chernenko), he replied: 'Yes, either that or the complete opposite!'

It was clear that something new had to be tried. The quasi-corporatism of the Brezhnev era – a style of rule which produced a lowest common denominator of agreement within the elite – would no longer work. The Soviet Union could not afford to try to 'muddle through' the remaining years of the 1980s and the 1990s in the way in which it had, in domestic affairs, muddled through the 1970s, for it was becoming increasingly evident that this would mean, as Seweryn Bialer put it, 'a process of "muddling down".'[2]

There remained, however, reactionary as well as reformist alternatives. The person within the top leadership team who could have personified the former tendency was Grigori Romanov, the former Leningrad regional party leader who by this time supervised the military and military industry within the Central Committee Secretariat. Like Gorbachev, he was a senior secretary (a full member of the Politbureau and a secretary of the Central Committee) at the time of Chernenko's death. Romanov did not control nearly as much of the apparatus or have as many friends as Gorbachev, and so he supported instead the elevation of another 'interim leader', the distinctly conservative 70-year-old Moscow party chief, Viktor Grishin, under whom the balance of power within the Secretariat could have been tilted in favour of Romanov and against Gorbachev.[3]

That Gorbachev was a far more skilful as well as a more appealing politician than Romanov and Grishin put together was a fact of no small importance. For if it be true that the changes of the last two years could not have occurred without an influential group of party members who not only support *but are pushing for* reform, it is equally clear that the Soviet system is one in which great power is vested in the office of General Secretary. Contrary to Western misconceptions and old-style Soviet propaganda, the party is *not* monolithically united. It contains people of very different ideas and personality types and embraces very distinctive opinion groupings and institutional interests.

It is of prime importance that a new General Secretary can change the correlation of forces – or balance of influence – among the competing tendencies and various informal groups. This is precisely what has happened under Gorbachev.

Gorbachev has achieved more personnel change in high places in his first two years than was achieved so soon by any other General Secretary in the Soviet Union's 70-year history. This was facilitated by the fact that Brezhnev had allowed the entire political elite to grow old together, and though a start to rejuvenation was made under Andropov (and slowed down under Chernenko), the process still had a long way to go. It would be an oversimplification to see all the new senior appointees as people whose ties are closer to Gorbachev than to any of his colleagues. Other senior members of the Politbureau, such as the *de facto* second secretary of the party, Egor Ligachev, and the chairman of the Council of Ministers, Nikolai Ryzhkov, have been successful in co-opting a number of their former colleagues and subordinates. But Ligachev and Ryzhkov are themselves part of the new top leadership team, men who were first brought into it under Andropov and who have risen still higher in the Gorbachev era. They are neither opponents nor clients of Gorbachev, but, rather, conditional allies.

Taken as a whole, the changes have been sufficiently sweeping as to greatly facilitate policy innovation. In some ways Gorbachev was fortunate in that a party congress (held every five years) was due within a year of Chernenko's death. This provided both a particularly authoritative platform for the enunciation of new policies and an opportunity to change the composition of the Central Committee. Against that, it is worth noting that Gorbachev has continued to strengthen his position in the meantime and a number of the new appointments to party and state offices in his second year are those which, when a party congress comes along, carry Central Committee membership virtually automatically.

Thus a Central Committee elected now would mean the departure of more survivors of the Brezhnev era than actually left the political scene at the party congress in early 1986. Even so, the Central Committee membership turnover was greater at that 27th congress than at any congress since Khrushchev's last – the 22nd congress of 1961. Whereas 87 per cent of surviving full members of the Central Committee elected at the 25th congress in 1976 were re-elected in 1981, only 59 per cent of those elected at the 26th congress in that year were re-elected in 1986.[4]

It is within the inner bodies of the Central Committee – the top leadership team who compose the full and candidate membership of the Politbureau or belong to the Secretariat of the Central Committee – that the personnel change has been greatest. Gorbachev's main power base lies within the Secretariat, a body which in practice wields only slightly less power than the Politbureau itself. Here the change has been dramatic. Of 12 Secretaries of the Central Committee, nine have been appointed to their posts since Gorbachev took over.

They include several key people who are particularly close to Gorbachev – among them, Alexander Yakovlev who oversees culture and propaganda within the Secretariat, who has been a strong proponent of the policy of glasnost and

who in January 1987 added candidate membership of the
Politbureau to his secretaryship; Georgi Razumovsky who
has a background in agriculture, career links to Gorbachev
and is in charge of the extremely important Central Committee department responsible for placement of party cadres;
and most recently (in January of this year) Anatoli Lukyanov
who overlapped with Gorbachev in the Law Faculty of
Moscow University in the early 1950s and who had been
heading since 1985 the General Department of the Central
Committee through which papers pass to the Politbureau – as
such, he was the nearest functional equivalent in the Soviet
system of the Secretary of the Cabinet in Britain.

There is only one woman in the top leadership team, but
that is one more than was there throughout the Brezhnev,
Andropov and Chernenko periods. Alexandra Biryukova
was promoted in March 1986 from the secretariat of the
Soviet trade unions to the vastly more important position of a
Secretary of the Central Committee. Gorbachev has
criticised the slow promotion of women within the party ranks
and there is no reason to doubt that he was responsible for this
particular appointment.

Neither quantitatively nor 'qualitatively' is Gorbachev's
position quite so strong in the Politbureau as it is in the
Secretariat. Whereas in the latter body, not only are three-
quarters of the members new, a majority of them would
appear also to be people of similar outlook to his own.
Among full members of the Politbureau, the turnover has
been substantial – of the 11, five have received this promotion
under Gorbachev – but less sweeping than the turnover in the
Secretariat. What is more, among them all, only the Foreign
Minister, Eduard Shevardnadze, looks as if he would go as far
down the road of reform as Gorbachev himself is prepared to
contemplate. Among the candidate members of the
Politbureau, Gorbachev's position is stronger. Here, as in the
Secretariat, the turnover has been 75 per cent. Of the eight
candidate members at present (March 1987), only two were in
that position when Gorbachev took over from Chernenko.

Only full members of the Politbureau may vote but, as in
the British Cabinet, votes are the exception rather than the
rule. The candidate members of the Politbureau and the

Secretaries of the Central Committee attend Politbureau meetings as of right and may speak. Hence, these 25 people constitute in a very real sense the top leadership team whose collective support the General Secretary needs, even though his political resources exceed those of any other individual among them and though his 'power to persuade' them is, on several counts, impressive.[5]

The reform wing of that top leadership team, on which Gorbachev himself should certainly be placed, will, however, be significantly strengthened when two or three more people, from the ranks of the Secretariat or from the candidate membership of the Politbureau, who share Gorbachev's political orientation can be promoted to full Politbureau membership. Though the Central Committee nominally elects these members, the process is, in essence, one of collective co-option by the Politbureau itself. Within it, the General Secretary's voice counts for more than anyone else's but his colleagues (with historical precedents in mind) are usually anxious to maintain checks upon his power. Though such sentiments can be understood, the cause of reform would undoubtedly be furthered by the elevation from candidate to full membership of Alexander Yakovlev and of the outspoken First Secretary of the Moscow party organisation, Boris Yeltsin.

The choice of Gorbachev as General Secretary (and the further changes in the composition of vital party and state institutions which followed) has also changed the correlation of forces among party influentials. Thus, people who already were known reformers and party members of some significance in Brezhnev's time, have come to enjoy substantially *higher* standing and to advocate more directly the economic reform and 'democratisation' of the Soviet system which they proposed in more cautious language in the 1970s or early 1980s. Many examples of such people could be cited, but for the sake of brevity four may suffice: Abel Aganbegyan, Tatiana Zaslavskaya, Georgi Shakhnazarov and Fedor Burlatsky.

Aganbegyan, an economic reformer of long standing, spent almost 20 years as director of the Institute of Economics and Organisation of Industrial Production of the Siberian Section of the Academy of Sciences, but was brought to Moscow to play a more central role in the elaboration of economic reform soon after Gorbachev became General Secretary.

His colleague in Novosibirsk, Zaslavskaya, produced for a high-level seminar in 1983 an analysis of economic and social problems – and of the obstacles to reform – too devastating to be published in full in the Soviet Union at that time, though it subsequently appeared abroad.[6] Now, however, one can see strong echoes of her analysis in the speeches of Gorbachev and she herself has achieved a greater prominence than ever before for her views as one of the boldest reformers.[7] She has had access not only to the party's main theoretical journal, *Kommunist*,[8] but also more recently to the pages of *Pravda* where she made a swingeing attack on the concealment of information from social scientists and compared the level of Soviet sociology unfavourably with that of Poland and Hungary, 'not to mention the developed capitalist countries.'[9]

Shakhnazarov, an innovative Soviet theorist both on international relations and on 'socialist democracy', who combines his academic role with a responsible job in the Central Committee apparatus, has been promoted from being one of a number of deputy heads of the Socialist Countries department of the Central Committee to the important post of First Deputy Head.[10]

Burlatsky, a bold reformer and man of broad-ranging talents who already in Khrushchev's time advocated competitive elections for deputies to soviets[11] and within months of Khrushchev's fall became the first advocate of a separate discipline of political science in the Soviet Union,[12] has achieved a greater prominence than he enjoyed even under Khrushchev[13] with plays on the Soviet stage and on television, a regular political column in the Writers' Union weekly newspaper (which he was first granted during Andropov's General Secretaryship) and a place in the Soviet entourage which accompanied Gorbachev to the Geneva and Reykjavik 'summits'.

Both within the higher ranks of the party apparatus and outside it, the people who have now come to the fore include far more with a commitment to reform than there were in positions of great power under Brezhnev or even under

Gorbachev's two immediate predecessors. It is worth emphasising that the changes which are now under way can hardly be considered a response to the activity of dissidents, for the dissident movement was already very weak by the time Gorbachev became General Secretary. It had been crushed. Thus, though it remains far less radical, the process of change within the Soviet Union is more akin to that in Czechoslovakia in the 1960s when the impetus for reform came from within the party itself than to that in Poland in 1980–81 when the Kania leadership retreated in the face of the 'extra-systemic' pressures of a spontaneous mass movement.

The Soviet context must, of course, be distinguished from that of Czechoslovakia too. The political cultures of the two countries remain very different and the strength of indigenous conservative forces in the Soviet Union is much greater than was that of their counterparts in Czechoslovakia. There are, moreover, complicating factors which even Soviet *reformers* must bear closely in mind. If in Czechoslovakia there was (and is) a relatively mild nationalities problem in the shape of strained relations between Czechs and Slovaks, there is in the Soviet Union – with over 100 different ethnic groups, many of whom have administrative responsibility for their own national territories – a much greater *potential* problem of fissure. Hitherto, this has not been allowed to get out of hand, but some devolution of political and economic powers could whet local (and thus, in many cases, national) appetites for greater autonomy.

For many reasons, therefore, the present time in the Soviet Union is a period of political struggle. How far the reform process will go the reformers themselves do not know. Since it is in part their relative open-mindedness and political realism which marks them off from their opponents, this is hardly surprising. For many of them, including Gorbachev, 'democratisation' is not just a slogan, but neither is it yet pluralist democracy. We should not expect to see in the near future the institutionalisation of autonomous groups (still less rival parties) capable of challenging the policies advocated by the top leadership of the Communist Party.

At the same time the 'diversity within monism' which is becoming ever more of a reality permits a substantial amount of informal group activity and some increasingly effective criticism. Soviet political commentators themselves point to the role of Russian creative writers in getting the party and government leadership to reverse a decision already taken to start work on a massive diversion of Siberian rivers for the irrigation of Central Asia.[14]

To the extent that a conscious broadening of the limits of the possible within the system is taking place – so that, to take a few examples, criticism of the Stalin era is once again appearing,[15] *Doctor Zhivago* is scheduled for its first-ever Soviet publication in the widely-read literary journal, *Novy mir*, in 1988, and demonstrations in Kazakhstan in December 1986 with strong overtones of ethnic animosity were promptly reported by the Soviet mass media – this may be interpreted as no more than progress towards a more enlightened authoritarian regime. Such a change – far removed from the totalitarianism of the Stalin era[16] and the unenlightened authoritarianism of the Brezhnev years – should not be dismissed as negligible. But in the period since the 27th party congress and especially at the very important plenary session of the Central Committee in January 1987, there have been signs of something more.

Gorbachev himself (and certainly the reform wing of the party intelligentsia) seems to regard a measure of political reform as desirable both in itself and as a necessary complement to economic reform.[17] Some elements of 'democratisation' have now been proposed by Gorbachev – in his January plenum speech – which, if fully implemented, would be quite a remarkable change from established Soviet practice. This is particularly true of his proposal that there be more than one candidate for party secretaryships (including first secretaryships) at all levels from the district up to the union republican, and that the elections be by secret ballot at meetings of the respective party committees. Rather more vaguely, he added: 'The Politbureau's opinion is that further democratisation should also apply to the formation of the central leading bodies of the party. I think this is wholly logical.'[18]

Some may view it, rather cynically, as an attempt by

Gorbachev to speed up the personnel change throughout the party and to get more of his supporters into key positions. In that context, his insistence that the party leadership retains its powers to select cadres could be seen as a safeguard against local party committees choosing opponents of reform. But it is hard to see why he should raise the issue at all unless he meant it to be taken seriously. One of the contributory factors to Khrushchev's downfall was his fixing compulsory percentage turnovers for the membership of all party committees from top to bottom – a move which induced feelings of insecurity within the very party apparatus on which his power rested. Many party secretaries may feel similarly insecure in the light of Gorbachev's recent proposals. A willingness to incur the costs of generating such dangerous emotion would appear to betoken a determination to implement a reform which would indeed enhance control 'from below' while not, of course, going so far as to abrogate control 'from above'.

In general, Gorbachev's speech to the January 1987 plenum was even more innovative and important than his political report to the 27th party congress in 1986. It was, perhaps, the most significant speech by a Soviet leader since Khrushchev's speeches demythologising Stalin delivered to the 20th congress in 1956 and the 22nd congress in 1961. Among the other important points Gorbachev made were that Central Committee plenums had for years been brief and formal and that they must from now on be so conducted that 'there can be no persons beyond criticism or people with no right to criticise' and that the promotion of non-party members to leading positions was an 'important aspect of the democratisation of public life.'

He also asserted that the authority of the soviets needed to be further enhanced (and this seems likely to involve the introduction of competitive elections for deputies to soviets, at least at the local level, though, needless to say, none of the candidates would be challenging the 'leading role' of the Communist Party). Of great importance was his reference to the crippling effect of the Stalin era on Soviet development when he observed that Soviet socialist theory had remained largely fixed 'at the level of the 1930s–1940s' when 'vigorous debates and creative ideas disappeared ... while authoritarian evaluations and opinions became unquestionable truths'.

Noteworthy also was his suggestion that a party conference
be held in 1988 to monitor the course of economic reform
and 'to discuss matters of further democratising the life of
the party and society as a whole'.

This last proposal was an important one. Party
conferences – second only to congresses in terms of party
authority – are rare occurrences; the last one was held in
1941. The significance of holding one in 1988 is that it keeps
up the pressure for economic and political reform. The
matters Gorbachev has put on the political agenda cannot
now be conveniently forgotten.

On economic reform, Gorbachev has emphasised that
only the first steps have so far been taken. One important
step was the publication this February of the draft law on the
enterprise which sets out the considerably enhanced rights
and greater autonomy of Soviet industrial enterprises and
associations. It embodies also the recently legitimated
principle of 'socialist self-management' (which for long was
regarded as a revisionist Yugoslav notion) whereby leading
personnel in factories are to be elected by a general meeting
of the work collective either by secret or open ballot, the
latter decision being left to the discretion of the meeting. Of
course, it remains to be seen how this draft legislation will be
eventually improved (it has been criticised by, among
others, Zaslavskaya) and, more important, implemented.

So far the goals of the more radical Soviet economic
reformers – explicit recognition of a role for the market as
well as for central strategic economic decision-making –
have been recognised only at the level of legalising
small-scale private enterprise (which means, *inter alia*, that
the Soviet Union is beginning to see its first private
restaurants). But of greater importance for the economy as a
whole will be the extension of the market principle into
areas of the socialised economy. Gorbachev clearly
recognises that the attempt to fix all prices administratively
is a nonsense, but so far his support for a market element
within the Soviet economy has been in the coded language of
advocating a greater role for 'commodity-money relations'.

That is doubtless because there is fierce opposition from
within the ministries and from many party organs to a
reform which attempts to combine real concessions to the

market with central planning (and the doubts almost certainly exist also at Politbureau level). If, however, as seems likely, Gorbachev goes on to consolidate his power still further, the chances of quite far-reaching economic reform will be better under the present leadership than they have been at any time since the fall of Khrushchev – and Khrushchev's reforms are no model, for they were hasty, inconsistent and ultimately ineffective.

In some ways Gorbachev's strategy is a high-risk one. It threatens more vested interests and arouses more immediate hostility than Brezhnev's consensus style of rule. But Gorbachev's answer (which he often expresses in a phrase familiar also in Britain) is: 'There is no alternative'. There are many in the West who dismiss the changes taking place in the Soviet Union as no more than cosmetic; if that is so, it is difficult to understand why they are encountering such fierce resistance and why pushing through what Gorbachev calls the 'reconstruction' of the Soviet system is such an uphill task.[19]

In his speech to the 18th Congress of the Soviet Trade Unions in February of this year, Gorbachev mentioned that the plenary session of the Central Committee eventually held in January 1987 had been postponed three times – evidently for lack of agreement on how the reform process should proceed.[20] It is often remarked that there is resistance at the 'middle levels' of the Soviet system to the Gorbachev 'reconstruction'. That is certainly true, but the middle levels alone could scarcely have held up the convening of a Central Committee meeting to hear the General Secretary's proposals if the policies embodied in them had from the outset received the unanimous backing of his Politbureau colleagues. It is clear that there is resistance and a struggle going on at *all* levels.

There is also a tendency to say that because there are still dissidents in prison and restrictions on emigration, nothing has really altered. It is right to be aware of what has not changed. The release of Andrei Sakharov from exile and of a number of other dissidents from prison does *not* mean that dissent has been institutionalised. It is, rather, an attempt to bring some of them – and this applies in particular to a man of Sakharov's great distinction and moral authority – back 'within the system', given that the boundaries of permitted criticism have been extended and there are articles now being published in the Soviet press which only a few years ago would have landed their authors in serious trouble.

Similarly, travel abroad – whether in the form of emigration or for a short trip – remains a privilege rather than a right. In conditions of relaxation of East-West tension, it is a privilege which under the present Soviet leadership is likely to be much more widely extended, but we are some way off the day when Soviet citizens are free to leave the country at will. To go on from this, however, to say in effect that unless everything has changed, nothing has changed is an abdication of responsible judgement.[21]

Gorbachev himself describes the process of reform and restructuring as 'irreversible'. As a politician, it doubtless makes a great deal of sense for him to do so; he has no need to give encouragement to his domestic foes. The outside observer must be more cautious and allow for the possibility that the current trend *could* be reversed. And doubtless many in the West – including some in the Reagan administration – would welcome a return to the old simplicities as well as to the days when they could rely on Soviet propaganda being more hamfisted than their own.

The reversal of the current trends and the defeat of Gorbachev would, however, be in the long-term interest neither of the people of the Soviet Union nor of the West. If (as, on the whole, still seems likely) Gorbachev does remain in office for years to come and, as previously long-tenure General Secretaries have done, strengthens his power and authority over time, this will open up new prospects within and outside the Soviet Union. By the end of the century Gorbachev will, at 68, still be younger than any previous General Secretary was when – for political or biological reasons – he demitted office. There is reason at least for hope that by that time the reform of the Soviet system will have made it qualitatively better than it has been hitherto and that opportunities will have risen (which should not be passed by) for a more constructive relationship with the West.

Notes

[1] Thus, the American Sovietologist, Jerry Hough, and I independently came to the conclusion while Brezhnev was still alive that Gorbachev was a future General Secretary and that he wished to undertake reform. See Jerry F Hough's chapter in Seweryn Bialer and Thane Gustafson (eds), *Russia at the Crossroads: The 26th Congress of the CPSU*, Allen and Unwin 1982, esp. pp 43-44; and Brown in Archie Brown and Michael Kaser (eds), *Soviet Policy for the 1980s*, Macmillan 1982, esp. pp 240-242, 244-245 and 269-270.

[2] Seweryn Bialer, *Stalin's Successors: Leadership, Stability and Change in the Soviet Union*, Cambridge University Press 1980, p 305.

[3] Rather remarkably, an article by the Soviet author, Mikhail Shatrov, in the journal, *Ogonek* (no 4, 1987, p 5) recently confirmed that there had indeed been an attempt to secure the General Secretaryship for Grishin and put a stop to the rise of Gorbachev.

[4] See Thane Gustafson and Dawn Mann, 'Gorbachev's First Year: Building Power and Authority' in *Problems of Communism*, vol XXXV, no 3, May-June 1986, esp p 4. Following the 'anti-party group' crisis of 1957, only 49 per cent of surviving 1956 Central Committee members were re-elected in 1961.

[5] Eleven full Politbureau members, eight candidate members and twelve Secretaries of the Central Committee do add up to twenty-five people because six of them hold full or candidate membership of the Politbureau jointly with a Secretaryship.

[6] See 'The Novosibirsk Report' in *Survey*, vol 28, no 1, 1984, pp 88-108.

[7] Indeed, as I noted two years ago, these echoes were already there in a speech Gorbachev delivered in December 1984 – three months before he became General Secretary. See Archie Brown, 'Gorbachev: New Man in the Kremlin' in *Problems of Communism*, vol XXXXIV, no 3, May-June 1985, esp. pp 18-19.

[8] *Kommunist*, no 13, September 1986, pp 61-73.

[9] *Pravda*, 6 February 1987, pp 2-3.

[10] I have discussed Shakhnazarov's views and role at greater length in my article, 'Soviet Political Developments and Prospects' in *World Policy Journal* (New York), vol IV, no 1, Winter 1986–87, esp. pp 72-74. In general the personnel change in the foreign policy establishments has been particularly great. For further details, see the above article, esp. pp 68-74, and F Stephen Larrabee and Allen Lynch, 'Gorbachev: The Road to Reykjavik', in *Foreign Policy* (Washington, DC), no 65, Winter 1986–87, esp. pp 10-13.

[11] On this, see an interesting interview (by Monty Johnstone) of Burlatsky in *Marxism Today*, February 1987, esp. p 15.

[12] See Archie Brown, 'Political Science in the USSR' in *International Political Science Review* vol 7, no 4, October 1986, esp pp 445-448.

[13] Burlatsky was at one time a speech-writer for Khrushchev and in the early 1960s he was a prominent member, and for a time the leader, of a group of consultants to Yuri Andropov who at that time headed the

Socialist Countries Department of the Central Committee.

[14] For example, Burlatsky in the interview cited above.

[15] On this, see, for example, Stephen F Cohen, 'An anti-Stalinist Tide is Flowing Again', in *International Herald Tribune*, 3 February 1987.

[16] Even under Stalin, the system did not precisely fit the 'ideal type' of *total* control from above. But if the concept of totalitarianism is ever to be applied to any actual society (and not only to a fictional Orwellian one), then the period of 'high Stalinism' (broadly speaking: 1934–1953) corresponds sufficiently closely to the style and character of rule captured by the concept as to justify its application to the Soviet Union in those years.

[17] For more detailed argument of this case before the January plenum took place, see Brown, 'Soviet Political Developments and Prospects', *op cit*, esp. pp 57-67 and 75-85.

[18] This major speech of Gorbachev to the January plenum is published in *Pravda*, 28 January 1987, pp 1-5, and in English in BBC, *Summary of World Broadcasts*, SU/8478/C1/1-37, 29 January 1987.

[19] For a recent account of some of the psychological and institutional resistance to the Gorbachev reforms, see the text of an interview given by Academician Tatiana Zaslavskaya to a Hungarian newspaper, translated and published in BBC, *Summary of World Broadcasts*, SU/8480/C1-6, 31 January 1987.

[20] *Pravda*, 26 February 1987, p 1.

[21] For one example, among all too many others, of such an oversimple response, see A M Rosenthal, 'How to Make This Glasnost More Interesting Than Ever' in *International Herald Tribune*, 3 February 1987.

Appendix: April 1989

The political change which has continued to take place in the Soviet Union in the two years since I completed the article published above seems to me to justify fully its tone of moderate optimism. I was, of course, concerned more with the political system than with the economy and that makes a difference. In the short term (that is to say, in Gorbachev's first four years) it is political reform, glasnost and the changed political and psychological domestic climate which, together with innovation in foreign policy and better and more constructive relations with most of the outside world, constitute perestroika's main achievements. This is quite a lot to be going on with. In contrast, however, the economy remains in the doldrums. The main difference with the past is that the extremely serious economic problems can be openly admitted and honestly analysed and that in itself is a necessary first step towards improvement. But until that improvement begins to be perceived by the Soviet consumer, reformers are going to feel less secure than their otherwise quite remarkable progress in shifting the balance of forces within Soviet political life would appear to merit.

Apart from the economy, the one other area where things have gone worse rather than better for reformers over the past two years is in national relations within the country. Writing in early 1987, I mentioned this as a major potential problem, one that makes the radical reform of the Soviet political system more difficult than it would have been in Czechoslovakia in 1968, had the Moscow leadership then taken a sufficiently enlightened view of Soviet long-term interests to allow developments in Czechoslovakia to take their course. Instead, by crude military intervention, they sentenced the Czechs and Slovaks to twenty years or more of discredited and oppressive government, while simultaneously strengthening the hand of conservative forces within the Soviet Union itself.

The potential problem of 1987 (which had already, however, manifested itself in ethnic unrest in Kazakhstan in December 1986) has turned into a series of overt and, in some instances, acute crises in different parts of the country involving loss of life in Armenia, Azerbaijan and Georgia. Political protest in the Baltic republics did not spill over into inter-ethnic violence but the manifestations of Estonian, Latvian and Lithuanian national consciousness and assertiveness were on a sufficient scale to make an impact in Moscow. The official response has been to promise a Central Committee plenum on the nationality question and, beyond that, the devolution of more political power to the republics. It is probable that nothing less than a fully-fledged federalism, going well beyond what the Soviet Union has had hitherto, will begin to satisfy feelings and desires which are by no means new but which in the changed political climate have been able to come out into the open. Devolving more power to the republics does not, of course, provide an easy answer to all the ethnic problems. The Soviet leadership does not want to so weaken the centre as to leave Moscow in the position it perceives the federal authorities to be in Yugoslavia, and it is aware that it still has a role to play as an honest broker between the titular nationality of a republic and minority nationalities within that same republic. This role, as the cases of Azerbaijan (and the ethnic Armenians in Nagorno-Karabakh) in 1988, and of Georgia (the tensions between the Abkhazians and the Georgians) in 1989 demonstrated, can be a vital and delicate one. Greater power (or even independence) for the union republics would not of itself dispose of the nationalities question. There is no once-and-for-all answer to the politics of ethnicity, but there is the beginning of a realisation in Gorbachev's Soviet Union that they require a constant sensitivity and responsiveness to grievances – political attributes which have hitherto been at best partial and at worst replaced by outright repression.

Economy and ethnicity aside, there have been real political advances over the past two years, especially in the realms of ideas, personnel change and even institutional change.[1] In the article published in *Marxism Today* in June 1987 I spoke of the recognition of different interests within Soviet society and of 'diversity within monism', while the notion of political pluralism remained, however, taboo. But the very next month Gorbachev used the term, 'pluralism', in a positive context,[2] and since then he and Soviet reformers more generally have developed the idea and spoken in favourable terms of a 'socialist pluralism' or a 'pluralism of opinion'.[3] Given the extent to which Soviet leaders and ideologists had devoted time and resources to criticising the notion of pluralism ever since they began to perceive it as a political threat during the 'Prague Spring', this represented a considerable ideological breakthrough, but Gorbachev and the reform wing of the party leadership still stop short of embracing 'political pluralism' – as distinct from 'socialist pluralism' – for that clearly has connotations of a competitive party system and one in which there is no guaranteed 'leading role' for the Communist Party. But now that the concept of pluralism has entered official Soviet political discourse, it has become open to a variety of interpretations and not all of those who use the term accept the same restrictions on its applicability as those embraced thus far by the top leadership.

The personnel change which has occurred over Gorbachev's third and fourth years as General Secretary, and the beginning of his fifth year, has – like that of the first two – been quite spectacular by the standards of the past, especially if comparison is made – appropriately – with the earliest years in power of previous General Secretaries. By March 1989, on the fourth anniversary of Gorbachev's accession to the General Secretaryship, only three out of the eleven full members of Chernenko's Politbureau (including Gorbachev himself) were still in the Soviet leadership, none of Chernenko's six candidate members were there (and though in the case of two of them, that was because they had been promoted, in the case of the other four it was because they had been pensioned off), and of the ten Secretaries of the Central Committee on the eve of Chernenko's death, only two – Gorbachev and Ligachev – were still in the Secretariat in March 1989.

Personnel change had been so rapid at all levels – whether that of the Central Committee apparatus, the republican and regional party organisations, senior military posts and ministerial office – that the Central Committee had come to contain a large number of functionless and, in not a few cases, disgruntled members. To remove Central Committee members in between the five-yearly Party Congresses is no easy matter, for the Party Rules stipulate that only Congresses have the right to change the composition of the Central Committee (other than at the margins when members are expelled for gross turpitude or new full members are co-opted from the ranks of those who are already candidate members). It was, therefore, quite a dramatic break with precedent when Gorbachev secured in April 1989 the removal from the ranks of full and candidate membership of the Central Committee and that of the Central Auditing Commission (the latter body also one that is elected at Party Congresses) a total of 110 people.[4] It was not done in breach of the Party Rules, for the members – who were mostly elderly and who had lost the jobs which had merited their Central Committee membership in the first place – signed a letter of resignation which the April Central Committee plenum duly accepted. But no-one imagined that the 110 had spontaneously and simultaneously decided that this was the time to give up their last important power – one that in a leadership crisis could have been of decisive significance – and so their departure was a signal success for Gorbachev and the reformist cause. At the same time an unusually large number of candidate members – 24 – to be promoted at any one time to full membership of the Central Committee received that elevation. Taken in conjunction with the overwhelmingly conservative character of many of those who departed, the pro-reform orientation of most of the new full members represented a further blow for opponents of perestroika.

It is worth noting what has happened to several of the people mentioned by name in my article in the two years since it was written. Two key supporters of Gorbachev within the leadership to whom I referred have continued their upward rise. By the summer of 1987 Alexander Yakovlev was already a full member of the Politbureau as well as a Secretary of the Central Committee, while by 1988 Georgi Razumovsky was a candidate member of the Politbureau and Secretary of the Central Committee. When the Central Committee apparatus was reorganised in October 1988 and six new Commissions were created, Yakovlev became Chairman of the Commission of the Central Committee responsible for international affairs and Razumovsky heads the no less important Commission for party construction and cadres policy, while continuing to be chief of the Central Committee department which supervises the party apparatus. The only woman in the leadership, Alexandra Biryukova, received a modest promotion, moving from a Secretaryship of the Central Committee to candidate membership of the Politbureau. Egor Ligachev, who could be described as 'the *de facto* second secretary of the party' in 1987, no longer occupies that position. He is still a full member of the Politbureau and Secretary of the Central Committee, but his supervisory responsibilities are now confined to agriculture and his political standing has declined.

Notable institutional change has also occurred in the Soviet Union within the past two years. The creation of new Commissions of the Central Committee has already been noted. At the same time the number of departments in the

Central Committee building was reduced from twenty to nine.[5] This included the abolition of all the branch economic departments except that of agriculture, suggesting a greater seriousness about reducing the party's role in economic administration. By the end of 1988 the numbers working in the Central Committee apparatus had been cut by approximately 40 per cent.

An even more important reform took place in the state structure – the creation of a new-style parliament and presidency and, above all, the introduction in 1989 of competitive elections for the legislature. The March 1989 elections for the 2,250 members of the Congress of People's Deputies (which in turn had to elect the 542 members of the Supreme Soviet, intended to become a vastly more serious legislative assembly than it had been in its previous incarnation) had numerous imperfections, but they were, nevertheless, the most important elections for a state body in the whole of Soviet history. A year earlier, it would have been difficult to imagine that the candidates most favoured by the party apparatus in the three major Soviet cities of Moscow, Leningrad and Kiev would actually be defeated, but this is precisely what happened.

Both in the territorial elections and in the elections of a third of the deputies by 'public organisations' a sizeable minority of deputies with independent minds were chosen by an electorate whose voting behaviour varied interestingly from one part of the country to another. While it remained conformist in Soviet Central Asia, in the Baltic republics support for candidates was closely linked to the extent to which they identified with the national cause. And in the Russian heartland, the results were quite remarkable. Not only was the maverick Boris Yeltsin elected for Moscow, despite the party leadership's efforts to scupper his chances, but in separate districts of Moscow the very independent-minded historians and political critics, Roy Medvedev and Yuri Afanasyev, topped the polls in competitive elections.

In some of the public organisations, it was only after a struggle that the views of the membership as a whole – rather than those simply of a narrow leadership group – were able to hold sway, but in one of the most interesting such cases, the Academy of Sciences eventually elected twenty deputies who included some of the most radical and distinguished reformers in the country. It is particularly notable that within their ranks was Academician Andrei Sakharov who for almost twenty years had been regarded as a dissident and who spent the first half of the 1980s in exile from Moscow. Other deputies from the Academy included proponents of far-reaching economic reform, such as Nikolai Shmelev, Gennady Lisichkin and Nikolai Petrakov as well as the space scientist, Roald Sagdeyev, and the jurist, Alexander Yakovlev (not to be confused with his Politbureau namesake) who has advocated the introduction of trial by jury in the Soviet Union.

Taken as a whole, the change of political climate and the concrete achievements in the field of political reform are as much as could reasonably be expected within the space of four years – and more than even most reformers dared to hope for within such a short space of time, if they recall objectively their expectations in March 1985. So far as the economy is concerned, however, reformers had hoped for more success by now, and until they get it, the continuing dominance of the reform tendency cannot be taken for granted. But if in 1987 those in the West who could not accept the very idea of any change for the better taking place in the Soviet Union were still saying that Gorbachev and the reformers wished to change nothing of any consequence, they are now increasingly conceding the seriousness of the reformist intent but insisting that those efforts are bound to fail. They were wrong before and they could be wrong again.

Notes

[1]For a fuller-up-to-date account of these developments, see my article, 'Political Change in the Soviet Union', in *World Policy Journal* vol VI, No 3, New York, Summer 1989.

[2] *Pravda*, 15 July 1987, pp 1-2, at p 2.

[3] See Archie Brown, 'Ideology and Political Culture' in Seweryn Bialer (ed), *Politics, Society and Nationality Inside Gorbachev's Russia*, Westview Press 1989, pp 1-40.

[4] *Pravda*, 26 April 1989, p 1.

[5] *Izvestiya TsK KPSS*, vol 1, no 1, January 1989, pp 81-86, esp. p 86.

Fedor Burlatsky

The State After Stalin

Fedor Burlatsky wrote this article as part of the debate in the build-up to the 19th Conference of the Soviet Communist Party in June 1988.

What kind of socialism do people need? Such a question, I am sure, will sound seditious to some. But if we think about it, this is the nerve centre of today's discussion. The *Pravda* editorial 'Principles of *Perestroika*' (April 5) touches upon this very pointedly: 'How can we speedily revive the Leninist essence of socialism, uncover and rid it of deformations, free it of that which fettered society and prevented the development of socialism to its full potential?'[1]

Lenin made a significant statement after 'war communism': 'We are re-examining all our viewpoints concerning socialism.' Clearly, we now have to engage in a similar task. Firstly, in order to go back to Lenin and overcome Stalin's legacy; and secondly, to state the interests and expectations of our people who have been building socialism over the last 70-odd years. People's experience in the other 14 socialist countries must be taken into account; and a realistic evaluation of the state of competitiveness with the capitalist world in an era of technological revolution must be carried out. It is in these points that, I believe, the essence lies of the new thinking concerning contemporary socialism.

When stating what we see our task to be today, we need to mention the article 'I cannot abandon my principles' in *Sovyetskaya Rossiya* (March 3) which cannot be seen as a mere expression of dogmatism. Rather, and bearing in mind

First published in *Literaturnaya Gazeta*, April 1988, this translation first published in *Marxism Today*, July 1988 that it was published before the 19th party conference, it can be seen as intending to consolidate the power of conservative forces.

Glasnost and people's freedom to express a range of opinions are inevitably accompanied during the initial period by emotional extremes, destructive repercussions and uncivilised polemics. This is because people do not come from a different planet, but developed under the same difficult conditions underpinned by the cult of personality, the excitement and disillusion of the 60s, and specifically, during a period of stagnation dominated by the legacy of an authoritarian-patriarchal political culture. So what? In politics, as it has been known since ancient times, there aren't only either absolutely positive or absolutely negative manifestations. It is always necessary to make choices in order to come to a decision that will bring better results. And can there still be doubts after we compare two methods: to reveal the problems or to conceal them?

Serious politicians, as well as any other people who deal with this responsibility, understand that if the problem is concealed it is then pushed inside and given a chance to grow to such proportions that it will become impossible to tackle it. But to reveal a problem means to start resolving it. Or is it the case that in the past, during the cult of personality period, planes did not have accidents, trains did not crash, national conflicts did not erupt? Of course they did. But silence fell on all of them, as in a cemetery. And now the country cries over the years and decades of silence. Glasnost is the people's mirror which they don't fear because, as the saying goes: 'Don't blame the mirror if your face looks crooked ...' Yes, the appearance of the society has to change and the mirror won't be blamed for what we see in it.

Conservative forces want to take advantage even of the specific asymmetry which exists between glasnost and the few concrete economic results. But the responsibility for the slow speed at which these innovative reforms are moving lies in the hands of these conservative forces. They resort to all means available to them, whether directly or indirectly, to oppose the development of co-operatives, family, collective and brigade contracting, individual efforts, which would not be costly and yet would yield quick results.

But the article in *Sovyetskaya Rossiya* is useful in one sense. It defends Stalin and his legacy in a defiant and straightforward manner. It seems that for the concealed opponents of perestroika the expediency would lie in finding a more balanced position, so to speak, to enable them to fight on two fronts – against the extreme anti-stalinists and against the outspoken Stalinists. But this hasn't happened: thus demonstrating that there is no alternative to perestroika. Brezhnev's stagnant and weak policies do not suit anybody any longer. And this is significant.

It is not difficult to understand why the opponents of perestroika have now come out into the open. They realised that perestroika is entering into a stage that can become irreversible, as it will turn into people's flesh and blood as well as our social relations. They felt this and decided to put up a fight against it, aiming at finding a base in the most backward social forces.

According to the article in *Sovyetskaya Rossiya*, the main point of discussion is Stalin's place in the history of our country. But this is not at all correct. This question was the reason for the struggle 30 years ago, at the 20th party congress. In essence, a straight answer was given then and it was published in Khrushchev's 'secret' speech. More facts are now becoming available, thanks to work done by the politburo commission of the Soviet Communist Party as well as by different research bodies, and which can be found in print and in academic literature. It seems that only the most backward people, those on the periphery of political debate, have only just started to open that chapter of our history.

In fact the main question is now a very different one, which was not given an answer in the 60s. It concerns the system of government which came into being during Stalin's period. 'We understood', Gorbachev has said,

> that the party has to show courage and will, and that it has to free itself from certain existing ideas about socialism which constitute the base upon which conditions such as the cult of personality can exist. It has to rid itself of old ideas about how to build socialism, but mainly, to free itself from everything which deformed socialism and constrained people's creative abilities.

Why and how has a distortion of socialism occurred in our

country? To understand this we have to start by
acknowledging that since the 1920s there have been not just
two conceptions of socialism but two models, which in
practice competed against each other.

The first one, 'war communism' (1919–21), was strengthened thanks to the cruel civil war, but also to a degree it
reflected quasi-anarchist views about the possibility of a
'leap' into communism. In practice it was expressed through
orders, force, depriving peasants of their produce and the
elimination of the normal exchange of the products of
labour.

The second model – the new economic policy or NEP
(1921–28) – was based on a commodity economy where
different types of enterprise competed with each other –
state, co-operative, private – and where peasants freely sold
their produce on the market and bought manufactured
goods in return. An important aspect of NEP was
democracy – inside the party, the trade unions and the
soviets as well as at local grassroots level – along with
struggle between different trends in the world of culture and
artistic creation.

Without entering into a debate about why and how the
NEP was overturned I want to point out that this struggle
has prevailed all through our history.

The point is that at the very inception of the movement for
emancipation there was a struggle between two tendencies:
the social democratic one (in our case, Bolshevism) and war
communism. The latter was very strong in our party. It
commanded a firm base in a backward consciousness and in
the authoritarian-patriarchal political culture of the masses.
Almost half of the members in the politburo of the party
central committee were at one time or another close to 'left
communism' ideas. In this context, special attention needs
to be given to the work of Bukharin and other leaders who
understood the meaning of Lenin's political legacy, and the
new approach to socialism. For behind this lies the question
of whether there was an alternative to Stalin's methods of
industrialisation, collectivisation and the consolidation of
the industrial and military might of our country.

It is easy to see how Stalin gradually – at first almost
imperceptibly – changed the emphasis and shifted the centre

of gravity in respect of Lenin's views. And the direction of these shifts becomes clear. Slowly but steadily it revealed itself – the apotheosis of violence. Revolution, collectivisation of the economy, management of culture and all other changes were for him equated with brutal force. This put a gloomy and grim seal on both the methods for the implementation of collectivisation and industrialisation and on the forms of struggle inside the party: in sum, on the entire process of socialist change. It is not at all surprising that during the early 30s Stalin, in his search for a parallel to his historical period, turned to such figures as Ivan the Terrible and Peter the Great. He wanted to draw from their experiences in order to justify the inevitability of the most gruesome methods resorted to in the name of the country's power.

But the analogy with Peter the Great in fact recoils on Stalin. Peter was not a socialist. He had to pull the country out of backwardness at any price. He was not at all concerned for the well-being and cultural development of the people. In other words, Stalin's understanding of the role of the state in our country was mostly drawn from Russia's past experience and not from marxist sources.

At the 18th party congress in 1939, in the wake of the horrendous bloodletting that took place inside the party and among the people, Stalin announced that the time for the immediate transition to communism had arrived. What exactly he meant by communism was not clearly explained: is it when everybody is well and fully fed or when there is equality for everybody – of what? – of needs, abilities, skills, opportunities? It was left unclear. But it was clearly stated that a whole generation had to be sacrificed to the future 'leap' into communism.

Stalin also simplified the problem of building socialism by equating the process of broad socialisation with state ownership.

At first enterprises were placed under state management, and then, in essence, the state took over the collective farms. This not only affected the economic sphere, but gradually spread over the entire spiritual life, the leadership of the cultural institutions, publishing houses, theatres, schools, universities, hospital and sports. If we also take into account the fact that state officials were not elected but appointed, it then becomes very easy to see the origin of bureaucratic management.

During the post-Stalin period our theory and practice on the whole contained two of Stalin's erroneous ideas: the belief in the absolute power of coercion and the temptation of a 'leap' into communism. Khrushchev was the last leader to still hope that 'the present generation will live under communism'. But until now there has remained unshaken the main Stalinist idea of 'state socialism'. I put this concept in inverted commas because of my recognition of its ambiguity, conditionality and inadequacy.

But it was Stalin and not Lenin, who put forward the theory that the state plays the decisive role in the building of socialism. Not the working class and its party, but the state, even if on its own it does not produce anything – no bread, no footwear, no engines or books. These are made by people and the state only regulates – for better or for worse – the process of production.

Though Brezhnev was the first of our leaders not to promise the building of communism in the life of one generation, he still believed in the omnipotence of the state, in its organisational possibilities. When he came to lead the country, he thought that the time had come to overcome Khrushchev's schemes, go back to the previous forms and everything would work just fine. He believed, more than any of our leaders, in the illusion of the 'organised response'. It is not a coincidence that during his rule the number of ministries and departments reached over a 100. And so far the belief in organisational solutions to real problems, which affects almost exclusively the upper echelons of the leadership, has not been abandoned. The task is, then, to create new conditions for each producer – be they workers, peasants or the intelligentsia – to stimulate their interest in the results of their labour, and to allow their own initiative.

The article in *Sovyetskaya Rossiya* aims at giving the impression that socialism is going through a deep crisis. But if we have to talk about the elements of this crisis, this relates not to present-day socialism in its entirety, but to one of its forms – 'state socialism'. This form is approaching its end, it is showing its lack of effectiveness in an era of technological revolution. In extreme situations, especially during the civil and the great patriotic wars, centralism and state coercion played their part in the mobilisation of resources and the concentration of forces. But now such a form hampers any move forward in economic, social and cultural life. And it has to change in a slow and well thought-out manner, into a new form which could be called 'public, self-managing socialism'.

This does not mean that the centralised form of state rule will disappear. A total 'dismantling' of the state – the idea is absurd, especially bearing in mind the ever more complex internal and international economic, communication and humanitarian links. But it means that a significant part of its power, functions and prerogatives will have to be ceded to civil society and its institutions. First of all to the labour collectives – at the factories, plants, co-operatives, institutes, unions, as well as to social organisations and other already new and existing institutions, which I am sure will start arising as perestroika moves ahead. Society has to take on much of what the state used to do, as it is choking under the burden of extremely complex tasks and bureaucracy.

Incidentally, capitalism went through different stages of its reconstruction: classical in the 19th century, state and then its state-monopoly form in the early 20th century, and now, due to the technological revolution, it is taking a new form which so far has not shown a clear shape. It still changes its skin and that is why, I am sure, it is taking such a long time to rot. And it has also to be said that in capitalist countries there are not that many dogmatic people, or real idiots who would like to go back to the times of Louis Napoleon, Bismarck or Hitler and Mussolini. This is one of the few advantages of the ideology of pragmatism which looks everywhere in order to get the best results.

Gorbachev stated that socialism is a society of people with initiative. State socialism deserves a severe sentence for its stifling of the initiative of working people. At first individual initiative was sacrificed for the sake of the collective, then it was the turn of collective initiative to be sacrificed for the sake of the ruling apparatus. Finally the initiative of those working in that apparatus was also stifled. This apparatus, built in a pyramid-like fashion, concentrated the initiative

more and more in the top echelons of power, and finally in
the hands of an individual leader and chief. So whatever
question the worker wanted to tackle they would have to
confront a myriad of hurdles built on orders, rules,
instructions and traditions. That is what made any initiative
into an offence. Who hasn't experienced this personally?

What is then the qualitatively new model of a more
effective, democratic and humanistic socialism? So far we
can only see some of its contours.

It is the planned commodity economy based on individual
cost-accounting by enterprises and a range of types of social
ownership – to raise the form of state property to a form of
public ownership by the whole people, and to develop
co-operatives, and family and individual enterprises. It is
economic competitiveness. It is the development of civil
society and the accountability of the state to the society. It is
the sharing of power, authority and functions between the
party, the state and the social organisations. It is the end of
uncivilised forms of bureaucracy and the structuring of state
management on the principle of 'the less, the better'. It is
the development of self-management, the formation of
social opinion as a factor in the political process, the
development of elections, the rotation of cadres, profession-
alism. It is the coexistence of a range of cultural trends, the
fostering of a socialist personality, the transcending of a
culture based on an authoritarian-patriarchal legacy and the
creation of a socialist one. All these changes aim at
strengthening socialism and public power.

It is quite clear that the development of modern socialism
will take a long time – not just a decade. But if not disturbed,
it will be decades of inspired effort by our people for the
benefit of our homeland and of each Soviet person.

So this is what the manifesto by the opponents of
perestroika has to confront. It has to face this powerful
social movement. The preparations for the forthcoming 19th
party conference raise the hope of a transition to resolute
action by all the forces of perestroika. Drawing from Lenin
we can say that a defensive position is the death of
revolution. Only a persistent offensive and the constant
strengthening of the position of the revolutionary reformers,
the unrelenting move towards a change in economic

principles and the democratisation of society will permit the isolation of the opponents of renewal and bring on to the side of reform all those who still are wavering. And only then will the present stage of perestroika become the starting point for its transition to a new, and higher stage.

Translated by Anna de Skalon

Notes

[1] This article was written in support of perestroika, as a response to an earlier article, 'I cannot abandon my principles', published on March 3 in *Sovyetskaya Rossiya*; the *Sovyetskaya Rossiya* article was widely interpreted as a manifesto for conservative opponents of perestroika.

Martin Walker

What is to be Done?

This article was written just before the 19th party conference in the summer of 1988.

Officially, of course, Lenin's historic question has already been answered. The strategic line for the Soviet future was agreed at the 27th party congress back in 1986. There is a consensus which runs through politburo, central committee, party and public alike, that the Soviet system needs a drastic economic reform, which in turn will require (and will impose) fundamental cultural and political transformations.

But that is like saying we all believe in Santa Claus. The Soviet elite now finds itself faced with the urgent and divisive questions of how much reform, how fast, in what fields, and what price in social disruption and internal unrest will finally have to be paid. If the strategic question of the need for reform is broadly settled, the arguments on the tactics of bringing those reforms to life have become dangerously bitter.

And so they should. These are the most fundamental questions the Soviet system has confronted since Stalin effectively abolished Soviet political thought 50 years ago. In the last few weeks, Gorbachev and his supporters have tossed every ideological preconception into the new arena of public debate. The role of the party in the modern state. The role of the state under *perestroika*. The nature and even the legitimacy of the Soviet leadership. Can democracy co-exist with Soviet socialism? The relative status of the elected soviets and the party machine. The need for the party to abandon its pretensions to economic management. All are being discussed in the press. Nothing is sacred. One of the

First published in *Marxism Today*, June 1988

party academics preparing drafts for Gorbachev's big speech to open the party conference on June 28 found himself, to his increasingly delighted surprise, writing that it was significant that Lenin had never been general secretary of the party, that the office from which the nation is ruled should not depend on the way Stalin hijacked the party bureaucracy 60 years ago.

Then he opened that day's copy of *Sovyetskaya Kultura* and found letters suggesting that Gorbachev's continued leadership was too important to be left to the party, and even to its central committee. Its 307 members, the party's ruling body, should have the power only to propose that he be fired, with the final decision to be taken by a national referendum.

That same issue carried an unprecedented debate between two Soviet intellectuals on Gorbachev's chances of survival:

> Activists prepared to fight for perestroika are still the minority of our people. This being so, the danger remains of a repetition of what happened in 1964 (when Khrushchev fell – *MW*) and in the following years. History shows that unsuccessful reforms are invariably followed by a counter-revolution.

To read the Soviet press these days is to fall off your chair with shock, to rub your eyes in disbelief three or four times before breakfast. Just to take examples that fell to hand this week:

> Our right-wing extremists are trying to get hold of our Afghan war veterans, making some kind of militant stormtroopers out of them. It is very useful to have in your ranks a well-disciplined group, believers in the cult of strength, converts to your ideology. There are symptoms of that happening now.

Alexander Prokhanov, the best known of the Afghan war correspondents, in *Literaturnaya Rossiya*.

> Under our centralised economic planning system, shortages of goods are not the exception, but the rule, an inevitable component of the system.

Nikolai Shmelev in *Znamya* magazine.

> There is no other country in the world where history has been deliberately falsified to such a degree as here in the Soviet

Union. First they falsified Soviet history, then they had to
falsify pre-revolutionary history ... Stalin's regime did not need
history as a science. He needed it as a servant of propaganda,
and to justify the crimes the regime committed. We learned to
give names to things that never belonged to them.
Totalitarianism was called democracy. Things not yet begun
were called completed.

Professor Yuri Afanasyev's speech at a party conference,
cited in *Sovyetskaya-Kultura*.

The view was deliberately inculcated that the general secretary
is always right, that his statements are the final word of truth,
and therefore there is no need to study or look into public
affairs. It is necessary only to quote the leader correctly'.

Letter on front page of *Pravda* by V Selivanov, a leading
official of Ministry of Aviation.

There are two main reasons for this flood of analytical,
rather than sensationalist glasnost. The first is that this has
always been the way the Soviet Union holds its debates in
the weeks leading up to a major political event like the 19th
party conference. In the days before the 27th party
conference in February 1986, copies of *Pravda* even sold out
before dawn one morning when the party daily printed a
famous letter complaining about the privileged and 'secret'
shops and hospitals available to the party elite. 'The queues
would soon disappear if the high-ups had to come and join us
standing in line', the letter asserted.

The second reason is that the chattering classes of the
Soviet Union are desperately worried that Gorbachev is
faltering, and his perestroika is dribbling into the sand. For
some of them, indeed for any one of the people quoted
above, this could have unpleasant consequences. But most
of them are patriotic or selfless enough to think of the wider
picture. As Gorbachev keeps arguing, there is no real
alternative to perestroika. It is probably the Soviet Union's
last chance. Without economic transformation, the country
will be unable to sustain its great power status. Were it not
for the financial damage the Reagan presidency has inflicted
on the US through monstrous defence spending and budget

deficits, you might almost say that the arms race is over because the West has won. There is an uncomfortable kernel of truth in that American jibe about the USSR being 'Upper Volta with rockets'. If it can no longer afford the rockets ...

Gorbachev himself put it bluntly at the last plenum of the central committee in February:

> The economic development rates were declining in our country and hit a critical point. But even those rates, as has become clear now, were achieved largely on an unhealthy basis, due to temporary factors. I refer to the trade in oil on the world market at the then prevailing high prices, and the totally unjustified intensification of the sales of alcoholic beverages. If we look at the economic indicators of growth separately from these factors, we will see that over four 5-year plan periods we knew no increase in the absolute growth of the national income, and it even began declining in the early 80s. That is the real picture, comrades.

And that is a devastating admission. For the past 20 years, if you exclude the state's revenues from vodka and exporting oil, there has been no growth in the Soviet economy.

There is one positive side to all this. Economic disaster created the consensus within the Soviet elite on which the reform movement has been based. The problem is that the consensus has little to do with Gorbachev. He inherited it from Yuri Andropov, the former KGB chief who succeeded Leonid Brezhnev as Soviet leader in 1982. Andropov's time in the KGB had left him little opportunity to build a personal following, a private political mafia within the central committee apparat. Instead, in order to build a faction that could balance and even challenge the famous Dnepropetrovsk Mafia of Brezhnev and Konstantin Chernenko, Andropov had to stage a series of take-overs of the political clans of others.

In the group of convinced reformers which coalesced around Andropov at the beginning of the 1980s, there were members of the old Frol Kozlov faction that dated back to Khrushchev's day. There were economic liberalisers like Dr Aganbegyan who had backed Kosygin. There were the Siberian technocrats who had gathered around Kirilenko.

There were Andropov's own security men, like the current foreign minister Eduard Shevardnadze, who rose from the police to run Georgia, and the career KGB man Geidar Aliev of Azerbaijan. Andropov's faction was an Adullam's Cave of Mr Cleans and anti-Brezhnevites, of puritans and economic liberalisers, of cops and technocrats.

Andropov seemed to have the knack of holding them all together, partly because he did not have long enough in power for the fault lines in his coalition to show, before the kidney disease took hold that was to kill him. There were, however, two other factors. First, the threat of the Brezhnev group helped keep Andropov's clan together. The Brezhnev mafia proved still influential enough to put Chernenko into the Kremlin after Andropov's death. Second, Andropov, as the former KGB chief, had a single buzzword around which his economic reformers could unite – discipline.

Within days of coming to power, the police were scouring the Moscow bars and public baths, checking documents. Heaven help the man without a good explanation for taking time off. KGB fraud squads swooped on the more openly corrupt sections of Soviet life, like the police force and the foreign currency stores and the traditionally Muslim republics of the deep south.

And the first few months of Mikhail Gorbachev's administration looked and felt remarkably similar. Once again, the catch-word was discipline. There was the clamp-down on vodka sales, the policy pushed through by Egor Ligachev, the teetotal puritan from Siberia. His credentials as a genuine reformer are not in doubt. Ligachev's first real achievement for the party was to help build Akademgorodok, the Siberian science city outside Novosibirsk, which became a kind of reformist think-tank in exile in the Brezhnev period. And every year, reform economists like Dr Abel Aganbegyan would visit Ligachev's fief of Tomsk for informal seminars, and out of friendship.

But for all Gorbachev's and Ligachev's intellectual commitment to economic reform, the stress in that first year of power was on discipline. There was the new law against unearned incomes, and the new anti-corruption drives. 30,000 clean young men from the Komsomol and the army were drafted into the police force in that first summer of

Gorbachev, to replace the waves of dismissals. Warned that his trial was imminent, former Interior Minister General Shchelokov shot himself in his dacha outside the city. And the net was tightening around his deputy, Brezhnev's son-in-law, Yuri Churbanov – who is now in Lefortovo prison. Suddenly, Muscovites stopped carrying a 3-ruble note inside their driving licence. The assumption was that you could no longer automatically bribe your way out of a traffic ticket.

But discipline was not enough. The more the new administration studied the figures, the more they realised they had inherited a disaster. It is not clear whether Gorbachev changed his mind in that first year in office, or whether (as I believe) he had been a closet democrat during all those years climbing the sclerotic party *apparat* of the Brezhnev era. But increasingly, Gorbachev began to argue that economic reform would depend on political reform, or as he told the central committee in January 1987:

'A house can only be put into order by someone who feels that he owns the place. Our perestroika is possible only through and with democracy. It is only this way that it becomes possible to give scope to socialism's most powerful creative force – free labour and free thought in a free country'.

It was at this point that the old Andropov coalition began to break down. It became clear that Gorbachev's vision of perestroika went far beyond a pure economic reform, which would transform the efficiency of Soviet shops and farms and factories, but leave everything else unchanged.

Over the past year, the basic distinction between Gorbachev's reformers and Ligachev's conservatives has become cruelly plain. The Ligachevs want economic reform in order that the Soviet system and the party can remain pretty much the same. The Gorbachevs know that unless Soviet society and politics are themselves transformed, there is little chance of economic revival.

But how many Gorbachevs are there? Of the full, or voting members of the politburo, I count three committed supporters; propaganda chief Alexander Yakovlev, foreign minister Eduard Shevardnadze, and agriculture chief Viktor Nikonov.

Prime Minister Nikolai Ryzhkov, leader of the Russian Federation Vitaly Vorotnikov, and the former Belorussian party chief Nikolai Slyunkov form a technocratic group somewhere in the middle, but tending for the moment to the Gorbachev side. Bear in mind, as these men will, that they are the obvious scapegoats if the economy stubbornly refuses to respond.

Some observers include among the technocrats the Leningrader Lev Zaikov, former head of the military-industrial complex and now Boris Yeltsin's replacement as Moscow party chief. But by temperament he seems to be gravitating more to the elder statesman, the three survivors of the Brezhnev era, former foreign minister Andrei Gromyko, Ukraine party chief Vladimir Shcherbitsky, and the old heavy industry man Mikhail Solomentsev.

Ligachev can count on the support of the KGB chief Viktor Chebrikov, and probably reckons he has the sympathies, if not the votes, of the remnants of the old guard. This means that the two groups in the middle, the technocrats and the old guard, hold the balance between the radicals and the conservatives. And so far, these central groups have gone along, sometimes reluctantly, with Gorbachev.

It would be unwise to focus too strongly on the personalities, or the head-counting. Nobody wants matters brought to a head, to a decisive vote that could lead to appeals to the 307 members of the central committee, as Nikita Khrushchev appealed to them in 1957 when he fell victim to a putsch in the politburo. Nobody wants politics to become that open, nor the confrontation to become that deadly. And the Soviet system has an enormous inbuilt capacity for compromise, thanks partly to a country so big that many provinces can exercise something close to autonomy over their affairs.

But the argument has now got out of hand, for three reasons. The first is that for Ligachev and Chebrikov, for many senior army officers and for a large swathe of public opinion across the country, perestroika has already gone too far. Witness the Crimean Tartars demonstrating in Red Square, the nationalist rumblings and demos in the Baltic states, the mass protests in Armenia, the pogrom in

Sumgait, and the recent unrest in Poland's Nova Huta steelworks and the Gdansk shipyards.

Second, we are probably closer now to a genuine proletarian revolution than at any time since 1917. At least in these early stages of perestroika, there is an unfortunate whiff of Thatcherism about the way the reforms are working on the ground. Most people in the country are on a similar level of basic pay, between 120 and 200 rubles a month. Teachers, doctors, and office-workers have to be content with that. Factory workers, blue collar or managerial, have traditionally had a bonus of 30-60 per cent for fulfilling the production plan. But in most factories, the man from Gospriomka, Gorbachev's tough new state quality control board, is rejecting products as they come off the assembly line. So the plan is not fulfilled. So the workers are not getting their bonuses.

At the same time, inflation is taking off, and goods are in ever shorter supply. We even have meat shortages these days in the hard currency shops. Sugar is rationed. Butter is rare. Prices in the new co-op stores are two and three times higher than the subsidised prices in state shops. The new co-op restaurants have few ordinary customers when the average bill is over R10 a head. And Gorbachev has given warning that the state subsidies of R60,000m a year on meat and milk and bread are going to be phased out.

He promises that this will be done in such a way that the Soviet poor, which means the pensioners, the unskilled, the single parents, students and the disabled, will not suffer. He says also that the 16m industrial redundancies that automation and modernisation will bring by the year 2000 will not lead to unemployment. We shall see. Personally, I believe him. But then I am not a worried Soviet worker facing a three hour queue for a bottle of vodka with a hole in my pay packet, an empty larder, and the prospect of being redeployed to another and possibly worse job.

In the meantime, the folk doing well out of Gorbachev's perestroika are the chattering classes, never terribly popular with the lads on the shopfloor. All this glasnost is exciting and fulfilling for the intellectuals, the media, the film-makers and novelists and playwrights and rock musicians. The current phase of economic reform is also very popular with black marketeers and get-rich-quick co-op entrepreneurs. We have our Soviet yuppies swopping video cassettes and IBM-compatible computer programmes on the street outside the Shabolovskaya electronics store.

Third, we now have the battlefield looming very close ahead. On June 28, the 19th party conference, the first such gathering for 47 years, opens in Moscow. Gorbachev wants to use this event to democratise the internal structure of the party, to get rid of 20 per cent of the central committee and ensure himself a majority on that body, and to make his perestroika irreversible.

He is being urged by his radical supporters in the Moscow think-tanks to deliver a speech that will stun the world. They have presented him with drafts which call for the removal of the party from economic administration, the retreat of the party to the pursuit of ideology, and the settings of grand strategic targets for society. Their drafts echo Lenin's call of 'All Power To The Soviets', on the grounds that as publicly elected bodies, the Soviets should properly outweigh the various committees of the party machine.

Gorbachev is a wily enough politician to know how far he can go, and whether that speech would be over the top. But it is already plain that he is determined to break the grip of the entrenched bureaucracy on the party machine by reintroducing Khrushchev's old rule 25. This was the rule which said party officials could hold a post for a maximum of two terms, the rule that broke the lifetime job guarantee of the party careerist. It was also the rule which in 1964 led Mikhail Suslov and Leonid Brezhnev to conspire together to topple Khrushchev in the name of the party cadres.

Can Gorbachev do it? That depends on the votes of the 5,000 delegates to the party conference. And the current battle is over the procedure under which those delegates are chosen. The fear is that if selected by the traditional method of 'election' at plenums of regional party committees, the old party machine politicians will be able to ensure a pretty conservative list of delegates. This is what Ligachev is fighting for within the central committee *apparat*.

Gorbachev and his allies are fighting for a radical list of delegates, by secret ballot and open election within the primary organisations of the party if they can, but by straightforward selection and nomination if they must. As I write, the battle goes on, and it will probably need to be resolved at a central committee plenum meeting late in May, just before the arrival of President Reagan for his Moscow summit.

Gorbachev is now in the tricky position of depending on the American President. His foreign policy successes and his image in the West are among Gorbachev's chief political assets. The central committee is unlikely to risk a Gorbachev resignation, far less a dismissal, on the very eve of the Reagan summit. Gorbachev is gambling that he can get his way.

The political suspense in Moscow these days is tangible. The city is full of rumour and gossip. There are outlandish claims that Ligachev tried to convene an emergency plenum on April 8, when Gorbachev was in Tashkent, but that the Minister of Defence General Yazov refused to release the aircraft. There is gossip of Gorbachev forcing a vote of confidence on the politburo, and Ligachev and the KGB's Chebrikov abstaining. I do not know the truth. But I do know that tales like these, repeated to me by respectable Soviet journalists, by East European diplomats and Soviet think-tank staffers, testify to a bizarre and dangerous mood of political crisis.

This is not a simple matter of the good guys versus the bad guys. Ligachev and the conservatives are genuine reformers, and they are not Stalinists. They honestly fear that Gorbachev is in danger of throwing the baby out with the bathwater, that the party machine has to remain intact and loyal if the country is to be hauled out of the economic mess. The problem is that by the cruel laws of politics, they may be forced to depend on the support of the real nasties, the Russian nationalists, the anti-semites, the Stalinists, the militarists – which is what happened to Brezhnev after 1964.

And against that, Gorbachev is offering the insubstantial and still inchoate vision of a Soviet democracy, while the economy still staggers and limps towards reform, and the workers and their families look at the prices and queues and pitifully-stocked shops and worry what will become of them.

I guess, or perhaps I hope, that there will be some kind of compromise reached before or during the party conference, that Gorbachev will tone down or perhaps delay his reforms, and the conservatives will remember the combination of hope and disgust that brought them into the original Andropov coalition in the first place.

The compromise after all, has held together during the three years of perestroika. Gorbachev is not the kind of man who thinks democracy can be imposed by totalitarian methods. And Gorbachev would not have been elected general secretary, and would not have got so far with his perestroika, without Ligachev's open support. By their very presence on the politburo, Ligachev and Chebrikov have legitimised the reforms so far, and have reassured the worried party barons in the regions. But that phase is over. The Andropov coalition is now at breaking point.

But as we gnaw at our fingernails and wonder whether Gorbachev can once again pull through, it is worth raising a cheer for the phenomenal progress he has made so far. It is not just the glasnost and the cultural thaw and the INF treaty and the retreat from the Afghan war. It is the mood of suspense, of nobody knowing what comes next, of people taking up public positions and holding real debates. The unpredictable has returned to public life. Real politics have revived in the Soviet Union. The effect is exhilarating.

Interview with Roy Medvedev

Moscow in Motion

Roy Medvedev was interviewed by Monty Johnstone in Moscow immediately after the Soviet Communist Party Conference in the summer of 1988.

What are your general impressions of the recent conference of the Communist Party of the Soviet Union? Do you think it represents a significant advance in Soviet society?
The conference certainly represents a significant step forward in what we can call the democratisation of our society. I think it was an interesting and important event. People followed everything that was published and shown on tv. Even though it wasn't shown in full on tv, those parts that were shown aroused great public interest. Ten or 20 years ago when party congresses took place people didn't bother to read the papers because they weren't interested in Brezhnev's reports and the speeches that followed them. This conference was different because there was real debate and controversy. The delegates' speeches were not all alike. Gorbachev's report was perhaps rather too long by Western standards though not by Soviet ones. He combined two reports in one. The conference revealed the different tendencies, points of view, trends and even factions in the party, although officially the existence of factions is denied.

Do you think they are sufficiently firmly formed to be called factions? Aren't they something rather looser?
They aren't of course factions as understood in common political vocabulary as something organised. They are political trends to be understood in a looser sense.

First published in *Marxism Today*, August 1988

**Do you think that these trends exist throughout the party or
only in any stable form in the leading bodies of the party?**
They are characteristic of the whole party at all levels. The
party is not responding uniformly to the process of
perestroika.

**Do you think that if one had to identify these tendencies or
trends with leading figures in them one could talk very
approximately of a Gorbachev trend, a Ligachev trend and a
Yeltsin trend?**
It is possible to speak of a Gorbachev trend and a Ligachev
trend but not of a Yeltsin one. Yeltsin doesn't represent any
particular trend now, though there are other people who
think the same way. But Yeltsin has shown that he is broken
as a politician and cannot lead any trend within the party.
There are very many different trends in the party but the
party conference represented three main tendencies. The
first one, if one wants to start with that, is the tendency of
the opponents of perestroika in general. They are people
who want to return to the past, people who are being thrown
out of social and political life by perestroika. There are very
many such opponents and they still have a huge influence on
the running of the country.

But they didn't express themselves openly at the conference.
They mostly kept silent. They were criticised at the
conference. I have in mind the top levels of the bureaucracy
– people whose activities symbolise stagnation and what we
refer to as the braking mechanism holding back perestroika.
They didn't reply to the criticisms. For example, the ministry
of finance was strongly criticised but the minister didn't
come into the discussion to explain his position to the
conference. The huge and extremely rich ministry of land
improvement and water conservancy also came under sharp
attack for doing a great deal of ecological damage to our
country, but that minister didn't say anything either.
    Although these people were represented at the confer-
ence they realised that if they spoke they would get a hostile
reception. Only one person from this tendency spoke at the
conference, and that was the writer Bondarev. He
represents that part of our literature which perestroika is

casting aside. People of a different level are now coming to the fore in our literature and in our culture generally. People like Bondarev and Markov were for 20 years the bosses of our literature. They formed a mafia which decided the policy of the publishing houses and determined who should and should not be published and what royalties they should receive. Now it is not these people who decide – they have lost power.

And the second trend?
The second trend is represented by people who are supporters of perestroika. They understand that our economy is in a critical state, as Gorbachev said. They want to restructure it but without glasnost, without press freedom, with democratisation but by old administrative methods and orders. They are people who come out against corruption and abuses and oppose the mafias. They are mostly honest Communists and Soviet people, but they have got used to the old ways of working. The most striking representative of this group is (party secretary) Ligachev, who himself organised the Nina Andreeva article.[1] But they won't achieve their objectives without using the levers of glasnost against the bureaucracy. Without a free press it is simply impossible to formulate a point of view.

This group embraces the majority of regional and city party secretaries, the majority of the apparatus. It was quite active at the conference where its attacks on the press were applauded. It is characterised by both innovation and conservatism, impulses to move forward and dogmatism. It combines both old stereotypes and new thinking. It occupies an intermediate position. It is the strongest group in our party but it does not dominate it because complete power in the party is not in its hands. In his conference speech Ligachev warned Gorbachev, and it was an unmistakeable warning: 'Without us you wouldn't have become general secretary of the party' – that is, without the votes in March 1985 of politbureau members Chebrikov, Gromyko and Solomentsev whom he named.

And the third tendency is Gorbachev's?
Yes, the third group can be called that of Gorbachev himself. This group strives for perestroika, for the reform of all

economic and political structures. I myself don't understand some of their reforms, for instance some of Gorbachev's conference proposals for changes in the political system. But at all events they are people looking for a way out for our country, for means to take it further forward. They want to give socialism a new face and make it more attractive. Their intention is to do so through democracy, glasnost and a relatively free press and through involving the whole people in the process of perestroika. And, you see, there is a conservatism to be overcome not only in the apparatus but also among ordinary people, among workers and peasants who need to be got to work better.

And Yeltsin?
Yeltsin represents vanguardism in the party. He doesn't represent a trend as such but only some individuals. He wants to push perestroika ahead more quickly, more energetically, but this is not realistic. Yeltsin is saying much that Gorbachev was saying at the beginning, but there is very little support for this now. Yeltsin's political collapse is due to not appreciating that if we start going too fast it will lead to the end of perestroika rather than its success.

In our conditions it is possible for perestroika to move forward fairly quickly but not by leaps. Politics is the art of the possible. Yeltsin always spoke of a time span of one to two years. When he went to a factory when he was Moscow secretary he used to say: 'I give you two years to fulfil perestroika here.' That sort of thing is not possible. And now we see that neither he nor any of the enterprises that he visited have achieved this goal.

How far do you think that in the interests of pursuing the politics of the possible Gorbachev has made certain compromises with Ligachev and his tendency, and how far would you see those compromises reflected in the conference decisions?
Gorbachev has always proceeded by means of compromises. There is no other road open to him. The leader of the party and the country emerges from the same stratum that represents the old elite and the previous epoch. Gorbachev was elected from among the Brezhnev elite. He is always

making compromises with Ligachev's group and even with the conservatives. But there are compromises and compromises: those which take things backwards and those which move them forward. Gorbachev has shown himself to be a master of compromises, and each of his compromises enables the country to take one step forward and sometimes more than one. The party conference represented another step forward.

Do you think that this compromise between Gorbachev and his trend, on the one hand, and Ligachev and his trend, on the other, is a long-term compromise which will last a number of years or a short-term one liable to break asunder in the foreseeable future?
Each compromise has its time span. I don't think the compromise between Gorbachev's and Ligachev's groups will last very long. But it is not excluded that it could last for two to three years. The main idea of this compromise is to defeat the other main group – the most conservative group of bureaucrats represented by the officials of the ministries and those departments of the central committee which deal directly with different branches of industry and agriculture like energy, construction and transport. They feed off that power and are often corrupted by it. We need to do away with these surplus parts of our apparatus. Ligachev and the regional party secretaries also understand that these are bureaucratic obstacles that need to be removed as they are hampering perestroika. It is quite unnatural that one-third of the adult population should be employed in performing administrative functions of one kind or another. It would be quite reasonable if the service sector were bigger than the industrial sector for instance, as this is a feature of industrially developed countries. But it is unacceptable that a third of the workforce should be employed in administration. In general the compromise is directed against the most reactionary bureaucratic section of the party and against the opponents of perestroika as a whole.

Do you think that in two to three years' time it might come to a showdown between the supporters of Gorbachev and those of Ligachev? Is there a danger that, as in 1964 against

Khrushchev, an alliance of different trends might be formed to get rid of Gorbachev? In this case an alliance of the Ligachev forces with the directly anti-perestroika trend taking advantage perhaps of the fact that the economic situation had not adequately improved?

Of course there are various possibilities. For instance, one of them is that anti-perestroika forces might consolidate themselves, win support from some of the forces now supporting perestroika and overthrow Gorbachev. But this is not the most likely possibility. It is more likely that the anti-perestroika forces will be thrown out as they don't respond to national interests. And there is a hope that people now associated with Ligachev's group will learn how to speak to people and how to work in a democratic way. Some of the secretaries of district party committees may learn some lessons which will enable them to work for perestroika in the proper way.

So, broadly speaking, Roy Aleksandrovich, you are optimistic about the prospects for perestroika?

I was optimistic when we were living through the worst times here. I said then that perestroika and changes of a completely new kind were possible in our country. It may then have seemed the least likely prospect, but there are many examples of what seems least likely coming about because basic national interests assert themselves. In that respect I am an optimist. I understand that Gorbachev personally might suffer a defeat. He might make a serious mistake, take a false step. A monetary reform or price reform that was unpopular might be used by demagogues against him. The country might again, for a short time, enter a period of stagnation but that would once again come to an end.

The election of Chernenko was an absolutely false step for the country. In the interests of a small group, time was lost which was precious for the country. For the sake of a fatally-ill man a whole year in the life of the country was sacrificed. Such a situation can no longer be accepted. Time is very important for the Soviet Union because such a great power cannot allow itself to fall behind countries like Brazil or South Korea. Ultimately the national interests of the country will carry the day.

What do you think of the reforms in the political system put forward in Gorbachev's report? How do you assess the proposal that in future first secretaries of party committees should be nominated as chairpersons of soviets?

Frankly speaking, I don't understand these proposals and I don't know how this system will work. It seems to me to be a reform in the spirit of Khrushchev when he thought that something needed doing but did not test it experimentally. I cannot imagine how it will work on the level of a city, a district, a region or a republic. I think the new system is simply impossible locally and will immediately show its ineffectiveness. Gorbachev argued for a separation between party and state organs with each getting on with its own work – the party concentrating on political strategy and policy and the soviets on economic and other matters. But combining the posts of party secretary and Soviet chairperson in one person will have just the opposite effect. It hasn't been thought through. It's just going to lead to confusion and the mixing up of functions. Moreover it's not realistic. I know in practice how people in these posts operate: even now they are overloaded with work.

Academician Abalkin in his conference speech expressed disagreement with this proposal of Gorbachev's. If I had been a delegate at the party conference I would also have voted against it. But many voted to accept it because they believe in Gorbachev.

What do you think of Gorbachev's constitutional proposals for setting up a Congress of People's Deputies meeting once a year and electing a president with considerable powers and a smaller two-chamber Supreme Soviet whose members would be full-time parliamentarians?

Maybe it is easier to imagine how the changes at the top will work because every leader of our party eventually became leader of the state. Stalin became prime minister. Khrushchev became prime minister. Brezhnev became president of the Supreme Soviet. Now Gorbachev will get the post of president with increased powers.

But I don't know how the new-style Supreme Soviet in Moscow will operate when even the present type of Supreme Soviet hasn't learnt to work democratically.[2] What will the

400-450 delegates do who will be full-time deputies of the
Supreme Soviet? Great Britain, for instance, has very old
parliamentary traditions which go back hundreds of years.
But here unfortunately people are not accustomed to such
things and they will have to learn a lot. It will take time.

**Next spring elections to the new Congress of People's
Deputies are due to take place. Do you believe they will allow
for contests between candidates with different platforms and
in a certain sense maybe even proto-parties? For instance, if
you have green candidates standing on a distinctive green
programme might this not represent something approximat-
ing to a green party and therefore a move towards the *de facto*
ending of the one-party system?**
There is no doubt that such 'informal' movements and
organisations will try to stand their own candidates in the
elections to the Congress of People's Deputies. They openly
say this. But I don't know whether they will be allowed to or
not. Under our system an electoral commission decides
which organisations have and do not have the right to put up
candidates. Such unofficial organisations have not been
allowed to stand candidates in the past. They were
considered undesirable elements in our society, and many of
their representatives were arrested or put under permanent
pressure by the authorities. Also, judging by the conference
resolutions, there are different sorts of informal groups –
useful and harmful. It is impossible yet to say what will
happen in the future and who will be allowed to stand.

**Some commentators have described the national question in
the Soviet Union as a 'time bomb' under the whole process of
democratisation. Do you foresee such a danger? Do you think
that solutions will be found to such problems as Nagorno-
Karabakh and the demands of the Baltic republics for greater
political and economic autonomy?**
I must say that I don't see the activisation of national
movements as a 'time bomb' against democratisation. It is a
factor for the development of perestroika. But there are
different types of national movement. In Azerbaijan, for
instance, they go on the streets with slogans like, 'Make
Ligachev general secretary', because they liked his speech

which said that Nagorno-Karabakh would always remain a part of Azerbaijan. In Armenia they demonstrate with different slogans.

'Lenin, Party, Gorbachev!'
Yes, as against 'Stalin, Brezhnev, Ligachev!' in Azerbaijan, I suppose! The situation in the Baltic republics is quite different. In Estonia, for instance, they've set up a very strong People's Front For Perestroika. They see in perestroika the guarantee for their national traditions and for democratisation.

Yes, there's obviously a big difference between these positive developments in the Baltic republics and the conflict that has developed between Armenia and Azerbaijan over Nagorno-Karabakh accompanied by prolonged strikes and inter-ethnic violence. If no solution can be found to this problem in the period ahead, is it not going to produce a backlash against perestroika with some people saying, as our driver was saying today, that in Stalin's times such disorders didn't happen?
It's not true that such things didn't happen in Stalin's time, though of course they were cruelly suppressed. What the driver said was the idealisation of Stalin's time. There were strikes, uprisings, urban disorders and mutinies in the armed forces. Because of the absence of glasnost people didn't know about them. Certainly it is essential to solve the problem of Nagorno-Karabakh one way or another. There are no problems for which no solution can be found. Maybe though some people will still remain dissatisfied, but that's only to be expected. However, it can take a long time to solve that problem, which is after all 1,600 years old.

But Gorbachev hasn't got that much time to solve it!
I can give no prognosis here. It is a regional problem. In the same way that the problem of Northern Ireland hasn't killed British democracy ...

But there are dangers ...
... the problem of Nagorno-Karabakh won't destroy perestroika. It is a problem that concerns only a small part of the Soviet population and it will be solved either by

compromise or by force. But in the end it will be solved.

Notes

[1] A long article which appeared in one of the central committee's papers, *Sovyetskaya Rossiya*, in March under the name of Nina Andreeva, a Leningrad chemistry lecturer, challenging the whole course of democratisation and glasnost. It was strongly attacked by *Pravda*.

[2] The present practice is for those elected to the Supreme Soviet to combine working at their normal jobs with fulfilling their duties as deputies and attending the sessions of the Supreme Soviet which normally meet briefly twice a year.

3. Making Perestroika a Reality
Economy, Democracy and Civil Society

Julian Cooper

The Soviet Economy in Transition

The reform process now underway in the Soviet Union represents an attempt to break with the system of economic management that has operated unchanged in its essential features for almost sixty years. What is at issue is not simply a technical matter of changing planning and management procedures, but a radical break with a particular conception of the socialist economy, and socialism in general, which formed under Stalin and which came to be seen as the sole form of true Socialism. Just as Gramsci declared that the October Revolution of 1917 was a 'revolution against Karl Marx's *Capital*', so we can say that the process of *perestroika* is a revolution against Stalin's Socialism.[1] While economic reform is central to this revolutionary break, a broader perspective is essential if the necessity for reform is to be understood and its prospects of success correctly assessed.

The imperatives of reform

It was in February 1986 at the 27th Party Congress that Gorbachev first declared that the economic mechanism could no longer be improved by partial measures: 'A radical reform is needed'. Prior to the Congress the task had been posed of achieving an 'acceleration of social and economic development', leaving open the question of whether this could be achieved by improving the operation of the existing economic management system. It was not until January 1987 that political change was presented as an essential condition for successful reform of the economic system. By the summer of that year a package of reform measures had been adopted. There began what is now known as the 'transition period', the difficult and contradictory process of replacing the old economic mechanism by the new, with the intention

117

that the latter would be fully in place in the 1990s.

Just as it has taken time to arrive at an adequate strategy of reform, so appreciation of the depth of the economy's problems, and their systemic roots, has also evolved since April 1985 when Gorbachev first posed the need for change in Soviet society. Indeed, as the reform process unrolls and practical experience is accumulated, the problems to be tackled appear ever more formidable. Thus we have a dialectic of perception, policy and practice, which to date has worked in the direction of progressive radicalisation of the reform process.

Almost all Soviet economists agree that the traditional economic mechanism in place from the beginning of the 1930s has exhausted its potential. Many also now regard this system of economic management as an integral component of a particular model of socialism which has reached the limits of its development. Some go further, questioning whether this model, at least in its classic form under Stalin, merits the designation 'socialist' at all.[2] It is the recognition on the part of the political leadership and wide sections of society that a historic limit has been reached that constitutes the principal imperative of reform. This exhaustion of the Stalinist variant of socialism is largely a product of its own internal contradictions, and to that extent the imperative to reform is domestic and intra-systemic in character.

But what makes the present conjuncture so fateful for Soviet development is the simultaneous appearance of a second, related, but relatively independent, imperative for change of a no less ineluctable character. For all its limitations, the Soviet economic system through several decades of 'extensive' development has brought the country to a level of development such that it too faces the challenge of the new productive forces emerging throughout the world economy. An awareness of this additional imperative for reform is clearly present and, it could be argued, provides the real force behind Gorbachev's frequently repeated conviction that 'there is no alternative'.

It was the prominent reform-minded economist Gavrili Popov, now editor of the country's main journal of economic theory (*Voprosy Ekonomiki*), who first introduced the term 'Administrative System' to encapsulate the essence of the economic and political system that emerged under Stalin.[3] The main features of this system are state ownership of all the basic means of production, a highly centralised system of economic management based on administrative commands, a dominance of vertical, top-down, economic and political relations, and effective power resting in the hands of an all-powerful state-party bureaucracy, with the General Secretary at its apex. In the Administrative System the state is everything, civil society nothing. Individuals are not active subjects of economic and political life, but subservient performers of commands from above: in Stalin's unfortunate, but apt, term, the mass of citizens were 'little cogs' (*vintiki*). Distrustful of creativity and talent, the leadership ceased to provide proper rewards to those with skills and abilities, leading over time to a general levelling-down in society. The mass social psychology formed under this system was one of passivity, resignation and envy.

Some Soviet writers have characterised this form of society that formed under Stalin as 'barrack room' socialism.[4] Others have gone further, bluntly describing it as 'totalitarian'. Disregarding the terminology, what these characterisations have in common is an appreciation that the form of socialism which has evolved in the Soviet Union from the end of the 1920s has simultaneously depreciated the role of the individual, and elevated to an extraordinary degree the role of the intermeshing Party and state bureaucratic apparatuses.

The economic mechanism of the Administrative System secured, at great cost, the industrialisation of the country. This was extensive development. Growth was obtained by investment in new production facilities on an ever-expanding scale, drawing in all available labour, and exploiting rapaciously the country's initially rich material and energy resources. The highly centralised administrative resource allocation system proved an effective means of securing the state's priorities, above all the build-up of both military strength and basic industries considered vital to the country's survival and independence from the capitalist world. Driven by an inherent 'investment hunger', the system, focused on the maximisation of current output in accordance with the centre's priorities, has as its characteristic mode of operation the reproduction of shortage.[5] With consumption a relatively low priority and a subordinate position for the individual at all levels (apart from the upper reaches of the apparatus), the system is unable to promote initiative, rapid technological innovation, and the efficient use of resources.

Notwithstanding attempts to reform it, notably in 1965, the Administrative System has proved extraordinarily resilient. Its essential mode of operation has not changed since the time of Stalin, testifying to its strong inner coherence and logic. Yet the system lacks the capacity to adapt to changed circumstances brought about by its own 'success'. Extensive development has been carried to the point of resource exhaustion. All reserves having been absorbed, the rate of growth of the labour force has steadily declined. While other industrial countries have been cutting back their production of steel and other basic, traditional products, in the Soviet Union expansion continues unchecked, costs rising sharply as raw material and energy reserves are depleted. Unable to secure rapid technological innovation except in the very highest priority sectors, the rate of adoption of new products is often desperately inadequate.[6] Even in the late Brezhnev years, large new factories were still being built regardless of the resource position: it is hardly surprising that the return on capital invested has shown a persistent downward trend. This pattern of growth has involved a squandering of non-renewable resources and incalculable damage to the environment.

This formidable, but increasingly insecure, growth of industrial strength has not been matched by a corresponding enhancement of living standards and welfare. Most Soviet citizens have seen a substantial improvement in their levels of consumption during the post-war years, but in absolute terms standards lag appreciably behind those of other industrially advanced countries. Welfare services were developed to secure a basic standard of provision for all, but from then on they were not improved sufficiently to keep pace with new demands. During the Brezhnev years expenditure on education, health and welfare services was inadequate. Social problems accumulated, but were not properly acknowledged; indeed, information on them gradually disappeared from public view. Two indicators serve as graphic illustrations of the position reached: life expectancy and infant mortality. By 1985 male life expectancy had fallen to 64 years, 7 years lower than the US level and 11 years lower than that of Japan.[7] The growth of alcoholism played a major role, but this itself was an expression of the general deterioration of morale induced by systemic failure. Against international trends, infant mortality rose, reaching levels far higher than in other industrially developed countries. In 1980 there were 27.3 deaths by the age of one year per 1,000 births, with a range from 14.5 in Lithuania to an extraordinary 58.1 in Tadzhikistan, the least developed Soviet republic. The national rate was five times that of Japan and two to three times that of USA, Britain, West Germany and the GDR.[8] Further continuation of these trends would have had very grave consequences for Soviet society.

On the threshold of a new era?

The new stage of development associated with changes in the productive forces of modern societies has been less the focus of recent Soviet discussion than the failings of the old model of socialism. However it is undoubtably appreciated as a forceful imperative for reform. In the West variously termed the era of post-Fordism, 'New Times', post-industrial society, or the 'Third Wave', in the USSR it is discussed in terms of the Scientific and Technical Revolution (STR). Here there is a certain irony. It was Soviet theoreticians who first introduced the concept of the STR and attempted to understand the significance for socialism (and the fate of capitalism) of automation and other major technical changes of the post-war years.[9] In a sense this theoretical exegesis was premature: under Brezhnev there was a widening gulf between Soviet reality and the conclusions of the theory of the STR. Abstract theorising about the STR became discredited and now that the 'revolution' is beginning to make itself felt as a powerful force for change, Soviet theorists are less confident than in the past about their ability to comprehend it.

It is the new information technologies that symbolise the technical element of the revolution in the productive forces, which in the view of some Soviet writers will lead to the formation of a new technological mode of production. While the Soviet Union's performance in robotics and flexible manufacturing systems is reasonably respectable by international standards, the level of achievement in computer production and application is markedly inferior. Advanced communications being essential if the new technologies are to have an impact throughout society, the state of the telephone system provides an illuminating indicator. In 1985 the number of telephones per 100 population was 11 in the Soviet Union, compared with over 80 in the USA and almost 55 in Britain: the present Soviet figure was attained in the USA by the end of the 1930s!

As Soviet writers have stressed, the new technological systems require for their creation and effective operation workers of higher educational standards and skills than required for traditional mechanical production. In so far as it promotes changes in the social relations of production and of the wider society, it is this human dimension to the transformation of the productive forces which is seen as most important in the unfolding STR. As Vasilchuk has argued for capitalist society, it is these changes which put on the agenda demands for greater democracy in economic life and for improved opportunities for creativity and self-expression. But as Vasilchuk also argues, the transformations now taking place cannot be seen narrowly in terms of the production sphere. Changes in consumption patterns and the use of leisure also play an increasingly important part in shaping the human potential of production.[10] This latter point is of particular significance for the Soviet Union. While general cultural and educational standards are relatively high, there is backwardness in the sphere of consumption; this not only deprives citizens, especially women, of free time, but also limits the ways in which it can be used and must now be regarded as a serious impediment to the unfolding of the STR.

In recent years Soviet writers have paid much attention to the evolution in the West of new management practices and economic arrangements. They appreciate the growing importance of adaptability and flexibility, and write with ill-concealed envy of the Japanese 'just in time' approach to production, knowing that it is out of the question in present-day Soviet conditions. Central to these innovations is the influence of increasingly diverse customer demands; but the Soviet economic system is one in which the producer not the customer reigns supreme.

The changes in the productive forces now taking place are increasingly global in scope. It is doubtful whether any major nation could isolate itself from this global process even if it so wished, not the least because the new technologies are vital to military capability. The conclusion is inescapable: the system has to change fundamentally if the Soviet Union is to go beyond the threshold of the New Era. But this second reform imperative also means that any change will have to be more radical than in 1965, when economic reform was last attempted. It also imparts to current developments an additional element of open-endedness and uncertainty, discomforting to those habituated to the 'tramline socialism' of the Brezhnev years.

Reform, modernisation and reorientation

The process of economic transformation now underway has several dimensions. It involves not only reform of the economic mechanism, but also the implementation of policy measures intended to change the structure of the economy and the priorities of its development. The latter can be summarised as modernisation and reorientation.

Reconsideration of property relations represents an increasingly important component of the reform. There is a move away from the forms of state ownership that have predominated for the last fifty years. Individual and family economic activity is now permitted, provided no outside labour is employed, and co-operatives can be organised in many fields. By the end of 1988 individual and co-operative economic activity employed almost two million people, and were beginning to contribute on a worthwhile scale to the provision of goods and services to the population. Co-operatives have also been formed to promote new technology and innovation, while in some cases, by the decision of their workforces, loss-making state enterprises have been taken into co-operative ownership.

In the state sector itself new forms are emerging, often introduced first on the basis of local initiative without official sanction from above. These new arrangements are designed to enhance workforce involvement, and overcome the alienation now acknowledged as a real feature of Soviet life. In practice state ownership tends to mean that no-one is owner, with a corresponding absence of a sense of responsibility. Enterprise share ownership schemes are spreading, shareholders receiving annual dividends dependent on performance. So far there is no provision for trading shares and while some economists favour the creation of a capital market of the type now developing in Hungary, this has not yet gained official support. Leasing arrangements are also being adopted, first of all in agriculture, but also increasingly in industry. For an agreed leasing fee, workers hire the productive assets and are then free to dispose of them, usually fulfilling contracts with customers or ministries. Leasing arrangements within the framework of collective and state farms have generated some remarkable gains in productivity, and the policy of allowing fifty year leases could open the way to major changes in the Soviet countryside. Given the rapidity and spontaneity with which share and leasing schemes have been taken up, it is likely that further new forms will emerge in the future.

The basic measures for the reform of the economic mechanism were set out in a package of decrees adopted in 1987, in particular the Law on the State Enterprise. The scope for autonomous enterprise decision-making is to be enhanced substantially. Instead of the previous directive plans determined by the State Planning Committee (Gosplan) and the industrial ministries, the enterprise itself now draws up its own plan with accounts of advisory control figures supplied by Gosplan. Apart from compulsory state orders for military supplies and other priority goods, the enterprise is in principle free to fix its own output plan on the basis of customer orders. As the administrative allocation of material and equipment inputs is progressively replaced by wholesale trade, the enterprise will have much greater freedom to choose its own suppliers. However, the precise nature of wholesale trade is a matter of controversy, as the State Committee for Supply envisages a closely regulated system rather than genuine market relations.

Central to the reform is the principle of self-financing: every enterprise will have to pay its own way. In future, only major new construction projects will be funded from state resources; technical reconstruction and modernisation will have to be financed from retained earnings. Failure to operate on a profitable basis may now lead to merger with a viable enterprise, conversion into a co-operative or, in the last resort, closure. A certain share of enterprise profit is paid into the state budget, the proportion determined by a so-called normative, fixed in advance for a five-year period. Similar normatives determine the allocation of the remaining profit between the enterprise funds for bonuses, housing and welfare measures, and investment, research and development. Economists are agreed that these normatives should be standardised at least by sector of industry, if not for the whole economy. The growth of the fund available for wages is also determined by a normative relating it to the growth of value added. These conditions are designed to provide a stable framework for enterprise decision-making and an interest in profitable operation strong enough to promote entrepreneurial initiative and active measures for cost reduction and innovation. If they so choose, enterprises can adopt a second, different model of self-financing, according to which the wages fund is a residual of total income once all other financial commitments have been met. This is a riskier option, but offers the prospect of substantial earnings if the enterprise is successful. It is an option increasingly favoured by the more radical reform-minded economists. With pay and bonuses linked more closely to enterprise performance, differentiation of earnings is set to increase and many now favour the adoption of a system of progressive income tax.

Greater enterprise autonomy and an enhanced role for profit will not work in the interests of society as a whole, or promote the efficient use of resources, unless there is a major reform of the system of prices. The non-market fixing of prices is one of the central elements of the Administrative System. Prices are essentially arbitrary in nature, reflecting neither the true conditions of scarcity of resources, nor the requirements of market equilibrium. It is recognised that price fixing must be decentralised to a substantial degree for the success of the new system, but such a move faces conservative opposition, in part fuelled by the not unreasonable fear that in conditions of overall market disequilibrium it will lead to serious inflation. It is also recognised that the system of retail prices has many irrational features and that the substantial subsidies on such items as food, in particular meat, and on housing and public transport represent a major burden on the state budget and foster the wasteful use of resources. Thus the low rents provide a revenue so modest that it is insufficient to cover even the cost of necessary repairs. This is a major factor accounting for the neglected and run-down appearance of much of the Soviet housing stock.

There is little doubt that changing the price system represents the most difficult and politically sensitive aspect of the economic reform. If Soviet citizens begin to perceive a general improvement in living standards as a result of economic reform, they may be willing to accept selective price increases. But in the absence of such positive development, the authorities will be anxious to avoid a popular reaction of the kind that occurred when prices were raised in Poland. But at some point a price reform must be carried out if the new economic mechanism is to operate effectively.

The new economic mechanism is intended to promote more rapid technological innovation. It is envisaged that in pursuit of profits enterprises, working in co-operation with a revitalised research and development system, will seek to create and adopt new products and processes. However, it is recognised that such entrepreneurial behaviour will be limited in scope in the absence of competition between enterprises. Economists acknowledge that competition, previously considered alien to the socialist economy, will be difficult to promote in Soviet conditions because of the highly concentrated structure of industry and the dominance of the ministerial system. In these circumstances, opening up the economy to the world market provides a means of injecting competitive pressure into the system. Measures adopted include the granting of direct trading rights to individual enterprises, the establishment of joint ventures with foreign firms, and moves towards the convertibility of the ruble, the latter being an essential, but extremely difficult, precondition for effective participation in the world economy.

Integral to the reform is a policy of overcoming alienation by creating conditions for active involvement of Soviet citizens in economic and social life. Given the historical legacy of a top-down system with limited active participation from below, it is understood that perestroika cannot succeed unless popular energies are released. The Law on the State Enterprise provides for the formation of councils of the labour force, with some decision-making powers relating to the activities of the enterprise, and for the election and periodic re-election of directors and other managerial personnel. The electoral principle has also been extended to other fields, including research institutes and higher educational establishments. More developed forms of participation in management are appearing at enterprises adopting leasing arrangements and also in the co-operative sector. In the agricultural sector, long-term leasing arrangements, within or outside the framework of collective and state farms, are regarded as vital to improve incentives and to restore a sense of responsibility eroded by decades of over-centralisation and bureaucratised management.

Taking the reform as a whole, it amounts to a serious move away from the traditional economic mechanism. Decentralisation will be greatest in consumer-related sectors, where market and quasi-market relations will have a role; least in sectors judged to be of strategic significance to the economy and the country's defence. However, as many reform-minded economists argue, the measures adopted to date may not be sufficiently radical to overcome the economy's problems and meet the challenges of the new stage of development of the productive forces. In particular, market relations and competitive conditions will probably have to be developed further and action taken to transform more decisively the structure and mode of operation of the central state economic agencies. But as the implementation reveals the weaknesses of the new arrangements, opportunities for further changes are constantly arising: the Soviet Union is only at the beginning of what could be a protracted process of economic reform.

Decades of extensive development and priority for traditional branches of heavy industry have left their mark on the structure of the Soviet economy: by modern international standards it is seriously deformed and backward. The new, advanced technology industries are relatively underdeveloped, consumer-related activities, and especially services, have suffered substantial neglect, and within the hypertrophied heavy industrial sector there are many enterprises with antiquated technology. According to a recent estimate, at least half the country's productive base is 'hopelessly obsolete' or surplus to real requirements.[11] The most advanced sector of industry, developed beyond the reasonable security needs of the country, is the defence sector. Structural change is thus a high priority, essential for achieving the social and economic goals of perestroika, including participation in the world market on fully competitive terms. The latter is a vital consideration as rapid modernisation of the economy will be impossible without imports of technology from the West.

The modernisation and re-orientation of the economy is now underway. Investment is being reallocated away from building new enterprises in traditional sectors to the re-equipment of existing facilities and the development of new industries, in particular micro-electronics and information technologies. Consumer goods industries and the so-called non-productive sector are now receiving a greater share of investment. The INF treaty and the cut-back in the armed forces announced by Gorbachev in December 1988 will lead to a one-fifth reduction of weapons production. The defence industry is now being engaged to an increasing extent in the production of equipment for the food and consumer industries and also in the manufacture of a wide range of consumer goods. The new circumstances are making arms factory conversion a matter of practical concern.[12] However, the task of changing the structure of the Soviet economy is formidable, and will inevitably extend over several five-year plans.

The transition period and its problems

To decide on a policy of reform is one thing; to implement it successfully quite another.[13] Gorbachev and his colleagues find themselves victims of perversity: as the perestroika unfolds the problems it is intended to tackle appear to get progressively worse. For most Soviet citizens the situation early in 1989 is no better than during the Brezhnev 'stagnation'. Washing powder, soap, toothpaste, razor blades and refrigerators are just some of the goods that disappeared from the shops during 1988, while in many parts of the country meat is rationed. Prices are rising: money being the sole commodity in abundant supply. These are phenomena of the difficult transition period between the old and the new economic mechanism.

During the first year of the reform the new planning and self-financing arrangements were adopted in about 60 per cent of industry. With limited development of wholesale trade (covering less than 15 per cent of all material and equipment inputs), and in the absence of price reform, the partial introduction of the new mechanism led to a somewhat faster growth of labour productivity and improved delivery contract fulfilment, but no dramatic breakthrough was achieved. Enterprise autonomy did not develop as intended because Gosplan and the ministries raised the proportion of obligatory state orders to such a level that directive planning was in effect maintained. But most serious was the appearance of problems in the financial sphere: inflation fuelled by a substantial budget deficit.

The country is now paying the price for a long-term neglect of financial relations. At the core of the Administrative System was resource allocation in physical, non-monetary terms. The rift between the primary, natural economy and the secondary world of value relations was reinforced by an ideology sceptical of, and at times hostile to, the role of market and financial relations in the socialist planned economy. In the absence of appropriate financial institutions and practices, limited decentralisation and self-financing, together with the development of coopera-tives and leasing arrangements, have increased inflationary pressure and made possible its open expression in rising prices. According to the economist Oleg Bogomolov, in 1988 prices of consumer goods and services rose by 5 to 7 per cent. It was victory for glasnost that the budget deficit was acknowledged for the first time, although much remains obscure. Officially put at 35 billion rubles for the projected 1989 budget, Soviet economists claim a real deficit of approximately 100 billion, rubles, equivalent to 11 per cent of gross national product, and in relative terms at least three times more serious than the US budget deficit. The serious disequilibrium in the economy represents a threat to the economic reform, as it makes difficult any decentralisation of price setting or the transition to wholesale trade in means of production.

Measures to restore equilibrium include reduced state budget outlays on investment, defence and administration, and more rapid elimination of subsidies to loss-making enterprises. Some actions run counter to the spirit of the reform, including restrictions on the scope of co-operative activity and new administrative price controls. At the same time, fearful of the economic and political consequences, the authorities have decided to postpone indefinitely the retail price reform. The political commitment to economic reform remains strong, but as the reform was extended to the whole of industry from the beginning of 1989, many economists were arguing that action must be taken to tackle what is widely perceived as the principal obstacle to successful reform: the entrenched power of the central state economic agencies, above all the industrial ministries.

The Soviet economic system is one totally dominated by the state. Most economic activity is undertaken within organisations subordinate to extremely powerful, hierarchically organised state ministries. Their dominance is such that they effectively dictate the pattern of economic development; the other central bodies, in particular Gosplan, but even the Council of Ministers, have only limited control over their activities. To some extent the political and legal reforms now underway will improve the situation, in so far as they offer the possibility of bringing the state economic agencies under more democratic political control within a framework of law. But this may not be sufficient to solve the problem of the ministries. Some economists argue that the only solution is the abolition of the ministries, bringing about what is now often termed a 'destatisation' of economic life. Breaking the organic link between the enterprises and the state, it is maintained, will permit genuine decentralisation of decision making, the social interest being secured through the use of indirect means of regulation rather than direct administrative control. Enterprises, in a variety of ownership forms, would then become independent, self-managed, financially self-reliant entities. Radicalisation of the reform in this direction may prove to be the only way in which the Soviet economy can adapt to meet the challenges of the New Era.

Conclusion

The bold attempt to reshape the entire economic system of the Soviet Union and to install a new model of socialism appropriate to contemporary conditions is an endeavour of historic importance. Its significance extends far beyond the borders of the USSR and Eastern Europe. The issues now being raised are in many respects similar to the concerns of the left in Western Europe and elsewhere, above all the fundamental question: what form of socialism, *if any*, is appropriate to the conditions of the world at the end of the 20th century? In the Soviet Union, the heroic, 'utopian' stage of development is nearing its end and it is not surprising that there are socialists in both East and West who are finding the process unsettling, or even alarming. Central to utopian conceptions has been the conviction that a complex, modern economy can be run successfully 'in the interests of society' according to a predetermined, detailed central plan with a minimum resort to market relations. But a simple truth can be derived from almost sixty years practice: it has been tried and it has failed. The imperatives of reform are ineluctable. Gorbachev is correct: there is no alternative.

To say that there is no choice but economic reform, is not to say that reform will succeed. The obstacles to change are formidable. The problems cannot be reduced to the malevolent obstruction of bureaucrats; they are more deep-rooted and systemic in character. Sixty years of the

Administrative System have produced entrenched structures of institutions and interests, with corresponding modes of thought, making change in the direction of decentralisation, democratisation and initiative from below extremely difficult. These structures have overlaid pre-existing, but enduring, forms and mentalities which, also, are frequently not favourable to reform, and exhibit significant national variation. A by no means trivial example of the latter is the historically formed social psychology of the Russian heartlands. In the words of two Soviet economists.

> a significant part of the population of the economically leading regions of the country, where there predominated less than a century ago patriarchal structures and an orthodox culture orientating the individual to the saving of souls through various forms of social philanthropy and charity, censuring any form of social struggle and competition, regards economic entre-preneurship just as before with distrust and hostility.[14]

In view of the unpropitious initial conditions and the diversity of social interests for and against genuine economic reform, one must expect difficulties, conflict, and possible reverses during what could be a protracted process of reform extending into the next century. But the central fact remains: a vigorous dynamic of internal renewal has emerged from the complacent immobility of 'developed socialism', and it is this which gives grounds for optimism that the process of reform will lead to the creation of a just, democratic and humane society truly appropriate to modern times.

Notes

[1] See A Gramsci, *Selections from Political Writings (1910-1920)*, Lawrence and Wishart, London 1977, pp 34-7. Gramsci was attacking dogmatic interpretations of Marx's work, which held that 'events should follow a predetermined course'. The action of the Bolsheviks, he argued, 'bears witness that the canons of historical materialism are not as rigid as might have been and has been thought'.
[2] Perhaps the most outspoken in this respect has been the historian Yuri Afanasyev: 'I do not consider the society we have created socialist, even of a "deformed" kind. These "deformations" refer to its very living

foundations, political system, production relations and absolutely everything else', *Pravda*, 26 July 1988.

[3] Notably in his review of the novel by A Bek, *Novoe naznachenie* (The New Appointment) in the popular science journal *Nauka i Zhizn* (Science and Life), 1987, no 4. See V Andrle, 'Beyond the Administrative System', *Detente*, No 12, 1988.

[4] Barrack room communism was Marx's term for the egalitarian society advocated by the early German utopian socialist Wilhelm Weitling. See Marx and Engels, *Collected Works*, Volume 6, Lawrence and Wishart, London 1976, p 598.

[5] The work of the Hungarian economist Janos Kornai provides an insightful analysis of the operation of the unreformed Soviet-type economy. 'Investment hunger' is his term. J Kornai, *Economics of Shortage*, North-Holland, Amsterdam 1980.

[6] Some output figures for 1985 illustrate this point: steel, USSR 155 million tonnes, USA 81; cement, USSR 131 m.t., USA 77; plastics, USSR 4.1 m.t., USA 22; personal computers, USSR 9,000 units, USA 4,024,000; video recorders, USSR 7,000 units, USA 12 million.

[7] *Agitator*, 1988, no 18, p 34. Female life expectancy in the same year was 74, more respectable by international standards.

[8] *Vestnik Statistiki*, 1989, no 1, p 54. There has been some improvement since 1980: in 1987 the rate was 25.4 (12.3 in Lithuania and 48.9 in Tadzhikistan).

[9] The term was first used by Bulganin at the July 1955 plenum of the Party Central Committee. For reviews of the STR debate see the author's 'The scientific and technical revolution in Soviet theory' in F R Fleron (ed), *Technology and Communist Culture*, Praeger, New York 1977, and 'The Scientific and Technical Revolution in the USSR', *Co-existence*, Vol 18, no 2, October 1981, pp 175-192.

[10] Y A Vasilchuk, *Nauchno-tekhnicheskaya, revolyutsiya i rabochii klass pri kapitalizme*, Moscow, Nauka 1980.

[11] D Lvov and S Glazev, 'Trudnosti khozyaistvennoi reformy', *Sotsialisticheskii Trud*, 1989, no 2, p 7.

[12] See *Detente*, no 14, 1989, for a discussion of the conversion issue.

[13] This section draws on the author's article in *Rinascita*, no 9, March 1989.

[14] D Lvov and S Glazev, *op cit*, p 12.

Stephen White

All Power to the Soviets?

'Radical reform' of the Soviet economic system has so far proved an elusive goal. Radical reform of the Soviet political system, however, has been advancing at an accelerating pace since the accession of the new General Secretary, and with especial urgency since the plenary meeting of the CPSU Central Committee in January 1987. Addressing that meeting, Gorbachev made clear that economic reform was conceivable only in association with a far-reaching 'democratisation' of the political system. Parasitic and consumerist attitudes, he noted, had been growing; party leaders had placed themselves beyond the reach of criticism; and some had become openly corrupt. Whole republics, regions and institutions had been affected. All of this, in Gorbachev's view, argued the need for a 'profound democratisation' of Soviet society, designed to ensure that ordinary people once again felt themselves to be in control of their own destinies. The further democratisation of Soviet society thus became the party's 'most urgent task'.

Gorbachev elaborated upon the reasons for these changes in subsequent speeches. Democratisation, he told the Soviet trade union congress in February 1987, was a 'guarantee against the repetition of past errors, and consequently a guarantee that the restructuring process is irreversible'. There was no choice – it was 'either democracy or social inertia and conservatism'. The June 1987 Central Committee plenum agreed with his proposal that a party conference – the first for nearly 50 years – should be called in the summer of 1988 to consider further democratising measures. In his address on the 70th anniversary of the revolution the following November, Gorbachev returned to the theme. Democratisation, he told his audience, was 'at the core of restructuring' and upon it depended the fate of

134

perestroika and of socialism as a whole. The changes already agreed represented the 'biggest step in developing socialist democracy since the October revolution'; further change would concentrate particularly upon the Soviets, which must 'completely live up to their name as sovereign and decision-making bodies'.

The fullest statement of the General Secretary's conception of democratisation, at the time of writing this article, was his address to the 19th Party Conference in June and July 1988. Gorbachev called for 'radical reform' of the Soviet political system, not just 'democratisation', and he regarded it as 'crucial' to the solution of all the other problems that faced Soviet society. The political system established by the October revolution, he told the Conference, had undergone 'serious deformations' leading to the development of 'command-administrative' rather than democratic systems of management. The role of the bureaucratic apparatus had 'increased out of all proportion' – there were, for instance, more than 100 central ministries and 800 in the republics – and this top-heavy structure was beginning to 'dictate its will' in political and economic matters. Many millions of working people, elected to state and non-state bodies, had been 'removed from real participation in handling state and public affairs'. Public life had become unduly governmentalised, and ordinary working people had become 'alienated' from public ownership and management. It was this 'ossified system of government' which was now the main obstacle to perestroika.

The Conference, after an extended debate remarkable for its plain speaking and lack of unanimity, duly adopted a series of resolutions calling for the further democratisation of Soviet society and reform of the political system. These proposals were carried further at Central Committee meetings in July and October, and contributed directly to a series of constitutional reforms in the late autumn. These established an entirely new electoral law and provided for changes in the constitution designed to strengthen the rule of law and democratic procedures more generally. A new structure of government was agreed, to come into being in the spring of 1989. New principles of political life were instituted, including a choice of candidate at elections and a full-time working parliament. A new constitutional review commission was established, as a step towards what Gorbachev called a 'socialist system of checks and balances'. And these were just the first stage in a whole programme of legislation which would later extend to the republics, local government, the press and trade unions. What, first of all, is the nature of these changes? And what significance do they have?

Reforming the political system

The political reforms that have now been agreed include, in the first place, an entirely new electoral law, approved on 1 December 1988. The faults of the existing system were apparent not just to outside observers but also, and apparently increasingly, to Soviet citizens themselves. Most obviously, perhaps, there was no choice of candidate, still less of party or programme. At the last national elections, in March 1984, not even this degree of choice obtained as one of the nominated candidates died just before the poll, leaving the remaining 1499 candidates to fight it out for the 1500 seats available.[1] Not all the candidates were party members, but they faced the electorate as a single slate of 'Communists and non-party people' and there was not the slightest differentiation among them in terms of programme or priorities. This, it was pointed out at the time, was more of a referendum on the regime than an election in the normal sense of the term.

Another very obvious fault was the way in which the deputies were nominated – only a small number of party-controlled organisations enjoyed this right – and the 'crude modelling' of the list of candidates so that it conformed to certain centrally-specified guidelines. This 'modelling' could be alarmingly precise. One local official, for instance, told *Izvestiya* what his 'programme' was in this respect: he was to ensure that 4.6 per cent of the successful candidates were enterprise directors, 1.1 per cent were to be employed in culture and the arts, and 45.9 per cent were to be returned for the first time. In another instance, reported by an emigré source, a notorious prostitute had to be returned as she was the only person in the constituency who satisfied the relevant criteria: female, aged between 35 and 40, unmarried, and a factory worker.[2] Apart from this, too few deputies lived or worked in the area they were supposed to represent, and the actual vote was a highly formalistic exercise in which electors had to do no more than drop their ballot paper, unmarked and even unread, into the ballot box to record a vote in favour of the single list of candidates.

Procedures of this kind inspired little confidence, even among those who had no wish to oppose party policy. As V Timofeev, a war and labour veteran, told *Izvestiya* in early 1987, existing arrangements hardly encouraged the discriminating exercise of one's political rights:

> You pull a pencil out of your pocket – everyone can guess your intentions. Young Pioneers or poll attendants are standing by the polling booth. If you go into the booth, it's clear you voted against the candidate. Those who don't want to vote go straight to the ballot box. It's the same at plant trade union elections and party election conferences. You can't even go off into a corner by yourself before a curious eye is peering over your shoulder.

Over-zealous local officials in some localities were occasionally reported to have gone so far as to remove the pencil that was supposed to be placed in the voting booth so that voters could, if they wished, cross out the name of the single candidate, and the level of turnout – over 99 per cent – suggested that many people must have voted on behalf of others, even allowing for official absentees and other factors.

There had been expressions of dissatisfaction with these arrangements for some time and Gorbachev, in his speech to the 27th Party Congress in February 1986, promised that the 'necessary correctives' would be made. A limited experiment took place in the local elections in June 1987, by which more candidates were nominated than seats available in about 1 per cent of all constituencies, and the same principles were applied in by-elections in January 1988 (to the USSR Supreme Soviet) and in October 1988 (to republican Supreme Soviets). The new electoral law, published in draft in *Pravda* on 23 October and adopted in final form on 1 December 1988, made these practices universal. The right to nominate has been extended to electors' meetings of 500 or more; and an unlimited number of candidates may be nominated. Deputies cannot hold governmental posts at the same time as they exercise their representative duties, and they are required to present 'programmes' to the electorate and have the right to appoint up to ten campaign staff. Electors, for their part, will have to cast an 'active' vote and make some positive indication of their preference on the ballot paper if it is to be considered valid. The new law was to apply to the next national elections, in the spring of 1989; the Central Committee, at its meeting on 28 November 1988, promised that those elections would be 'unlike all those that had preceded them'.

The process of political reform has also extended to the Soviet state. The central objective here is 'All power to the Soviets', and more generally a shift of political authority from party to state institutions. The Soviets, it has been argued, served as the basis of a system of genuinely socialist democracy during the revolutionary years, but very soon afterwards fell prey to bureaucratisation and over-detailed regulation by party committees. One problem was the often honorific character of membership of the Soviets. In the Supreme Soviet elected in 1984, one writer calculated, up to 39 per cent of the deputies were represented by virtue of the public position they occupied. They were balanced by large numbers of manual workers, leaving very few deputies to represent the white collar professions. Would it be so bad, the writer asked, if there were fewer milkmaids and party secretaries in the new Supreme Soviet, but rather more popular and articulate economists, historians, actors and writers?[3]

Another contribution to the discussion came from three prominent jurists, Barabashev, Sheremet and Vasilev, writing in the leading legal journal *Sovetskoe Gosudarstvo i Pravo*. Surveys, they noted, had found low levels of satisfaction with the work of the Soviets, and even deputies themselves appeared to be unsure of their own usefulness. There had been encouraging signs recently, such as the criticism and amendment of legislation that had taken place in the Supreme Soviet, 'probably for the first time in its history', in the summer of 1987. But deputies were allowed access to legislation only in its final stages, and the brevity of Supreme Soviet sessions (just two or three days at a time) was such that even the annual plan and budget could hardly be seriously discussed. Nor had the Supreme Soviet ever exercised its constitutional right to hear a report by the Soviet government, the USSR Council of Ministers. (The last such report, according to a writer in *Pravda*, was in 1935.)[4] The situation at lower levels was much the same, with local Soviets limiting themselves very largely to the formal approval of decisions taken beforehand by their executives.[5]

There was very general agreement among contributors to the discussion, which extended through 1987 and 1988, that the Soviets should become (as Barabashev, Sheremet and Vasilev put it) 'genuine centres of elaboration and adoption of all major state decisions in the field of legislation and administration'. This meant, for instance, that deputies should be chosen for their professional qualities rather than their social origins, and that they should be able to devote much more time to their representative duties. A more radical view, put by the jurist Boris Kurashvili in the party theoretical journal *Kommunist* in May 1988, was that nothing less than 'Soviet parliamentarianism', modelled in part on Western liberal democracies but also on the forms of government that had existed in the USSR itself in the 1920s, was likely to be adequate. Kurashvili also favoured a 'separation of powers', involving a constitutional court with the power to strike down decisions of the Council of Ministers, a system of smaller, full-time Soviets staffed by salaried politicians, and the greatest possible access for the media and members of the public to their proceedings.

A number of these proposals found favour in Gorbachev's speech to the 19th Party Conference a month later, and have again found reflection in the package of constitutional amendments that was approved by the Supreme Soviet on 1 December 1988, after some weeks of public discussion. These have established a Committee of Constitutional Supervision (not quite a court) to monitor the legality of government actions. Judges are to be elected by higher-level

Soviets and are to hold office for ten years at a time rather than five in order to strengthen their independence and contribute to the development of a 'socialist law-based state'. Local Soviets, similarly, are to be elected for five-year terms rather than for two and a half years at a time; their officers are to be elected by secret ballot from a plurality of candidates, and are to hold office for two five-year terms at the most. Local Soviets, in their work, are now required to 'take account of public opinion'; they must submit the most important issues of national or local significance to public discussion, and they must 'systematically' inform the public about the decisions they have taken.

The centrepiece of the new changes, however, was undoubtedly the formation of an entirely new representative body, the Congress of People's Deputies, which was based in turn upon the Congresses of Soviets that had exercised governmental authority in the 1920s. The Congress of People's Deputies was to be elected by the population at large in three different ways. Ordinary constituencies, as before, would return 750 members; national-territorial areas such as the union republics would continue to return a total of 750 members; and they would be joined by a wholly new group of deputies, again 750 in number, who would be elected by a wide range of social organisations, including the Communist Party, the trade unions, and women's councils. (Precise norms were to be established in the election law rather than in the Constitution.) The Congress of People's Deputies, which was to meet annually from 1989 onwards, would in turn elect from its membership a much smaller Supreme Soviet of 542 members, which was to meet for two three or four-month terms every year. The Congress was also to elect to an entirely new post, the Chairmanship of the USSR Supreme Soviet, which (it was understood) would normally be combined with the post of party leader.

The Communist Party has itself undergone a process of political reform, the substance of which was agreed at the 19th Party Conference in mid-1988. The central thrust of these changes was, as *Kommunist* put it in an editorial in January 1988, that there should be a kind of 'division of labour' in which the party would stand aside from direct management of the economy and exercise a much more general co-ordinating role. The discussion that preceded the conference saw very widespread support for changes of this kind. There were calls, for instance, for party officials to spend more time working with ordinary people and less time in their offices, and for all party bodies from the Politburo downwards to present annual reports.[6] It was argued that there should be party conferences every other year, as in Lenin's time, and that the existing membership, recruited to a large extent during the Brezhnevite years of stagnation, should be reaccredited and if possible reduced. There was also a good deal of concern about the way the party's own finances were handled, with calls for elected bodies at all levels to present proper income and expenditure accounts. They knew more about the finances of Ronald Reagan and the British Royal Family, as one speaker at the Conference complained, than about the income and expenditure of their own party.

Perhaps the most widely supported proposals, however, were that there should be a choice of candidate at all elections to party office, and that positions of this kind should be held for a limited period. Under the existing system of recommendations from above, wrote one contributor to the discussion, party posts were filled not by election but by appointment, and often for life. Instead of this there should be a 'periodic renewal of elected and nonelected cadres', with maximum periods of tenure. Other correspondents suggested that two or three continuous terms of office should be the limit, and some called for the restoration of the compulsory turnover rules that had existed under Khrushchev. Selection must also be by secret ballot from among a larger number of candidates than places available. There might even be age limits, such as 65 for Politburo and Secretariat members. And there should be changes in the party's own bureaucracy: it should be smaller, and should less obviously duplicate the ministerial structure.

There was a related discussion of party recruitment policy. Greater attention, it was urged, should be paid to the purely political qualities of new members, and less notice should be taken of their social origins. Party officials were given 'percentages' by their superiors which they had to fulfil at all costs, and this often led them to press workers into the ranks provided they were reasonably sober and had a respectable work record. It was much harder, given this approach, for professionals to join the party, and party branches became dominated by manual workers and pensioners, not by those who were advancing scientific-technical progress or the other priorities of *perestroika*. The position of pensioners in particular provoked a lively discussion. Some thought they should be excluded altogether, but others took a quite different view ('a Communist doesn't retire'), and argued that the older generation was not a 'ballast' but a pool of experience and tradition. It should, however, be made easier for those who wished to do so to withdraw voluntarily from the party, for example if their health was poor, and this might be accomplished by a periodic process of re-registration.

Several more sensitive issues were raised in the discussion, including the operation of the party-controlled *nomenklatura* appointments system. The current 'closed' system, which too often protected the incompetent and corrupt from the consequences of their actions, came in for repeated criticism. Why, for instance, should the politically well-placed have more comfortable flats, special shops, special hospitals and even (a labour veteran from Krasnodar complained) special cemeteries? There was a strong case, others argued, for separating party membership entirely from the tenure of leading positions, in order to avoid membership becoming no more than a 'meal ticket' or a source of privileges. It was also suggested that the 'party maximum' on earnings of Lenin's time should be revived, and that a Committee on Party Ethics along the lines of those that had existed in the 1920s might be established.

Most of these themes found a place in Gorbachev's speech to the Party Conference on 28 June 1988. Democratic centralism within the party, he complained, had become bureaucratic centralism. The rank and file had lost control over the leaderships that spoke in their name; and an atmosphere of comradeship had been replaced by one of commands and subordination. The conference agreed that the party's whole existing membership should be reaccredited, so that the unworthy and inactive should be removed from its ranks. A less 'bureaucratic' approach to membership was to be adopted, with more emphasis being placed upon the personal qualities of new recruits rather upon than their social background. Central Committee members, it was agreed, must also be involved in a more regular way in the work of the leadership, and this has now been provided for with the formation of six new commissions covering party affairs, ideology, the economy, agriculture, international affairs and law reform. These, it appears, will guide the work of the central party bureaucracy, which has itself been reduced in size and in some of functions it performs.[7]

Party officials, moreover, like their state counterparts, are to be elected by secret ballot from a choice of candidates, and they are to hold office for no more than two five-year terms in a row. There was some discussion on this point at the Party Conference. The well-known actor Mikhail Ulyanov, for instance, argued strongly against 'changing horses in midstream'. In the end, however, it was agreed that there should be no exceptions, not even for Gorbachev. As Georgii Arbatov, director of the USA and Canada Institute of the Academy of Sciences, pointed out, if such a rule had been in operation in earlier years Stalin would have had to retire in 1934 (actually 1932), and Brezhnev would have had to step down in 1974, long before he became decrepit. Rules of this kind will however come into operation without retrospective effect, allowing Gorbachev (if re-elected) to hold the party leadership for a further ten years after the next Congress in 1991.

Political reform and models of socialism

Even those who espouse the cause of political reform accept that, even under the most favourable circumstances, its full implementation will be a matter of many years or even decades. A full legislative machinery had still, by early 1989, to be put in place: legislation on local government and the courts was still pending, and so too was legislation on voluntary societies and the press. Both are essential if an autonomous citizen-based politics is to be developed, but both could be framed in a manner more likely to constrain than to facilitate the *de facto* freedom of expression which had been achieved over the preceding years. Even if a set of broadly liberal measures was adopted, reformers still acknowledged that the development of a Soviet-style socialist pluralism would require many years of experiment and habituation. The development of a rule of law in capitalist countries, a *Pravda*/Institute of State and Law symposium pointed out, had been 'shaped over the centuries'; a 'socialist law-based state' would hardly be easier to establish.[8] Among the most important of the attributes it was necessary to develop was a willingness to listen to one's opponents and where necessary compromise with them: Burlatsky was one of the first to point to the need in this connection to 'learn democracy', rather than to resolve differences (as some extremist groups had done) by open street conflict.

Institutional change is nonetheless important, in the view of both reformers and traditionalists; Gorbachev, addressing the Polish Sejm in July 1988, admitted that he had not himself appreciated at the outset quite how important it would be. The legislation adopted in the late autumn of 1988, to be followed by further reforms in the course of 1989, provided grounds for both an 'optimistic' and a 'pessimistic' assessment of the likely consequences of such changes. In the 'optimistic' view, which is close to that of Gorbachev himself, a process of political change has been set in motion which has already provided the USSR, for the first time since the 1920s, with a set of political institutions capable of expressing a wide range of popular aspirations and focusing them on the conduct of government. The new full-time Supreme Soviet, in particular, will scrutinise legislation much more closely than any of its predecessors. There will probably be several readings of each bill, as in the parliamentary democracies. There will be more frequent and vigorous questioning of ministers, and the Soviet government will be required to give a periodic account of its stewardship. A more elaborate committee structure will be established than in the old Supreme Soviet, with both 'committees' and 'commissions', and these are likely to extend their scrutiny to the organs of security (including the KGB) as some contributors to the constitutional debate suggested.

There will almost certainly be divided votes – these, indeed, had begun to occur even in the old unreformed Supreme Soviet; and a wider range of viewpoints will be expressed, including (for the first time) those of religious organisations, whose representation is explicitly provided for under Article 39 of the new Election Law. Deputies, who will have emerged from a competitive struggle for the popular vote, are likely to press the interests of their constituents more vigorously than in the past, and they will be assisted, if suggestions made in the debate are heeded, by a proper library and information centre, researchers and even personal computers. The two chambers of the new Supreme Soviet will emphasise different spheres of policy, ending their previous uniformity, and the whole nation will be involved in their proceedings by means of radio and tv broadcasts and free access for all interested citizens. The reform process, seen in this perspective, is part of a much wider movement of democratising change: Poland, for instance, has embraced competitive elections and party reform, Hungary has provided for the formation of independent political parties, and even Mongolia has adopted a package of reforms including competitive party ballots, a choice of candidate at state elections and a critique of the 'cult of personality of Choibalsan'.

The experience of earlier Soviet reforms, however, also provides grounds for a more cautious judgement. The new electoral law, for instance, has opened up the political process to a wide variety of groups, but the burgeoning 'informal' movement received no formal recognition, in part at least because of its lack of an all-union representative structure. Nomination meetings in ordinary constituencies must be convened by the local Soviet and electoral commission, and can proceed only if at least 500 voters are present; this effectively excludes most rural settlements. Nominations, in any case, must be approved by constituency pre-election conferences, and these are likely to remove particularly controversial candidates. There will be no choice of party; legitimate political discourses will have to limit itself to what Gorbachev has called a 'socialist pluralism of opinions'; and all candidates will have to accept the existing constitution and laws. Surely, some contributors to the debate suggested, they might reasonably wish to change at least a few of them?

The principle of democratic centralism, moreover, will continue to apply: contributors to the constitutional debate suggested some modification, allowing deputies, for example, to appeal to higher-level bodies against unfounded decisions, but no changes of this kind were formally considered. The new post of Chairman of the USSR Supreme Soviet, which is to be held in conjunction with the party leadership, even raises the possibility of the revival of a 'dominant leader' system of a kind that (it is now suggested) led to the violation of rights and stagnation of earlier decades. There has been widespread criticism that the party has been lagging rather than leading in the process of reform; most instructively, the new regulations on party elections, issued after the Party Conference, largely recapitulated those of 1962. Reformers are already looking to the 28th Party Congress, due in 1991, to remedy some of these shortcomings.

The popular response might ordinarily be expected to determine which, if either, of these two perspectives came closer to reflecting the future course of events. It appears unlikely to do so in this case for reasons that will be familiar to students of earlier Soviet (and indeed Russian) history; everyone is 'for' the reforms in principle, but no-one does very much about it. Surveys certainly suggest that the changes so far introduced are popular. Researchers in the Ukraine, for instance, found that a very high proportion of the voters they asked – from 81 to 95 per cent – favoured the limited experiment of 1987 by which more candidates were nominated than seats available in a small number of constituencies. A much larger poll, conducted by the Institute of Sociological Research and the Institute of State and Law of the USSR Academy of Sciences, found that 58 per cent of those asked were in favour of the electoral experiment before it had taken place, but that 77 per cent were in favour after they had actually taken part. A very large-scale national poll conducted by the Central Committee's Academy of Social Sciences nonetheless found that, although 75 per cent believed more glasnost and democratisation of public life was necessary, only 30 per cent were actually willing to take an active part in such a process. Comparable findings have been reported elsewhere.

In these circumstances the future of political reform is likely to depend, as so often in the past, upon the balance of political advantage within the party and state leadership. The position in this respect is rarely possible to define with any certainty and is constantly changing. A reasonably clear 'reformist' perspective is at least available in the speeches and writings of senior members of the leadership such as Alexander Yakovlev and Vadim Medvedev as well as Gorbachev himself. For Yakovlev, for instance, the key issue is to establish a mechanism for 'sensibly, legally and dynamically reconciling all the legitimate interests existing in society'. His speech in Vilnius in August 1988 emphasised 'common human interests' in which both East and West should co-operate, such as international security and conservation of the environment. Speaking in Perm in December 1988, Yakovlev emphasised that for Lenin, at least after 1921, socialism was a 'society with commodity production, a market, competition, money [and] democracy', and himself urged the establishment of a 'developed socialist market'. For Medvedev too the market was 'irreplaceable' and there was much to learn from both social democracy and capitalism in the elaboration of an 'up-to-date conception of socialism'.

Gorbachev set out his own vision of such a 'new image of socialism', cleansed of the deformations of the Soviet past and open to the constructive achievements of other countries and social systems, in the conclusion of his speech to the 19th Party Conference. A still more ambitious programme of reform has been set out by party intellectuals like Tatiana Zaslavskaya and Boris Kurashvili. For Kurashvili, for instance, a Soviet society of the future was one in which there would be a variety of forms of property and very little direct party or state control of economic activity. Inner-party democracy would be restored within the CPSU, primarily through party-wide discussions and voting on major issues. There would be open discussion of competing political platforms, and 'real power' would be restored to the Soviets. There would be a proper separation

of powers, republics and local areas would have greatly
increased authority, and all citizens would have the legal
right to obtain unclassified information. In international
affairs there would be an era of 'social and class
reconciliation' and 'growing co-operation', leading ultimately
to a synthesis of the best features of both capitalism and
socialism. Lenin's remarks on this subject, he suggested
boldly, were 'not always satisfactory'.[9]

A very different vision of the Soviet future has however
been put forward by influential members of the leadership
such as Egor Ligachev, Lev Zaikov and Viktor Chebrikov.
For Ligachev, for instance, speaking in Gorky in August
1988, the CPSU was an unapologetically 'ruling' party
There was no room for a multiparty system or political
opposition, nor would there be any copying of Western
market and property forms, with their unemployment and
inequality. Socialism, he insisted, had the capacity to
develop 'on its own foundations'. In foreign affairs, equally,
there could be no retreat from 'class' positions, and no
'artificial "slowdown"' in the social and national-liberation
struggle'. Chebrikov and Zaikov, in further speeches, have
expressed particular concern about the growth of nationalist
and 'informal' associations. Chebrikov, for instance, told an
audience in Cheboksary in April 1988 that the espionage
services of foreign states were behind the 'nationalist
aberrations' that had been occurring in the USSR. In a
speech in Kishinev in February 1989 he attacked the
'so-called informal associations', accusing them of instigat-
ing 'anarchy' and 'destabilisation' and in some cases of
'attempting to create political structures opposed to the
CPSU'. The party, he hinted ominously, could not remain
indifferent to such developments.

Positions of this kind, moreover, appear to command
considerable support within Soviet society, and not simply
among elderly officials. Nina Andreeva, a Leningrad
chemistry lecturer, was perhaps the most celebrated of those
who contributed to the debate before the Party Conference;
her open letter to *Sovyetskaya Rossiya*, 'I can't forgo
principles', complained of the exaggerated attention that
was being paid to the Stalinist past and warned that attempts
were being made to undermine the party's leading role. Nor

was Andreeva alone in her concerns. There has been widespread resentment, for instance, at the profiteering that has been engaged in by some co-operatives, and at higher prices, food shortages and housing and transport difficulties. The attitudes of local party officials are of particular importance if democratisation is to have any chance of success; and if the 19th Party Conference is any guide they have very mixed feelings about it. Speaker after speaker at the Conference attacked the 'demagogic' and 'anarchic' groups that were making use of the slogan of glasnost, and the press came in for sustained criticism for its sensationalism and even 'destabilisation' of Soviet society. The strongest pressure was for legislation which would make the press legally accountable for its excesses, not for measures which might extend the boundaries of 'socialist pluralism'.

The prospect for Soviet democratisation are therefore open, changing and ambiguous. There is popular support for political reform – but not necessarily if it appears to lead to economic hardship. Leading reformers acknowledge that, even under the most favourable circumstances, there can be no short-term transformation of the society or even of the political system. Opponents of reform make little attempt to defend Stalinism as such (Nina Andreeva's family suffered directly during this period, as did Ligachev's), but they believe in modifying the methods of central control rather than abandoning it altogether, and they have little faith in reformist notions of a Soviet self-managing socialism, seeing it as a recipe for public disorder and perhaps for challenges to the integrity of the state itself. The background is one of serious and intractable economic difficulties and openly assertive nationalism, and even international agreements may have been won, if anxious readers' letters are any guide, at too great a cost in terms of domestic security.[10] It is in such difficult circumstances that an attempt is being made to construct a political form of an unprecedented kind which combines Leninism with some elements of Western-style limited government; perhaps the only certainty, at the outset of this experiment, is that the fate of world socialism as well as of the Gorbachev reforms hangs in the balance.

Notes

[1] See Stephen White, 'Noncompetitive elections and national politics: the USSR Supreme Soviet elections of 1984', *Electoral Studies*, vol 4, no 3, 1985.

[2] Mark Azbel, *Refusenik*, Houghton Mifflin, Boston 1981, p 154.

[3] *Izvestiya*, 29 April 1988, p 3.

[4] *Pravda*, 23 November 1988, p 2.

[5] *Sovetskoe Gosudarstvo i Pravo*, no 5, 1988, pp 3-13.

[6] For a detailed account, with references, of this very interesting debate, see Stephen White, 'Gorbachev, Gorbachevism and the Party Conference', *Journal of Communist Studies*, vol 4, no 4, December 1988.

[7] The membership of the commissions is given in *Pravda*, 29 November 1988, pp 1-2.

[8] *Pravda*, 2 August 1988, p 1.

[9] *Moscow News*, 5 June 1988, p 13.

[10] See for instance *Pravda*, 13 January 1989, p 3, for some misgivings about the decommissioning of the Krasnoyarsk radar station in response to Western criticisms.

Mary Buckley

What Does Perestroika Mean for Women?

Since Gorbachev became General Secretary of the CPSU in March 1985, women in the Soviet Union have been asking increasingly pointed questions about the difficulties they face at home, at work and in political life. As glasnost has increased its strength, women have become less afraid to speak out and editors more willing to print what they say. Topics which had been censored out of the Soviet press in the past, such as prostitution, the lack of contraceptives and extremely high abortion rates, are now acknowledged as problems. Although limited debate about female roles had taken place under Brezhnev, the boundaries of permitted discussion have broadened considerably since 1985. By 1987 and 1988, extremely bold remarks, by past Soviet standards, were being made about women's lives. The philosopher Olga Voronina went so far as to argue that 'men have created the world for themselves' and called for an end to 'patriarchal attitudes of man towards women'.[1] In Voronina's view, the 'spiritual progress' of the USSR depends upon a change in male/female relations, and upon a restructuring of the domestic division of labour.

Not all supporters of perestroika, however, agree with Voronina's interpretation of its significance for women and for the USSR. While like-minded thinkers hope for a transformation of male-female relations in a direction of greater equality, particularly in housework and childcare, others recommend that female labour, rather than male, should come out of the workforce and return to the home if an efficient perestroika of the economy results in rationalisation and job losses. These very different arguments about the implications of perestroika for women

151

come from advocates of perestroika, not critics. But how they interpret perestroika differs. The first argument assumes that the process of perestroika embraces women's liberation as well, and that perestroika increases the potential for positive changes in women's lives; the second argument, with a narrower focus, concentrates on a more efficient running of the economy as perestroika's main goal, paying no special attention to women's interests. By the end of the 1980s, these were the two most prominent arguments which linked perestroika and the '*zhenskii vopros*' ('woman question'). The first made a conscious link between them, concerned to examine how women could benefit from perestroika; its advocates were overwhelmingly women. The second linked them in a more instrumental fashion because women comprise 51 per cent of the labour force, and any discussion of the reorganisation of the workforce is incomplete without reference to female workers.

Other arguments about perestroika, particularly those on democratisation, carry implications for women's roles, but frequently fail to draw specific conclusions about the consequences of political reforms for women. Fedor Burlatsky's criticism of the 'period of stagnation' and the legacy of an 'authoritarian-patriarchal political culture' could be extended to an analysis of how authoritarian systems of government have a differential impact on the political participation of women and men.[2] Burlatsky, however, does not explore this; nor does he ask how the development of initiative by the people after years of stifled aspirations makes any difference to women's liberation. By implication though, a self-managing socialism would offer women and men a more active role in it and give space for the evolution of non-party informal women's organisations.

Similarly, recent statements on up-to-date notions of socialism by Vadim Medvedev, Politburo member and Chair of the Central Committee's Ideology Commission, carry implications for women, even if he does not directly address what they are. The 'qualitative renewal' and 'stepped-up dynamism' of socialist society in a direction of 'socialist pluralism', in which various social, national and occupational groups express their interests, implicitly gives a revitalised role to women.[3]

As has often been the case in the past, some contemporary visions of political change exclude specific reference to the woman question, subsuming it under the 'human question' and thereby playing down differences between the sexes. This can be explained only in part by a traditional partriarchal culture; it also has precedent in the Russian socialist tradition which, before and after the Revolution, viewed separate institutions for women as divisive of working class unity, as a distraction from class struggle, as a threat to revolution and as pandering to self-indulgent 'bourgeois feminism'. Such fears are much weaker today, especially since women's organisations are relatively powerless, no longer seen as a serious threat to socialism. So should female philosophers in the 1990s wish to link the significance of socialist pluralism to women's organisations or connect social dynamism to women's liberation, there is currently no ideological barrier stopping them. An extension of the arguments put forward by Burlatsky, Medvedev and many others could lead in this direction.

This chapter puts current ideas on the 'woman question' in historical context, discusses their significance and evaluates their implications for transforming Soviet socialism and women's roles within it.

The historical context

Immediately after the Russian Revolution the Soviet State proclaimed equality of the sexes in law, years ahead of most Western capitalist countries. For over seventy years this commitment has been reiterated under Lenin, Stalin, Khrushchev, Brezhnev, Andropov, Chernenko and Gorbachev. The official Soviet line has always been that only socialist society can guarantee women's liberation and that the USSR was the first state to declare equality of the sexes in law, to protect motherhood through maternity grants and to promote equal opportunities in education, in the workforce and in political activity. Early commitment to an ever-expanding system of kindergartens and creches was designed to enable women to join the workforce without worrying about childcare.

But although the Soviet state has been officially
committed to equality of the sexes since 1917, apart from
lively debates about emancipation in the 1920s, there have
been few uncensored discussions about the meaning of
equality and how best to promote it. In 1930, under Stalin,
the 'woman question' was declared 'solved'; allegedly,
equality of the sexes already existed. Views about women's
liberation were silenced.[4]

Then in 1956 at the 20th party Congress, Khrushchev
noted that women were promoted to top jobs 'with timidity'.
As part of his policy of destalinisation, Khrushchev wanted
to draw the people back into political activity. He noticed
that women played a much smaller role than men in politics;
so he asked why. He promoted the *zhensovety*, or women's
councils, to involve women in activities outside the home.
Issues concerning women, such as maternity leave,
kindergartens, and queues began to be discussed again.

It was not until the late-1960s, when falling birth rates and
labour shortages caused Brezhnev concern, that the woman
question was pronounced 'unsolved'. As a vital 51 per cent
of the labour force, Soviet women were needed in economic
production; but smaller family size in the Russian republic,
Ukraine and Baltic states of Estonia, Latvia and Lithuania
posed a serious problems for future labour supply. Outside
the Muslim areas of Soviet Central Asia and the Caucasus,
one-child families were becoming the norm. Throughout the
1970s a lively debate raged in Soviet academic journals and
in the press about female roles.[5] The main question was how
could women best combine production with reproduction.
Soviet sociologists pointed out that this combination was
difficult so long as women endured a 'double burden' or
'double shift' of a day in the labour force topped with
cooking, cleaning, washing, ironing, queuing for food and
childcare. On average women worked a thirteen- to
fifteen-hour day. By contrast, Soviet men did paid work,
topped with meagre 'help' at home, generally less than five
hours a week. At night, women slept one hour less than men
due to additional chores. This debate about female roles was
approved 'from above' and did not arise from women's
groups pressing for changes 'from below'.

So the way in which women's lives have been discussed in

the Soviet media and in scholarly journals has changed over time. Economic and social policies have also altered over the years, with various implications for workers and mothers. The New Economic Policy from 1921 to 1928 brought unemployment to the new Soviet state, and women suffered more than men. Cultural attitudes considered it appropriate that men should remain breadwinners. Similar attitudes after the Great Patriotic War (1941-45) led women to be replaced by men in the positions of authority they had taken while men were away at the front, such as running collective farms. These forms of female subordination to men were not seriously challenged by the CPSU, although muted female complaints were made, particularly in the 1920s against female unemployment, in the journal *Kommunistka* (Communist Woman).

Traditional notions of 'women's work' and 'men's work' have persisted from 1917 through to the present. However, these notions began to be questioned during the 1930s when job opportunities expanded as Stalin attempted to catapult the USSR into becoming an advanced industrial nation through Five Year Plans; they were challenged most directly in the early 1940s when women were needed in the war effort. Thus, at times when it has suited the Soviet state for economic and defence reasons, traditional stereotypes of 'appropriate' female behaviour have been played down. Although marxist ideology supports an active role for women in the economy in order for women's liberation to be achieved, this element of ideology has been stressed more in some periods of Soviet history than it others. The extent of debate has also varied.

Debate under Gorbachev has broadened, although there are still limits to what can be said. Male violence towards women awaits serious discussion, as does the effect of traditional gender role stereotypes in children's books on socialisation patterns. While some topics remain unmentioned, others receive only cursory treatment. For instance, the existence of prostitution and its links to a growing number of cases of syphilis and AIDS has been deplored in several newspapers, but the reasons for the development of prostitution under socialism have not been rigorously analysed. The role of pimps and Madams has been condemned, as has the corruption surrounding prostitution, such as thefts from clients; but as yet there has been no attempt at the level of theory to suggest how prostitution is relevant to the woman question under socialism or how perestroika will affect it.[6] No-one in the 1980s has tackled the relationship between prostitution and socialist development. Alexandra Kollontai moved in this direction in the 1920s, linking prostitution to the New Economic Policy, unemployment among women and an expanding business community.[7] Kollontai's argument, however, would be an awkward one to pursue today since many economists see an inspiration, even justification, for perestroika in NEP. If Kollontai was right, then by implication an increase in prostitution is likely if perestroika proceeds. Notwithstanding this theoretical omission, more was said about prostitution in 1987 alone than in the entire half-century from 1930 to 1980. To expect more, so soon, is perhaps unrealistic.

Despite varying depths of analysis according to topic, numerous fresh questions relevant to the woman question have been posed since 1987 – a year which can usefully be seen as one in which the growing strength of glasnost marked a turning point in the sorts of questions asked about women's lives. Among the new questions being asked by women are: why are boys rather than girls encouraged to study technical subjects?[8] why are noise and dust levels so high in the textile industry, putting women workers under strain and resulting in pulse rates of over 90 beats a minute?[8] why are infant mortality rates higher than in capitalist countries, and increasing in rural areas?[10] why are contraceptives poorly developed, and condoms in such short supply? why is the abortion system so humiliating and degrading for women? why are so few women promoted to top jobs? why did only five women make speeches at the 19th All-Union Conference of the CPSU in 1988?[11] Increasingly, Soviet women are focusing on how the Soviet system works to their disadvantage. In the past, many differences between the sexes were glossed over since the stress fell on 'equal opportunities' for men and women in the economy and politics rather than on 'unequal results' in housework, childcare, jobs and promotion. Now attention is shifting to 'unequal results'. In the past, emphasis was put on what socialism provided for women. Now women, protected by glasnost, are examining what socialism has failed to offer and ways in which women are treated differently. Their views found an outlet in January 1987 at the All-Union Conference of Women which was held in Moscow to ask what perestroika meant for women and how women could best contribute to it. Since then, women have expressed a range of opinions in the press and in women's magazines.

Will women benefit from perestroika?

So far it has been women rather than men who have voiced the most critical views about the aspects of equality and liberation that socialism has denied them. It is women, rather than men, who advocate what must change in society to make their lives less stressful, richer, more purposeful and equal. Many male advocates of perestroika ignore the relevance of reform to the 'woman question'; at best, they reiterate past party lines on policies affecting women; and at worst, they view female labour as a resource to be used or discarded depending upon the needs of the economy. Thus the emphasis of different interpretations of perestroika matters very much for the woman question. Those who give centrality to the political end of women's personal fulfillment and equality ask how perestroika can move Soviet society towards a realisation of these goals; those who value a more efficient economy, ask how women, as a labour resource, can bring it about.

So, despite being able to ask these more open questions about why women under socialism suffer some disadvantages which men do not, it remains open to question whether women will necessarily gain from perestroika. Glasnost has given women the opportunity to express views about injustices against them, but since they are conspicuosly absent from top jobs in decision making, are these views likely to make any difference? Some women hope that they will, while others are more sceptical.

Developments since 1985 have certainly been complex, often pulling in seemily different directions. Quite radically, at the 1987 All-Union Conference of Women, Valentina

Tereshkova, the outgoing chair of the Soviet Women's
Committee, argued for a perestroika of Soviet men and
called for male participation in housework and childrearing.[12] Yet in the same year at a conference in Sweden on
perestroika, the Soviet economist V Kulikov argued that in
future years women should come out of the labour force,
rather than men, in order to soften the impact of future
unemployment, a likely result of perestroika in the
economy.[13] If successful, perestroika means streamlining,
efficiency and new technology; these will lead to a shedding
of workers in traditional industrial sectors. White-collar
work also has room for rationalisation; many tasks are
duplicated and over-staffing is a well-known problem. In this
context of a drive for efficiency and a 'shake-up' of inert
bureaucratic structures, some economists believe that it is
appropriate for female labour to be 'restructured' into the
home. Demographers who would like to see a stronger
upturn in the birth rate agree. In 1987 G Sergeeva suggested
that in those parts of the country where small families were
the norm, a section of the female labour force could usefully
leave their jobs and devote time to reproduction. That way,
job shortages and falling birth rates could be tackled at the
same time.[14]

This is not the sort of 'restructuring' that many Soviet
women support. Although there is backing among women
for increased opportunities for part-time labour, mainly
because of the flexibility it allows young mothers, they are
not in favour of a general withdrawal of large numbers of
women from the workforce. Zoya Pukhova, the new Chair of
the Soviet Women's Committee, forcefully made this point
in her speech to the 19th party Conference in June 1988. She
pointed out that:

> Recently, pages of magazines, the radio and television have
> often expressed the view that woman loses her looks from the
> overload at work and at home, that she does not have time to
> rear children. From this comes unhappiness at home and the
> number of divorces increases. Then comes this conclusion:
> woman must return home.[15]

In firm response, Pukhova asked whether this conclusion
was just: it was important for women to fulfil themselves

through work and an active social life. Confining women to the home would go against equality. She added that 80 per cent of Soviet women had said 'no' in response to a questionnaire which asked whether they would stay at home if money was not a problem. The forcefulness of Pukhova's point indicates that there is probably strong and widespread support for the idea that women should return to domestic lives. This is consistent with the patriarchal tradition that Burlatsky criticises, and in keeping with the many Soviet academic and popular writings which have long held the view that domestic chores and childrearing are 'natural' for women and 'unnatural' for men. 'Psycho-physiological' differences between the sexes have made women soft, emotional, gentle and caring, and men strong, intelligent and determined. These characteristics, runs the argument, fit the sexes for different social and political roles.[16] While recent sociological writings have challenged these rigid stereotypes and have adopted more modern concepts, such as the notion of 'egalitarian families', traditional beliefs die hard.[17] Even Gorbachev has argued that it is time to return to woman her 'truly female destiny', since socialist development has not left her enough time for housework, childrearing and family life.[18] But Gorbachev's speeches and writings reflects different views about female roles, which appear contradictory. Alongside his remarks about 'truly female destiny', he repeated his commitment to the promotion of more women into top jobs.

In 1986, in keeping with this, Alexandra Biryukova was promoted to the Secretariat of the Central Committee of the CPSU. In 1988 she was further elevated to the Politburo, the top decision-making body of the party. Critics, however, view this as a token gesture. Women are markedly absent from top jobs and Biryukova's promotion is an exception to the general pattern. Nevertheless, she is the first woman to sit on the Politbureau for thirty years and this should not be dismissed as entirely insignificant. Neither, however, should it be praised as part of a renewed commitment in the USSR to policies promoting women.

In this context, some Soviet women are beginning to challenge the male domination of Soviet politics – a challenge without precedent under Khrushchev and

Brezhnev. In a stern critique of the absence of Soviet women
from top jobs in politics, Larisa Kuznetsova, a journalist on
women's issues, recently argued that women are 'elbowed
out' of leading positions and given roles of 'political extras'.
She regretted that 'we have reached a point where every
other man is a head of department, and the entire top
echelon is male, while women basically follow their orders;
they are yes-women'. She stressed that it was not just the
proportion of women who were elected to representative
bodies that was important, but 'the presence among them of
leaders able to raise their voices, not just their hands. We
have a dense forest of raised hands'.[19] Here Kuznetsova is
referring to the high percentage of Soviet women elected to
the Soviets. The local soviets are over 50 per cent female and
the All-Union Supreme Soviet is over one-third female.
However, the women on the soviets generally have much
less powerful full-time jobs than their male counterparts,
and are less frequently nominated to stand as candidates for
a second term. For example a study of the 1985
Azerbaijan Supreme Soviet shows that 85 per cent of its
female deputies had low status jobs, compared to 25 per cent
of male deputies. So despite the fact that 39 per cent of its
deputies were female, just a minority of these held
important jobs in party and state institutions. Among the
deputies of the 1980 Azerbaijan Supreme Soviet who
were re-elected in 1985, 1 per cent were women and 83 per
cent were men. Female deputies were thus handicapped by a
brief tenure.[20] Research shows that this is the general
pattern.[21] Although women have a high, if weak, profile on
the soviets, they are generally absent from top positions in
the party. Just 4.6 per cent of Central Committee members
are women, and even these women are noticeable by their
low status jobs.[22] Women and men have very different
political profiles both on the soviets and in the party.

Kuznetsova's remarks are one of the boldest public
challenges made by a Soviet woman about women's political
roles in the entire history of the Soviet state. They would
have resulted in labour camp under Stalin and earned
Kuznetsova the pejorative label of 'enemy of the people'.
Under Khrushchev and Brezhnev too, they would have led
to harassment by the KGB and arrested for 'anti-Soviet

agitation and propaganda'. The Soviet tendency has always been to praise large numbers of women on the soviets as a shining example of equality in practice and as a sign of superiority over Western parliaments. Before Gorbachev, the absence of women from top party posts was rarely mentioned; nor was the political weakness of the soviets, relative to Western parliaments. The fact that men on the soviets generally held proportionally far more high status jobs than women was also taboo. Kuznetsova's 'dense forest of raised hands' refers to this.

Curiously, alongside permission for views such as Kuznetsova's to be published, comes official support for beauty contests. In 1988 the first beauty contest was held in Moscow. It was a joint venture of several Soviet enterprises and foreign firms including Burda Moden, Sans Souci and Cartier. The decision to hold the event every year was reported in the Soviet press as 'one that is highly favoured by the majority of the male population'.[23] Up until today, features of Soviet socialism admired by socialist feminists in the West have included the official reluctance to package women in the media as sex objects and the ban on pornography. Feminists have praised the way in which the Soviet system focuses on the achievements of women at work and does not judge women by appearance or sex appeal.[24] Until 1988 it could not have been anticipated that the Soviet press would report that

> 'Miss Moscow-88' is good looking, long-legged (she is 176 cm tall), and slim (weighs 53 kg). A rare stroke of luck for a girl of seventeen just making her first steps into the big world. Her diamond watch, a present from Yves Saint Laurent, is a fine momento of the happy event.[25]

While some in the USSR support beauty contests, dream of possessing stylish clothes and want to wear Italian shoes, French perfume and 'imported' make-up, others criticise the emphasis on external beauty as superficial and as 'un-socialist'. Yet in a society where off-the-peg clothes have usually not been glamorous, tasteful or geared to consumer choice, the desire to be better dressed is understandable. This desire grew stronger during the 1970s due to increasing numbers of Western tourists in the USSR wearing clothes which Soviet citizens envied, but could only obtain on the black market. Aspirations to dress well are further encouraged by perestroika with its emphasis on the production of goods to meet consumer demand. Also understandable is the higher status given to 'imported' goods over 'ours' of lower standard. Since 1928 Soviet economic development gave priority to heavy industry. Although the clothing industry dates back to pre-revolutionary days, it has never been a privileged sector and has produced functional rather than elegant designs. Other consumer items which Western women taken for granted, such as tampons and sanitary towels, have never been produced in the USSR. Even in the 1980s, Soviet women feel lucky if they can find scarce wadges of cotton wool as inadequate substitutes. Leading difficult lives characterised by the 'double burden', it is not surprising that Soviet women value the opportunity to look nice or fantasise about more glamorous life styles.

These diverse developments may appear contradictory. At the same time that some Soviet women are calling for a more assertive presence of women among top leaders, many are seeking nicer clothes. While some women are emphasising the need to change male/female relations, and to give women the opportunity to develop the full range of their abilities, others put value in material possessions and external appearance. Those who are concerned with women's liberation under socialism cite Lenin's remarks about the stifling and petty nature of housework. Those whose praise beauty contests thank Yves Saint Laurent for diamond watches. Marxist ideology and consumerism sit uneasily side by side.

But the tension between female achievements and female appearance is perhaps less acute than often claimed. Concern about appearance does not automatically mean that achievements at work are unimportant. The issue need not be one of 'either' job 'or' pleasing appearance. One vital element of self-determination and individuality for women is the freedom to choose how to dress. There is no reason why women could not, nor should not, pay attention to both. A problem only exists for women's liberation when women devote a disproportionate amount of time and energy dressing solely to suit what they think will please the opposite sex, rather than themselves.

A more resilient contradiction, however, does exist between women's liberation under socialism and beauty contests. A show which packages women wholly as sex objects is exploitative, demeaning, distasteful and utimately a form of oppression over women since it encourages men to value sexual suggestion to the exclusion of other personality traits and abilities. Yet many Soviet women were keen to participate and many viewers enjoyed the event. The freedom that glasnost brings inevitably finds various forms of expression and produces developments which take different, often controversial, courses. Beauty contests have emerged in a society which has historically restricted discussions about sex. The puritanism, some would say prudery, of Soviet society, and the past repression of sexual topics, may have contributed to the keenness of some for beauty contests. Supporters are probably aware that such events are common in the West, and it is revealing that Western firms were involved in the organisation of 'Miss Moscow-1988'. Joint ventures with Western firms, one element of perestroika, may lead to the adoption of more controversial ways associated with Western lifestyles. Some may fear that pornographic magazines and films will be the next logical step. The political issue for guardians of ideology such as Vadim Medvedev will then be whether developments are 'healthy' and 'morally sound' rather than 'at variance with the principles of socialism'. Medvedev has argued that 'socialist pluralism' must not extend to practices which undermine socialism.[26] Soviet women's groups may choose to interpret pornography in different terms, but they have yet to formulate their arguments or define what is 'morally unsound' for women's liberation.

Current soviet policies for women

In 1985 and 1986 Gorbachev outlined his leadership's initial policy priorities for women. These were: first, support for combining motherhood with participation in the labour force; second, increasing opportunities for part-time work; third, the promotion of more women to senior positions; and fourth, the revival of the *zhensovety*, or women's councils. This package was not a radical break from the past and does not merit the label 'reform' as do Gorbachev's policies for the economy and soviets. The hallmark of policies for women is continuity with the past, not change in a new direction. Brezhnev had stressed the first priority, with the second and third also being put on the agenda during the 1970s, but with less prominence. Khrushchev, too, had discussed the first and third priorities, but gave the 'double burden' less serious attention than it received two decades later. As already mentioned, the 'solved' status of the woman question persisted under Khrushchev, limiting examination of it. The fourth priority was a revamped policy of the Khrushchev era.

Thus Gorbachev's policies for women represent an increased commitment to past polices. What differed by 1987 was the political context in which these policy priorities were located. The growing strength of glasnost allowed women to ask how Soviet socialism had failed to implement official policies for women in the past, whether perestroika would result in their more effective implemention, and whether policies adequately met women's needs. The new political context means that discussion about women's issues was freer and less stifled. But it did not mean that the Soviet leadership was drawing up new policies for women specifically designed to promote women's liberation or to reform traditional thinking about gender roles. Rather, by mobilising the Soviet people to discuss the significance of perestroika for the different groups to which they belonged – whether the trade unions, Komsomol, journalists or social scientists – the new Soviet leadership was by extension encouraging women to reflect upon what economic and political reform meant for their lives. The results of this general mobilisation for women depended, to a large extent, on what women themselves had to say.

The main policy for women, of official support for combining motherhood with participation in the labour force, dates back to the early years of the Soviet state, to Bolshevik policies before the revolution of 1917, and to the writings of Engels, Lenin, Kollontai and Armand. Backing takes several forms. There is general accep tance in the

USSR that women do, and should, work. Equally women are viewed as incomplete without children. To ease these two roles, working mothers have the benefit of maternity leave, extended in 1986 to 18 months. There are discussions about soon extending it to two years. Commitment has also been given to expanding the network of creches and kindergartens. Although state provision of childcare facilities has always been part of Soviet policy, it has lagged behind demand. Leaders generally renew past pledges to increase supply in every five year plan. Queues for kindergarten places have often meant that some children cannot be looked after in childcare facilities, especially in rural areas. And often the *babushka*, or grandmother, has not wanted to take on her traditional role of child-minder for her daughter. Thus some Soviet mothers have to stay at home. In Muslim areas, more women choose to stay at home.

Since the 1960s questionnaires have shown that some Soviet women, usually young mothers, would like to work part-time. Some considered that they could make child-care arrangements to cope with part-shifts, but not full ones. Others in full-time jobs desired to reduce their loads, not necessarily because their children lacked kindergarten places, but often because they wished to lead less stressful lives. Others still wished to see more of their offspring, or were dissatisfied with the quality of care in kindergaratens where children became ill more frequently than 'home children'. Whilst some demographers backed part-time labour for women, in the hope that it would lead to larger families, some economists pointed out that the economy needed women to work full-time. Managers in industry were similarly reluctant to put women on part-shifts, since their main concern was that the workforce reached its output targets. Time and motion studies, however, showed that productivity generally slackened off in the afternoon and that it would be more efficient to have different workers in the morning and afternoon shifts than the same worker all day.

In supporting part-time labour for women, the current Soviet leadership meets the requests of some mothers and wins the approval of demographers. If perestroika results in the laying off of some workers, part-time labour may also win the backing of more economists and managers. It is unlikely, however, to receive eager applause from women who wish to retain full-time jobs, and who fear that an escalation in part-time work for women could reinforce their low-status at work. As it is, female labour is concentrated in low-paying jobs at the bottom of job hierarchies. On average, Soviet women earn two-thirds of the male wage. A spread of part-time jobs for women would reinforce this pattern rather than correct it.

But at the same time, official CPSU policy wants to promote women. It is sensitive to their general absence from important positions in politics and industry. However, many qualified women have traditionally resisted upward mobility beyond a comfortable point for different reasons. In an interview in Moscow in the early 1980s one very able female economist said 'Politbureau work is not for women. It is so hard. Women do not need that too'. Some women place higher personal value on the responsibilities of childcare and home, view politics as 'dirty' and as a world not worth dabbling in. The very absence of women also makes it rather uninviting. Childcare and the career of husbands complicate the picture further. Women may be pleased to be promoted in their local area, but are often unwilling to move around if this means disruption for the family. Social pressures also dictate that men should not hold positions which are less responsible than those of their wives. On top of this, promotion to responsible posts is decided through nomenklatura lists. Party committees have lists of names to match lists of jobs. Should a job become vacant, the list is consulted. The little evidence available from archives, suggests that women tend to be left off nomenklatura lists. Moreover, informal male networks tend to screen women out.

With democratisation, however, perhaps women will feel encouraged to participate more actively in politics. With more open discussion about women's problems, a growing number of women may see a stronger need for women to represent women. Oddly, feminist groups have not, so far, been among the informal organisations to establish themselves. The most widespread representation of women has come about in the workplace through the officially revitalised *zhensovety*. Gorbachev called for their revival to promote perestroika among women and to defend women's interests.

Women's organisations in the 1980s

At the 27th party Congress in 1986 Gorbachev announced that the *zhensovety* should be revived.[27] By April 1988, 236,000 *zhensovety* had been formed.[28] Workplaces are encouraged to set up their own women's council, which is run by a group of women as small as eleven or larger than twenty. These organisers are elected by the female workforce, whose interests they represent. The work of the *zhensovet* is broken down into sections. These vary according to *zhensovet*, but common sections include 'production', 'daily life and social problems', 'children', and 'culture'. 'Production' sections concentrate on problems at work, such as working conditions and health protection. 'Daily life and social problems' is broader, ranging from setting up shopping facilities in the workplace to providing counselling services for couples who think they would like to divorce. The responsibility of this section extends to delivering food to elderly women who once worked in the factory and who have no-one to care for them. The section concerned with 'children' pays attention to kindergarten facilities in the workplace and does work with children's homes. 'Culture' covers a broad brief and includes arranging entertainment for workers. The aim of sections is to cater to local problems. What problems are important is, in part, decided by women workers who respond to questionnaires sent out by the women's council. The *zhensovet*, however, liaises with either the party committee or trade union within the workplace. Thus the determination of the importance of particular problems has to take into account the views of members of these more powerful organisations. For instance, one party policy is to promote happy families and to deter divorce. For this reason, members of the *zhensovet* will encourage workers to think again about separation.

The provision of shopping facilities in the workplace is clearly a popular demand among women workers. The opportunity to place food orders reduces the time spent queuing after work. While critics may view this as reinforcing women's responsibility for shopping rather than serving to challenge the traditional domestic division of labour, they cannot deny that such services in all workplaces – for women and for men – would make daily life much easier. Once this and other basic services have been set up, women could use the *zhensovety* to push for more female representation in factory decision-making. However, it is early days yet, and how women use the *zhensovety* depends very much on their own aspirations. Biryukova has argued that women should harness the *zhensovety* to tackle questions of concern to them. But at the 19th party conference, Pukhova made clear that two problems existed: firstly, male members of the CPSU were often indifferent to the *zhensovety* and did not take them seriously; and secondly, women themselves do not always use the *zhensovety* to their advantage. How the *zhensovety* develop depends, to a large extent, on what working women want to make of them.

How the *zhensovety* take advantage of the reformed electoral system will become clearer as the process unfolds. The new system will result in 2,250 deputies elected to the Congress of People's Deputies – and 750 of these will be from social organisations (including 75 seats nominated by the *zhensovety*). The Congress will meet just twice a year and elect a smaller group of 542 to form a more active parliament. It remains to be seen how many female deputies will be elected to the Congress and subsequently named to the soviet. A female presence is guaranteed through seats allocated to the *zhensovety*, but how many constituencies and territories nominate and elect women cannot be predicted.

The number of women eventually chosen in the constituency elections depends firstly upon how many women are nominated to stand; secondly, upon the consent of elections commissions for women's names to go forward onto the final list of candidates – commissions act to vet a long list of nominations and to reduce it to a short list of candidates who can stand for election; and thirdly, upon the final choice of voters. It is possible that fewer women than men will stand for election and that male candidates will be favoured by voters over female. The fixed quotas according to sex of the old soviets at least guaranteed a female presence, even if it was a weak one in terms of job status. Election commissions may work with the notion of female representation in mind, but cannot fix election results in their favour. Thus, the extent of female representation in the Congress depends to a large extent on the voting behaviour of Soviet citizens. However, if the percentage of women falls but women deputies are more assertive than Kuznetsova's 'yes-women' of the past, this may be an advance for women. It depends very much on who the women are and which causes they choose to champion.

Some difficulties in the nominating procedures for social organisations are already evident. Larisa Kuznetsova's name was put forward in 1989 by the *zhensovet* in the Central Aerohydrodynamic Institute, only to be tossed out by the Moscow regional *zhensovet* – one administrative level up in the *zhensovety* hierarchy. Kuznetsova, it turned out, could not be nominated by a *zhensovet* because she was not herself a member of a women's council. The Soviet Women's Committee at the apex of the hierarchy confirmed this. Article 18 of the new Electoral Law stipulates that deputies chosen by the women's councils must be drawn from among their own members. Complaining to *Moscow News*, two members of the *zhensovet* which nominated Kuznetsova asked why 'this kind of discrimination' existed against women and pointed out that the same restriction did not apply to the trade unions. They called upon the Central Election Commission and the election commission of the Soviet Women's Committee 'to decide how to eliminate this contradiction'. Otherwise, they argued, 'the women's movement can lose many potential deputies – active supporters of perestroika'.[29]

This example illustrates how women are taking initiative in the electoral process and contesting restrictions which limit their freedom of action. If several women like Kuznetsova were allowed to be nominated, and then succeeded in winning the final approval of the *zhensovety* for the new Congress, they could collectively set out to defend women's interests and to make the link between perestroika, necessary changes in male/female relations, and a restructured domestic division of labour. This, potentially, could give ideas about women's liberation a more public outlet and help to demonstrate that it is a political issue.

Conclusion

Perestroika and glasnost carry several implications for women's lives. Successful perestroika in the economy, yet to come about, will mean efficiency, higher prices, more consumer goods and job losses. Reflections on the rationalisation of the workforce have already resulted in suggestions that a withdrawal of some women from their jobs could soften the impact of unemployment. But most families need two wages; in fact, two wages are often not enough and workers sometimes top up their main salary with a second job. Price increases likely to result from price reforms, which are a necessary element of perestroika as currently conceived, will make two incomes even more essential. Single women rely on paid work, and single-parent families desperately need wages since state help is insufficient.

Aside from economic necessity, most women do not want to give up their jobs. Their reasons include personal fulfillment, participation in the collective and economic independence. With high divorce rates in the USSR, albeit falling slightly, many women are wary of increasing their dependence on husbands. Although questionnaires show that women would like more children than they manage to produce, these survey results should not be taken as indications that women would necessarily bear more if they left their jobs.

On the positive side, perestroika – if successful – will result in more consumer goods that citizens want. If women took more active advantage of 'socialist pluralism', they could exert pressure for tampons to be produced. In this sphere, joint ventures with Western firms would guarantee a large and ready market for a desperately needed product. Up until now, however, many Soviet women have complained that a range of sorely needed goods are not appearing. Moreover, queues are worsening and many items are becoming scarcer. All women get is a 'spate of male perestroika eloquence'.[30] The patience of some has been tried to the point that they argue, as one Muscovite did to me in 1987, that 'all this information generated by glasnost is very nice. But I would rather have goods in the shops than glasnost'.

Of course, not everyone feels this way. Women gathering at the All-Union Conference of Women in 1987 optimistically supported perestroika. One asked,

> Who suffers most in society from the negative aspects of our life? Women. And because of this we shall indeed be the main strength of perestroika – we have a vital interest in it.[31]

Pukhova also expressed this opinion at the 19th party Conference, arguing that the success in solving the problems of women's lives depended upon the success of perestroika, and the success of perestroika depended upon women's contribution to it. While some Soviet women are sceptical that perestroika will improve their lives, and eye price increases with anxiety, others pin stronger hopes on perestroika for a brighter future and applaud the results of glasnost.

Glasnost has certainly allowed space for a freer expression of ideas about gender roles. These ideas, however, embrace a broad spectrum of thought. Some arguments have moved in more feminist directions, while others champion traditional roles for women. Going into the 1990s, the 'woman question' is more open-ended than it has been since 1917. Supporters of equality of the sexes may most readily agree with the conclusion reached by Kuznetsova that 'we need to abandon patriarchal habits'.[32] Without doing so, large numbers of women are unlikely to be appointed to top jobs and men are unlikely to share equally in domestic labour and childcare. Yet whether the *zhensovety* will extend their work to embrace an attack on patriarchy has yet to be demonstrated.

What, then, would be indicators of progress for the 'woman question' under perestroika? For Voronina and Kuznetsova it will be an attack on chauvinistic attitudes towards women, a restructuring of the domestic division of labour, a more humane abortion system, the widespread availability of contraceptives and a more active female presence in political arenas.

Important turning points in attitudes would include recognition that working women should not automatically take more responsibility for housework and childcare than working men and that women should be respected in the workplace. These and other attitudes could be examined by social scientists in survey questionnaires over time. Evidence of a more humane abortion system would include a greater privacy for women, respect for the dignity of the client by medical staff, the provision of clean sheets and the use of anaesthetic. A general availability of contraceptives, perhaps through joint ventures with Western firms, would offer women a choice of birth control technique, and might reduce the enormous abortion rate. The development of sex education in schools, which has already begun, is a step in the right direction. Now that AIDS has spread to the Soviet Union, men have begun to protest that they can catch the disease from prostitutes and that condom machines are needed on the streets and in stations.[33] Because men have a more direct interest in condoms than ever before, perhaps contraception will be taken more seriously by economic planners.

In politics, positive change could be gauged by percentage increases in the numbers of women promoted to top jobs. The record for the Politbureau and Secretariat so far remains grim. However, analysis of the composition of the new Central Committee named in 1991 at the 28th party Congress will indicate the extent to which the current leadership is seriously committed to putting more women on nomenklatura lists and increasing the extremely low 4.6 per cent female presence. Central committee membership is a useful barometer of promotion in political and economic decision making. The female profile on the new Congress of People's Deputies will also reveal information about the willingness to nominate, select and vote for women to the new parliament. How female candidates act and what political programmes they support may show the sorts of initiative women are prepared to take. The role of the *zhensovety* could be crucial here. If women deputies organised themselves informally outside the soviet and became indirectly accountable to the women's councils, they could work out a programme for the advancement of women's interests. This is probably best done through the *zhensovety* since currently they constitute the only broadly based organisations for women. As already mentioned, no informal organisations of women to pursue women's interests have yet blossomed, despite the political space for these. But this aspect of 'socialist pluralism' could still flower and does have a precedent in underground feminist groups which formed in 1979.[34] The emergence of women's informal groups would be an indicator of growing concern among women about the promotion of women's liberation and equality of the sexes.

It was Lenin who wisely cautioned that equality in law is not equality in life. This remains the case today. Although Soviet women enjoy equality in law, their daily reality illustrates inequalities at home, at work and in politics. While perestroika and glasnost have already led to changes in this reality, they do not guarantee a speedy solution to the woman question. As early Bolshevik women such as Alexandra Kollontai and Inessa Armand recognised seventy years ago, the path to women's liberation under socialism is 'long and thorny'. Moreover, it is a struggle that women must wage more actively for themselves.

Notes

[1] Olga Voronina, 'Muzhchiny sozdali mir dlya sebya', *Sovyetskaya Zhenshchina*, no 11, 1988, pp 14-15.
[2] Fedor Burlatsky, 'The State After Stalin' *Marxism Today*, July 1988, pp 30-33, reproduced in this volume, pp 85-93.
[3] *Izvestiya*, 6 October 1988.
[4] For more detail about discussions of women's liberation in nineteenth century Russia and in the early Soviet years see Richard Stites, *The Women's Liberation Movement in Russia*, Princeton University Press, 1978. For analysis of women's changing economic, political and social roles see Gail Lapidus, *Women in Soviet Society: Equality, Development and Social Change*, University of California Press 1978.
[5] For information about this debate refer to Mary Buckley, *Soviet Social Scientists Talking: An Official Debate About Women*, Macmillan 1986. Analysis of changing ideological lines on women can be found in

174 *The Soviet Revolution*

Mary Buckley, *Women and Ideology in the Soviet Union*, Harvester-Wheatsheaf 1989.

[6] *Sovyetskaya Rossiya*, 12 March 1987; *Sovyetskaya Rossiya*, 19 March 1987; *Komsomolskaya Pravda*, 19 September 1987; *Nedelya*, no 12, 1987, p 15.

[7] Alix Holt (ed), *Alexandra Kollontai: Selected Writings*, W W Norton, New York, 1977.

[8] *Isvestiya*, 1 February 1987.

[9] L Telen', 'Kakaya zhe ona, zhenskaya dolya?', *Sotsialisticheskaya Industrya*, no 18, 22 January 1988.

[10] *Vestnik Statistiki*, no 12, 1986, p 71; *Izvestiya*, 1 February 1987.

[11] Larisa Kuznetsova, 'What every woman wants?' *Soviet Weekly*, 26 November 1988, p 15. I am grateful to Jim Riordan for drawing this article to my attention.

[12] *Bakinskii Rabochii*, 31 January 1987.

[13] *Dagens Nyheter*, 11 January 1988. I am grateful to Riitta Pittman for this reference.

[14] G P Sergeeva, *Professionalnaya zanyatost' zhenshchin: problemy i perspektivy*, Ekonomika, Moscow 1987.

[15] *Izvestiya*, 2 July 1988.

[16] Boris Zagrebelnyi, *Formirovanie otnoshenii sotsial'nogo ravenstva zhenshchin i muzhchin-kolkhoznikov v usloviyakh razvitogo sotsializma*, candidate degree dissertation abstract, Kiev 1977, p 1; A E Kotlyar and S I Turchaninova, *Zanyatost zhenshchin v proizvodstve*, Moscow 1975, p 6.

[17] O B Bozhkov and V B Golofast, '*Razdelenie truda v gorodskoi seme,*' *Sotsiologicheskie Issledovaniya*, no 4, 1986, pp 68-75.

[18] Mikhail Gorbachev, *Perestroika i novoe myshlenie dlya nashei strany i dlya vsegomira*, Politizdat, 1987, Moscow, p 117.

[19] Kuznetsova, *op cit*, p 15.

[20] Mary Buckley, 'Female Workers by Hand and Male Workers by Brain: the Occupational Composition of the 1985 Azerbaijan Supreme Soviet, Reserach Note', *Soviet Union*, vol 14, no 2, 1988.

[21] Ronald J Hill, 'Continuity and Change in USSR Supreme Soviet Elections', *British Journal of Political Science*, I January 1972, pp 11-12.

[22] For further details, see Genia K Browning, *Women and Politics in the USSR*, Wheatsheaf, 1987.

[23] *Sputnik*, December 1988, p 32.

[24] Barbara Holland (ed), *Soviet Sisterhood*, Fourth Estate, 1985 p 10.

[25] *Sputnik*, December 1988, p 30.

[26] *Izvestiya*, 6 October 1988.

[27] For discussion of the *zhensovety* under Khrushchev and Brezhnev, see Browning, *op cit*.

[28] *Sovyetskaya Zhenshchina*, no 4, 1988, p 18.

[29] *Moscow News*, no 3, 1989. Thanks to Jon Bloomfield for this reference.

[30] Kuznetsova, *op cit*, p 15.

[31] *Bakinskii Rabochii*, 31 January 1987.

[32] Kuznetsova, *op cit*, p 15.

[33] *Komsomolskaya Pravda*, 28 October 1987.

[34] Information about these groups can be found in Alix Holt, 'The First Soviet Feminists', in Barbara Holland (ed), *Soviet Sisterhood*, pp 237-265.

Dennis Ogden

A Union of a New Type?

The issues of republican rights and the division of powers
have been thrown into sharp relief by the recent crisis of
national relations in the Soviet Union. This is partly a result
of a tension between the formalities in the constitution of the
USSR and the reality.

In form the soviet state is a federation of 15 member-
republics varying in size from the Russian Soviet Federative
Socialist Republic (RSFSR), with more than 140 million
people, to Estonia with 1.5 million. According to the Soviet
constitution, each republic is 'a sovereign Soviet socialist
state' which 'exercises independent authority on its
territory'.

In reality, the Soviet Union has since the early 1920s been
a highly centralised state in which the central, all-union
government regulates every significant aspect of the life of
the member-republics. The all-union government ensures
the implementation of 'a uniform social and economic
policy', drafts plans for economic and social development,
compiles the budget, controls the monetary and financial
system, fixes taxes and lays down prices and wages policy.
Central, all-union ministries in Moscow control the most
important branches of industry, including most major plants,
wherever they are situated. The all-union government lays
down the guidelines for the exploitation and conservation of
natural resources. It controls foreign trade and economic
relations.

The constitution enshrines the right of each republic
'freely to secede'. But there is no mechanism by which it can
be implemented. Indeed, federal unions rarely permit
secession: the American Union did not permit the secession

176

of the southern states, and the Soviet Union would likewise seek to preserve its integrity. Genuine federalism, like genuine socialism, proved incompatible with the 'administrative-command' system, the form of 'barrack-socialism' which emerged in the Soviet Union in the 1920s and '30s. In the words of sociologist and political commentator Fedor Burlatsky, 'we did not have a Leninist federation'.[1] Just as current discussion of the forms of socialist ownership, planning and management contains echoes of the debates of the 1920s, so too the current discussion of the nature of socialist federalism, republican rights and the division of powers carries echoes of debates which took place when the Soviet Union was first formed in the early 1920s.

The socialists of the Russian Empire had opposed a federal solution to its national problems. Their vision was of a tsarist empire transformed into a democratic, socialist and unitary republic, though with autonomy for areas of distinctive national character. They were internationalists, not nationalists, believing in the unity of the working people of all nationalities and creeds in the struggle against autocracy and capitalism. They believed large unitary states to be more in keeping with modern trends and more advantageous from the point of view of economic progress and the interests of the labour movement.

The Programme of the Russian Social-Democratic Labour Party, forerunner of today's Communist Party of the Soviet Union, at the same time proclaimed 'the right of self-determination for all nations forming part of the state', defined by Lenin as the right to free secession and independent statehood. Lenin defended this right against Rosa Luxemburg, who contended that 'in a society based on classes, the nation as a uniform social-political whole simply does not exist'.[2] He defended it, too, against fellow-Bolsheviks like Bukharin, Pyatakov and Radek, who then saw national and socialist aspirations as incompatible and the demand for self-determination as a concession to the divisive forces of nationalism.

Lenin also underlined that the demand for self-determination was put forward *not* in order to 'recommend' secession, but on the contrary, to facilitate and accelerate the *democratic* association and merging of nations ... not because we *favour* secession, but only because we stand for *free*, *voluntary* association and merging as distinct from forcible association. That is the *only* reason' (emphases in original – DO).

The British historian of the October Revolution and the early years of the Soviet Union, the late E H Carr, saw this 'combination between the recognition of a formal right of national self-determination and the recognition of a real need for unity in pursuit of common social and economic ends' as 'the essence of the Bolshevik doctrine of nationalism'.[3]

It was in spring 1917, against the background of the upsurge of national movements in many of the non-Russian regions of the Russian Empire following the February Revolution and the overthrow of tsarism, that Lenin began to speak of 'a union of free republics'. The concept of a 'voluntary and honest union of the peoples of Russia' was embodied in the Declaration of the Rights of the Peoples of Russia issued by the new Soviet government shortly after its accession to power. 'We are told that Russia will disintegrate and split up into separate republics, but we have no reason to fear this', said Lenin in December, 1917.

We have nothing to fear, whatever the number of republics. The important thing for us is not where the state border runs, but whether or not the working people of all nations remain allied in their struggle against the bourgeoisie, irrespective of nationality.

The concept of a federal union was enshrined in the Declaration of the Rights of the Working and Exploited People published in January 1918, which proclaimed the establishment of the 'Russian Soviet Republic' on 'the principle of a free union of free nations, as a federation of national republics'. It was for 'the workers and peasants of each nation to decide independently at their own representative Congresses of Soviets whether they wish to

participate in the federal government and in other federal
Soviet institutions, and on what terms', said the Declaration,
which became the basis for the first Soviet constitution, that
of the RSFSR. The concept of 'a federal union of states
organised on the Soviet model' was incorporated into the
Soviet Communist Party's first post-revolutionary programme adopted at its Eighth Congress in March, 1919. But
federal union was still seen as 'one of the transitional forms
to complete unity'.

A number of 'states organised on the Soviet model' were
set up in many parts of the former Russian Empire in the
months following the October Revolution. Some, like those
in Estonia, Latvia and Lithuania, were overthrown by
counter-revolution and foreign intervention. By 1921, when
the civil war was largely over and most of the foreign
interventionist armies had been withdrawn, there were six
Soviet republics on the territory of the old tsarist empire: the
RSFSR itself, together with Armenia, Azerbaijan,
Belorussia, Georgia and the Ukraine. Each was formally
independent, with many of the attributes of sovereignty: a
constitution, a government, an army and, in some cases, its
own currency and financial system and diplomatic and
consular relations with foreign powers.

The relations between the republics had evolved in
response to the needs of a bitter and protracted civil war
and resistance to foreign intervention; they bore the imprint
of hastily contrived *ad hoc* military and economic
arrangements designed to achieve the unity of leadership
and effort that the circumstances of the time demanded.
They had taken shape during a period in which government
assumed the character of what a resolution of the
Communist Party's Tenth Congress in March 1921 – the first
to be held in conditions of peace – termed a 'military
proletarian dictatorship', in which the Communist Party had
taken over the functions of the Soviets and itself undergone
a process of 'extreme organisational centralism' and
'militarisation'.

During the civil war and foreign intervention, 'national'
Communist Parties had been created in the non-Russian
republics – sometimes in the face of strong opposition from

leading Bolsheviks, both Russian and non-Russian. In appearance independent (the representatives of some attended early congresses of the Comintern), they were in reality component parts of the All-Russian Communist Party, in which they had the status of regional organisations. This is still the case today.

Thanks to its size and relative military and economic strength, the RSFSR had from the outset played the dominant role in the relations between the republics. Except in the case of Armenia, which, having no financial resources of its own, was in September 1921 incorporated into the financial system of the RSFSR, they were in 1920–21 linked to the RSFSR by bilateral military and economic treaties. Under the terms of these treaties, many of the key commissariats of the republics, including those of Defence, Finance, Railways and Foreign Trade, and also their National Economic Councils, were amalgamated with those of the RSFSR.

The obscurity and ambiguity of the relationships were highlighted by speakers at the Tenth Congress. 'Certain comrades, entire institutions like the Central Committee follow one line, while the People's Commissariats follow another', said Vladimir Zatonsky, a Ukrainian delegate. Zatonsky warned against the growth of what he described as 'a kind of Russian red patriotism'. There were those, he said, who 'consider themselves as Russian, sometimes as Russian first and foremost. It is not so much Soviet power and Soviet federation that they value, as 'Russia One and Indivisible', he said, recalling the old Tsarist slogan.

A Congress resolution called for 'a federation of Soviet republics founded on their common military and economic cause'. It declared that 'in isolation not a single Soviet republic can consider itself secure against economic exhaustion and military destruction at the hands of world imperialism'. The resolution at the same time warned against 'the special danger and special threat' of great-power, chauvinistic attitudes. Russian communists who had grown up as part of a 'great-power' nation, and had not experienced colonial repression, often belittled the significance of national characteristics, and took no account of the distinctive features of the class structure, way of life and history of other nationalities. In this way they vulgarised and distorted the party's policy on the national question.

Encroachments by RSFSR commissariats and officials upon the prerogatives of the republics gave rise to friction. Following protests from the Ukraine, the Communist Party's Politbureau on 10 August 1922 instructed the party's Organisation Bureau to set up a commission 'to study the question of the relations between the RSFSR and the independent national Soviet republics'. The commission was made up of representatives of the Central Committee of the All-Russian Communist Party and of the Central Committees of the Communist Parties of the republics.

Stalin, from April 1922 the party's General Secretary as well as People's Commissar for Nationalities, drafted a resolution which envisaged the incorporation of all five republics into the RSFSR as autonomous components. His proposal hence became known as Stalin's 'autonomisation' plan. The draft was circulated to the Central Committees of the Communist Parties of the republics for discussion. Those of Armenia and Azerbaijan approved it, but the Central Bureau of the Belorussian party called, in effect, for the continuance of the existing forms of relationship based on bilateral treaties; the Ukrainian Central Committee did not discuss the matter.

The Central Committee of the Georgian Communist Party discussed Stalin's draft in an atmosphere already tense as a result of friction on a wide range of other issues affecting the republic's sovereignty. It rejected Stalin's plan, declaring that

> union in the form of the autonomisation of the independent republics proposed on the basis of Stalin's theses is premature. The unification of economic efforts and general policy is necessary, but with the preservation of all the attributes of sovereignty.

Tatar and Bashkirian Communists who discussed Stalin's plan not only rejected it, but also called for the dissolution of the RSFSR and the transformation of its autonomous components into formally independent national republics.

Although it had the support of only two of the five

non-Russian republics, Stalin's plan was nevertheless approved by the Organisation Bureau's commission. It was sent to Lenin, by this time no longer involved in day-to-day political leadership. Lenin rejected the fundamental concept upon which Stalin's plan was based – that of the incorporation of the non-Russian republics into the RSFSR. He instead proposed that the RSFSR and the other five republics should enter 'on an equal basis, into a new union, a new federation', a 'Union of Soviet Republics of Europe and Asia'. He also proposed the creation, alongside the governing Central Executive Committee (TsIK) of the RSFSR, of a new body, a 'federal, All-Union Central Executive Committee of the Union of Soviet Republics of Europe and Asia', to represent the interests of the republics.

Stalin accepted Lenin's concept of the entry of the RSFSR into a new union on equal terms with the other republics, depicting it as no more than a minor amendment to his own proposal. He was later to describe proposals to abolish the republics as 'a reactionary absurdity'. But he opposed the creation of a new All-Union Central Executive Committee, arguing that the Central Executive Committee of the RSFSR should take on the functions of an all-union body. He described Lenin's proposal for the creation of a new body to represent the interests of the republics as 'national liberalism'.

The Communist Party's Central Committee approved a proposal for the establishment of what was to become the Union of Soviet Socialist Republics (USSR) at a meeting which Lenin was unable to attend on 6 October 1922. Its governing body was to be a Union Central Executive Committee made up of representatives of the Central Executive Committees of the republics in proportion to their populations. Its executive body was to be an all-union Council of People's Commissars (Sovnarkom), with all-union commissariats of Foreign Affairs, Defence, Foreign Trade, Railways and Posts and Telegraphs. The Commissariats of Finance, Food and Labour of the republics, as well as their Economic Councils and 'central organs of struggle against counter-revolution' were also to be subordinated to the directives of corresponding all-union bodies. A commission was set up to draft the appropriate legislation for submission to a Congress of Soviets. Its proceedings were marked by protracted and at times heated debate about republican rights and the division of powers between the governments of the republics and the proposed new all-union government.

The Declaration and Treaty establishing the USSR were approved by the First Congress of Soviets of the USSR on 30 December 1922. Both documents were at the time seen as constituting the basis for further discussion. Republican representatives were still seeking additional guarantees for the sovereignty of the republics, said the Bolshevik military leader Mikhail Frunze, a member of the Ukrainian delegation.

Lenin was on the same day dictating his memorandum on *The Question of Nationalities or 'Autonomisation'*, in which he challenged the centralising philosophy which he saw as underlying the new union.

> It is said that a united apparatus was needed. Where did that assurance come from? Did it not come from that same Russian apparatus which we took over from tsarism and slightly anointed with Soviet oil? There is no doubt that that measure should have been delayed somewhat until we could say that we vouched for our apparatus as our own

he wrote. He went on to speak of the possibility of a much looser form of association:

> We should not in any way exclude the possibility that as a result of this work we shall not take a step backward at our next Congress of Soviets, i.e., *retain the union of Soviet socialist republics only for military and diplomatic matters* (my emphasis – DO).

This memorandum – in which Lenin also charged Stalin with political responsibility for 'a truly Great-Russian nationalist campaign' against the leaders of the Georgian Communist Party, whom Stalin and his associates dubbed 'national deviationists' because they championed the sovereignty of their republic – gives the lie to the contention contained in the classic text of Stalinist historiography that the Soviet

Union came into being in the form in which it did 'on the proposal of Lenin and Stalin'.[4] Differences on this matter, and on the 'Georgian affair', were among the reasons prompting Lenin to urge in January 1923 that 'the comrades think about a way of removing Stalin'. It is one of a number of documents, now attracting much attention in the Soviet Union, which were dictated by Lenin in the last weeks of his active political life, in which he charted a way forward for the Soviet Union radically different from that which it was in fact to take after what many Soviet historians now see as a virtual *coup d'etat* engineered by Stalin and his associates at the end of the 1920s.

The contents of Lenin's memorandum were made known to delegates to the Communist Party's Twelfth Congress in April 1923 (though it was not to be generally published in the Soviet Union until after Stalin's death). Calls for a looser form of association between the Soviet republics were voiced in particular by Georgian and Ukrainian delegates. A Congress resolution stressed the 'absolute necessity' for the continued existence and development of the republics. They should retain the financial and budgetary powers necessary to enable them to act independently in the economic, administrative and cultural fields, and have their own military formations. The creation of the Soviet Union was 'the first experiment of the proletariat in regulating the international relationships of independent countries', it said, and 'a test for the Soviet apparatus'.

But the first Constitution of the USSR which emerged from the debates of 1922–3 exemplified the widening gulf between policy and practice, between word and deed. Despite formal safeguards for the rights of the republics, a comparison of the 26 clauses of the December 1922 Treaty and the 72 clauses finally incorporated into the constitution ratified in January 1924 demonstrates the ascendancy of centralising forces.

The responsibility for this rests not with the remnants of the old tsarist state apparatus to which Lenin had referred, but with the Communist Party. It was, for example, the Central Committee's constitutional commission which in the final stages of the discussion introduced amendments which restricted the powers of the republics with respect to industrial management and the conclusion of concession agreements with foreign companies, and which enhanced the overriding authority of central bodies.

The form of association enshrined in the 1924 constitution had many of the formal features of a federal structure. It was created by agreement between formally independent states, and formal recognition was given to their continuing sovereignty. An indirectly elected All-Union Congress of Soviets in its turn elected an All-Union Central Executive Committee as its standing body, with two chambers, one of them made up of representatives of the republics and other national entities forming part of the Union. There was provision for a division of powers between the central authority and the governments of the member-republics, and formal provision for the right of secession. Though neither the words 'federal' nor 'federation' appeared in the constitution as a definition of the form of association which it established, it was frequently described as such in contemporary speeches and documents.

But the facade of federalism could not obscure an accelerating centralising momentum, for which the domestic and international circumstances of the time were congenial; this momentum was, furthermore, fostered by a centralised party structure and an ideology strongly influenced by centralist concepts, and it received a powerful new impetus as a result of the political and economic processes which took place in the late 1920s and '30s. Accelerated industrialisation, based exclusively on one form of social ownership – state ownership – and on centralised, increasingly detailed planning and wholesale collectivisation, was imposed in large measure by force upon a peasantry which constituted some 80 per cent of the population. This led to the emergence of an 'administrative-command' system which was as incompatible with federalism as it was with democracy.

The Soviet Union's second constitution – the so-called 'Stalin Constitution' of 1936 – replaced the indirectly elected All-Union Congress of Soviets by a directly elected Supreme Soviet with two chambers. One, the Soviet of the Union, was elected on a constituency basis; the second, the Soviet of Nationalities, was made up of representatives of the republics and other national entities – 25 (increased to 32 in 1966) from each Union Republic, 11 from each Autonomous Republic, 5 from each Autonomous Region and one from each National Area. The Supreme Soviet met twice a year for sessions normally lasting four or five days. Its proceedings were formal, largely confined to the ratification of measures placed before it. Those of the Soviet of Nationalities in no way differed from those of the Soviet of the Union.

At all levels the authority of the Soviets had been usurped by the party apparatus. Power was in the hands of Stalin and his associates at the head of that apparatus. Even in formal terms, the division of powers set out in the 1936 Constitution left the republics and other national entities little voice in the management of their own affairs, or in the shaping of the policies of the Union. The constitution was amended in 1944 to enable Union Republics to have their own military formations and, subject to the overall supervision of the central government, to enter into direct relations with foreign countries, conclude international agreements and exchange diplomatic and consular representatives; however these rights have been exercised only by the Ukraine and Belorussia, both of which are members of the United Nations Organisation.

The division of powers and the rights of republics were not significantly altered by the adoption of the current constitution, which dates from 1977. This defines the Soviet Union as 'an integral, federal, multinational state formed on the principle of socialist federalism'. Moves to enhance the economic and budgetary powers of the republics undertaken at the end of the 1950s had changed little, and the right of republics to have their own military formations was omitted. During the discussion which preceded the adoption of the 1977 constitution there were proposals further to restrict the rights of the republics, or even to abolish them, thus transforming the Soviet Union into a unitary state. These were rejected, but they indicated the existence of anti-federalist, centralising trends which have deep roots in the history of the Soviet Communist Party's nationalities policy.

Nagorno-Karabakh

Symptoms of a crisis in national relations surfaced in December 1986, less than two years after the election of Mikhail Gorbachev as Communist Party general secretary, and the inauguration of perestroika, glasnost and democratisation. Demonstrations and inter-communal violence erupted in Alma-Ata, the capital of the Central Asian republic of Kazakhstan, following the replacement of Dinmuhammed Kunaev, the secretary of the republic's Communist Party, by a Russian, Gennady Kolbin, amid allegations of large-scale corruption and abuse of power. Widely reported and discussed as a consequence of glasnost, the events in Alma-Ata had a profound effect upon the public discussion of national relationships. The Politbureau noted 'distortions' of nationalities policy, and spoke of the need to 'eradicate patronage and selection on the basis of clan, tribal or local affiliations and friendship'. The Communist Party newspaper *Pravda* spoke of 'complex and intricate' opposition to reform, and to the existence of 'protection rackets and tribal mafias'.

In summer 1987 Crimean Tartars demonstrated in the Red Square in support of their long-standing demand to return to the homeland from which they were deported in 1944. They secured the appointment of a top-level commission to investigate their grievances. In the Baltic republics of Estonia, Latvia and Lithuania there were demonstrations calling for the rehabilitation of the victims of Stalinism, the filling in of the 'blank spots' of history and the publication of the secret protocol of the Soviet-German Non-Aggression Pact of August 1939, seen as having played a key role in the incorporation of the three republics into the Soviet Union in 1940.[5]

In February 1988 demonstrations and strikes in support of the demand for the transfer to Armenia of the administration of the Nagorno-Karabakh Autonomous Region (NKAR), a predominantly Armenian enclave administered as part of Azerbaijan since the early 1920s, began in Stepanakert, the region's capital. They were to continue throughout most of the year under the leadership of an 'informal' committee. Similar protracted demonstrations and strikes in support of the demand for the transference of the administration of the

NKAR to Armenia also began in Erevan, the republic's capital. Those, too, were under the leadership of a broadly representative, *ad hoc* 'informal' committee.

There is a history of ancient animosities between Armenians and Azerbaijanis: Armenians have a Christian, Azerbaijanis a Moslem, mainly Shiah, tradition; Azerbaijanis were nomadic herders ruled by khans, Armenians were farmers and traders, with a merchant élite influential throughout Transcaucasia and beyond. Nagorno-Karabakh has for centuries been a source of friction between the two peoples. In December 1920 the Bolshevik leaders of Azerbaijan, where Soviet rule had been re-established in April of that year, greeted the establishment of Soviet rule in Armenia with the declaration that Nagorno-Karabakh should have 'the complete right of self-determination'. The view that Nagorno-Karabakh should be part of Armenia was twice – first in June 1921 and again in July – endorsed by *Kavbureau*, the body then responsible for the implementation of Communist Party policy in Transcaucasia.

But the Azerbaijani leaders backtracked, fearing a nationalist backlash in their own republic. They opposed the transfer of Nagorno-Karabakh to Armenia and demanded that the matter be referred to Moscow. *Kavbureau* also changed its position, declaring that Nagorno-Karabakh should remain part of Azerbaijan. Many, even before the days of glasnost, attributed *Kavbureau's volte face* to behind-the-scenes intervention by Stalin.

By contrast, Nakhichevan, a similar though larger Azerbaijani enclave within Armenia, enjoys the higher and somewhat better defined status of an Autonomous Republic administered as part of Azerbaijan. The special relationship between Nakhichevan and Azerbaijan was set down in a treaty concluded between Soviet Russia and the Turkey of Kemal Ataturk in March 1921.

The 1988 call for the transference of the administration of Nagorno-Karabakh to Armenia was supported by the region's Soviet and also by the Supreme Soviet of Armenia. But it was rejected by the Supreme Soviet of Azerbaijan, where counter-demonstrations lasting many months took place in the main square of the republic's capital, Baku. Nationalism has many faces, and its ugly face was seen when more than 30 died in an anti-Armenian pogrom in the industrial city of Sumgait, some 20 miles north of Baku on the shores of the Caspian Sea.

The Presidium of the USSR Supreme Soviet, the standing body whose 39 members include representatives from each of the Soviet republics, discussed the Nagorno-Karabakh issue in March 1988 and again in July. The Presidium, whose terms of reference include the approval of any changes in the boundaries of republics, acknowledged that the national rights of the Armenians of Nagorno-Karabakh had been infringed. (Its representative in the region was later to declare that nowhere else in the Soviet Union had he encountered such neglect and disregard for the fate of people.) But it rejected the call for the transfer of the region's administration to Armenia. This position was subsequently endorsed by the Supreme Soviet itself, on the grounds that, under the terms of the Constitution of the USSR, a republic's territory could not be changed without its consent.

Mr Gorbachev argued that the *status quo* had to be retained because good ethnic relations required that there should be neither winners nor losers. But the retention of the *status quo* meant that there were both winners and losers – Azerbaijan, which continued to administer a region to which it had little claim in terms of history or ethnic composition, and the Armenians of Nagorno-Karabakh, who remained the victims of historical injustice. Mr Gorbachev frequently indicated his view that the dispute was the work of 'anti-perestroika forces, part of the vigorous reaction to perestroika on the part of corrupt groups', seeking to divert attention from corruption and maladministration. Many senior party and government officials in both republics were dismissed and expelled from the Communist Party. 'Anti-perestroika forces' and 'corrupt groups' certainly had a hand in events in Alma-Ata, but Mr Gorbachev was guilty of a serious misjudgement in seeing them as the instigators of events in Stepanakert and Erevan, where the demonstrators carried the slogans of perestroika, glasnost and democratisation.

In July 1988 a programme of investment and other measures to promote the economic, social and cultural development of Nagorno-Karabakh was launched. A team headed by Arkady Volsky, a senior Communist Party official, was sent to the area in an attempt to bring about a negotiated settlement. One of his first achievements was to bring about a meeting of the secretaries of the Communist Parties of the two republics – the first for 15 years. But the dispute continued. It became acute in autumn 1988, with outbreaks of violence and widespread intimidation as a result of which more than 200,000 people in both republics were forced to leave their homes. More than 40 were killed in inter-communal clashes. Troops were deployed and a curfew and state of emergency proclaimed in many parts of Armenia and Azerbaijan.

Even natural disaster did not blunt the bitter animosity: following the Armenian earthquake there were reports of 'congratulations' telegrams sent to Armenians from Azerbaijan, and of Armenians turning back relief convoys from Azerbaijan.

In a move unprecedented in the history of the Soviet Union, Nagorno-Karabakh was in January 1989 temporarily placed under a form of direct rule by the all-union government in Moscow, though remaining an Autonomous Region within the republic of Azerbaijan. Arkady Volsky became chairman of a Special Administrative Committee appointed by the Presidium of the Supreme Soviet of the USSR, while local government bodies in the region were suspended.

National tensions

The crisis in Nagorno-Karabakh has roots that go far back into history. Other symptoms of the crisis in national relations have roots in more recent history and are part of the legacy of Stalinism. The mass deportations of the Crimean Tartars, Meskhetians and other nationalities in 1944 and the large-scale arrests and deportations in the Baltic republics, particularly in 1940, 1941 and 1949 were among its specifically national manifestations. Other manifestations, such as the famine in the Ukraine in the early 1930s (the consequence of large-scale requisitioning and the disruption caused by coercive collectivisation) had a national dimension.

The vulgarisation and distortion of the party's policy on the national question, against which the Tenth Congress had warned in 1921, became a key component of Stalinism. It led to the distortion of the history of the Soviet Union and its peoples, to forms of 'national nihilism', the underestimation of national issues, complacency and an insensitivity often accompanied by the 'Russian red patriotism' to which Zatonsky had referred at that same congress.

The political mechanisms of the 'administrative-command' system offered no channel for the expression or redress of national grievances or the solution of problems of national relationships. The Soviet of Nationalities was a cypher. The republics, and especially the smaller national groups, are inadequately represented in 'all the organs exercising real power', according to Burlatsky.[6]

Kalmyk poet David Kulgutdinov has written:

> When I look at the Central Committee I do not see a single Kalmyk, not a single Buryat, not a single representative of the Kabardino-Balkhars or of other peoples. They are represented by Russians who as a rule do not know the language of those in whose name they attend the meetings. It is an offence to national feeling.[7]

The processes of industrialisation and urbanisation which have changed, and are still changing, the face of the Soviet Union have a national dimension. The industrial development of Kazakhstan has led to migration which has made Kazakhs a minority in their own republic. Industrial development in the Baltic republics – most of it undertaken by all-union ministries in Moscow – which many in the republics see as ill-considered and unnecessary, has led to an increase in Russian migration which many Estonians, Latvians and Lithuanians see as a threat to their national identity.

Increasingly, plans for irrigation schemes and atomic power stations encounter opposition couched in national terms. Proposals from ministries in Moscow to develop phosphorite deposits in the Pandivere Uplands in the south-east of Estonia, blighting rich agricultural land and disrupting the water regime over one-third of the republic's territory, became a catalyst in the movement for republican rights in the spring of 1987. Campaigns to restore historic monuments and re-vitalise decaying villages have also taken on national tints; founded to preserve the monuments of Russian history, *Pamyat* (Memory) has become a vehicle for strident Russian nationalism and anti-semitism.

There are fears of linguistic and cultural assimilation, and a tension between non-Russian languages and Russian as the medium of communication between all the peoples of the Soviet Union. As industrialisation got under way in the Tsarist Empire, it was said that 'capitalism speaks Russian'; so, too, did the 'administrative-command' system. Some non-Russian languages, especially those which acquired a script only in the years of Soviet rule, find the pressure of Russian difficult to withstand. In the 1979 census more than 16 million non-Russians said Russian was their mother-tongue, while more than half the non-Russian population said they spoke it fluently. By contrast, less than 5 million Russians – 3-4 per cent of the total – knew a language of the non-Russian peoples. Russians are seen as unwilling to learn other Soviet languages, or to have their children taught them, even when they live in non-Russian areas.

Other issues – bureaucracy, excessive centralisation, chronic shortages of foodstuffs and consumer goods, housing problems – can also have a national significance. Some 95 per cent of the Soviet Union's industrial output is controlled by all-union ministries in Moscow; only 7-9 per cent of the industrial output of the Baltic republics, for example, is controlled by the republics themselves. Estonians, Latvians and Lithuanians complain about what they see as the buying up of their foodstuffs and consumer goods by Russians, and there have been proposals to limit the sales of such items to non-residents; Russians meanwhile are only too well aware that the *per capita* output of foodstuffs and consumer goods in their own republic is among the lowest in the Soviet Union. The attacks upon Meskhetians by Uzbeks in June 1989 were said to have been sparked by disputes about strawberry prices.

Arkady Volsky sees social injustice as the main cause of the growth of national movement:

It is not a matter of ethnic or historic roots. A national movement appears above all where and when social justice is violated, when favourable conditions and privileges are created for the representatives of one nationality, while every kind of obstacle is put in the way of the development of the language, traditions, education and professional advancement of another.[8]

In a book published at the end of 1987, Mr Gorbachev noted the achievements of Soviet national policy. But he stressed that

this does not mean, however, that national processes are trouble-free. Contradictions are typical of any development, and they occur here as well. Regrettably, we used to stress our really considerable achievements in the solution of the nationality problem, and stressed the situation in high-flown terms. But this is real life with all its diversity and all its difficulties.

Improved educational standards and economic modernisation lead to the emergence of national intelligentsias and the growth of national awareness, to the growth of a nation's natural interest in its historic roots, he wrote.

It sometimes happens that in the process a certain section of the people descend to nationalism. Narrow nationalist views, national rivalry and arrogance emerge. If negative phenomena emerge in this highly sensitive sphere of human relations, they emerge not just of themselves, but as a consequence of red tape, and lack of attention to people's lawful rights.[9]

The spring and summer of 1988 saw the emergence of Popular Front and other 'informal' movements in many parts of the Soviet Union. Uniting communists and non-communists, conservationists and cultural and religious groups, they were born of the growing realisation that it was necessary to campaign for perestroika, glasnost and democratisation, and to involve wider sections of the public in political activity, hitherto largely the preserve of Communist Party activists.

The Baltic republics were in the forefront of these developments. Popular Front movements in Estonia and

Latvia and the *Sajudis* movement in Lithuania campaigned for the extension of republican rights and the protection of their national cultures and environment. They demanded the recognition of Estonian, Latvian and Lithuanian as the 'state languages' of the republics – 'the language of inter-ethnic communication for those living in the republic', in the words of the Latvian Popular Front. There were calls for restrictions on the influx of migrants into the three republics, and for the expulsion of those already there. Candidates supported by these movements won the majority of seats in the Baltic republics in the March 1989 elections.

The debate in the Baltic republics became wide-ranging. Economists argued that the republics should, like factories under perestroika, become self-managing, self-supporting and self-financing. In Estonia, there were proposals that the republic should have its own currency, which should be convertible, and that it should gradually shift towards western trade partners, inviting western banks and companies to finance the re-structuring of Estonia's economy.

In all three republics anti-Soviet currents emerged, attacking socialism, recalling with nostalgia the republics' interwar regimes and demanding immediate secession from the Soviet Union. In a Latvian constituency during the March 1989 election, Janis Dobelis, an advocate of immediate secession, secured 31 per cent of the votes, compared with the 51.3 per cent won in the same constituency by Janis Vagris, the secretary of the Latvian Communist Party.

The Russian-speaking communities – in Estonia they make up about 28 per cent of the population, in Latvia about 33 per cent and in Lithuania about 9 per cent – have set up their own movements: in Estonia the *Interdvizhenie* (Intermovement) and the Joint Council of Work Collectives (largely based at plants under all-union management), the *Interfront* in Latvia and *Edinstvo* (Unity) in Lithuania. Like the Popular Fronts and *Sajudis*, they affirm support for perestroika, glasnost and democratisation. Points of difference relate to the issue of 'state languages', citizenship and residence in the republics, quotas of national representation in the Soviets, aspects of the status of the republics and their rights, and the role of the Communist Party in broad organisations.

Commenting on the emergence of ethnically-based movements, with the implicit danger of inter-communal conflict, Janis Vagris observed that

> each has its pluses and minuses. There are differences of approach to particular questions, but at the same time their programmes have much in common. On the main issue their aspirations coincide. They want the acceleration of perestroika, and we are trying to help them find surer roads to that objective.[10]

Attempts at reform

The Communist Party's 19th Conference, which opened at the end of June 1988, became a milestone on the road to perestroika, glasnost and democratisation. The first such conference since 1941, it approved proposals for the first major re-structuring of the Soviet political mechanism since 1936. For the first time for many decades the issues of national relationships, republican rights and the division of powers were discussed in a major public party forum.

> Today we speak about the growth of the national awareness of all the nations and peoples of our country, about manifestations of national feeling (the manifestations sometimes being in a deformed way). All these are topical questions and they have to be solved,

Mr Gorbachev told the conference.

> We will also have to think about the forms of further developing ties between republics, and strengthening their rights, including their representation in the central state bodies.

The conference adopted a resolution which spoke of the need to re-structure the political mechanism in order 'to strengthen and develop the Soviet federation on democratic principles'. The rights of the republics should be extended, and the division of powers more clearly defined, it said. Legislation relating to the republics and other national entities would need to be revised and the constitution amended.

The resolution called for the re-vitalisation of institutions dealing with national relations, in particular the Soviet of Nationalities. It proposed the creation of a special body to deal with national relations – in effect, a successor to the Commissariat of Nationalities headed by Stalin and wound up in June 1923 on the grounds that it had fulfilled its purpose. The resolution spoke of the establishment of a research institute to study ethnic problems. The conference approved a Politbureau proposal, mooted earlier in the year by Mr Gorbachev, to convene a special meeting of the Communist Party's Central Committee, to consider national relations, scheduled for June 1989.

The draft amendments to the Soviet Constitution approved by the conference, incorporating the proposals for the re-structuring of the central political mechanism, were published in October 1988. They envisaged the creation of a new 'supreme organ of power', a Congress of People's Deputies, one-third of whose 2,250 members would represent the republics and other national entities of the Soviet Union; its standing body would be a smaller, new-style two-chamber Supreme Soviet meeting in spring and autumn for sessions each lasting 3-4 months. It is a structure in some respects echoing that of the 1920s and early '30s.

In the Baltic republics, and to a lesser extent elsewhere, the draft amendments were seen as reinforcing the centralism already inherent in the constitution. 'They were greeted with caution or open criticism. Many voiced disenchantment, seeing them as incompatible with the letter and spirit of the 19th Party Conference', a Lithuanian deputy told the session of the Supreme Soviet convened to consider them. 'According to its own figures, *Sajudis* collected more than 1.8 million signatures (a figure equivalent to half the population of Lithuania – DO) in support of the demand that they be not discussed'. Similar demands were voiced in Estonia and Latvia. The atmosphere was exacerbated by what was seen as tendentious, selective and inadequate reporting of developments in the Baltic republics in the central and local

Russian-language press, and by counter-charges from the Russian-speaking communities that their views were not adequately reflected in the republics' media.

On 16 November 1988 a special session of the Estonian Supreme Soviet adopted a Declaration on the Sovereignty of the Estonian Soviet Socialist Republic. Under its terms, amendments to the constitution of the USSR would apply in Estonia only after they had been approved by the Estonian Supreme Soviet and appropriate changes made to the republic's own constitution. The Declaration also asserted the primacy of the laws of Estonia in its territory. The session also approved a Law containing a series of amendments to the Estonian Constitution. One said that all-union legislation should come into force in Estonia only after it had been registered with the Presidium of the Estonian Supreme Soviet, which would have the right to suspend or limit the application of all-union legislation in Estonia. Another made the land, mineral wealth and other natural resources of Estonia, as well as factories, transport, communications and banks on the republic's territory the exclusive property of Estonia. A third introduced private property as a form of ownership recognised by the Estonian Constitution.

Both the Declaration and the Law were rejected as unconstitutional by the Presidium of the USSR Supreme Soviet. According to the Constitution of the USSR, the sovereignty of the Soviet Union extends to all its territory, and all-union legislation is effective throughout Soviet territory. The USSR Constitution envisages two forms of socialist property – state property, defined as that of the whole people, and collective or co-operative property; there is no provision for private ownership of the means of production. The land and natural resources, factories, communications, banks, etc, are defined as state property – that is, the property of the entire Soviet people, not of a particular republic.

Addressing the Presidium, Mr Gorbachev argued that the transference of natural and other resources to the exclusive ownership of Estonia would undermine the integrated economic system of the Soviet Union and make it impossible to pursue a uniform social and economic policy, to distribute production forces rationally and create integrated transport systems and power grids. All the regions of the Soviet Union are interdependent, he said. Estonia depended upon oil, ferrous and non-ferrous metals and many types of machinery from other republics; it received raw materials at prices below world levels and did not have to pay in hard currency. It in its turn supplied other republics with the products of its light industry, electronic equipment, household goods and foodstuffs.

Private ownership

> is the basis of the exploitation of man by man, and our revolution was carried out for the purpose of eliminating it and turning everything over to the people. The attempt to restore private property is a step backwards, and it is a profoundly erroneous decision

he declared. But Mr Gorbachev also noted the abuse and maladministration which had given rise to 'this crisis – I shall call things by their proper name'. It was necessary 'to see the legitimacy of the many real issues which Estonia has come to face and which demand a solution ... This shows once again that we have a problem of harmonising the centre and the republics'.

Republican rights and the division of powers featured prominently in the discussion at the special session of the Supreme Soviet of the USSR called in December 1988 to consider the draft amendments incorporating the proposals for the re-structuring of the central political mechanism. Mr Gorbachev rejected the view that the amendments reflected a tendency towards excessive centralism. But he acknowledged that some had been badly formulated. Substantial changes had been made, he said. The final text included provision for the right of republics to challenge all-union legislation and the decisions of all-union bodies through the newly-created Constitutional Review Committee, and also provision for republican representation on the committee. The number of representatives from each Union Republic in the new-style Soviet of Nationalities was increased from the seven envisaged in the original draft to eleven. A proposal from a Latvian deputy that representation in the new Soviet of the Union should also take account of the size of the electorate in each republic was accepted. So, too, was a proposal from a Georgian deputy that there should be mandatory consultation with the republic concerned in the event of the proclamation of martial law or a state of emergency in any locality. A proposal envisaging the possibility of referendums on a republican and local as well as countrywide basis was also accepted.

But a proposal from Arnold Ruutel, the Chairman of the Presidium of the Estonian Supreme Soviet, that republics should be free to decide for themselves whether they should introduce Congresses of People's Deputies, or should only have a directly elected, continuously functioning Supreme Soviet was rejected. The grounds for the rejection were that such a matter was not purely local and would violate the principle of the uniformity of governmental structures in all republics, which was enshrined in the Constitution of the USSR. The terms of reference of the Congresses were however left to the republics. A proposal by a Latvian deputy that groups of deputies from the republics should vote separately on issues of vital concern to the republics, and that such measures should be deemed adopted only if they secured the affirmative vote of all groups was likewise rejected, securing only 23 votes, in the main those of deputies from the Baltic republics. The revised package of amendments was approved with 1,334 votes in favour, five against and 27 abstentions. The votes against and the abstentions came from deputies from the Baltic republics.

In preparation for the second phase of the re-structuring of the political mechanism, the Supreme Soviet set up a working party including deputies from all the republics to draft proposals regarding the division of powers and the rights of the republics. The committee's terms of reference included the provision that any proposals should take into account the need to ensure the uniformity of the basic principles governing the political, economic, social and cultural development of the Soviet Union and the management of its economy as an integrated whole. Its proposals should enable the central government to organise the country's defence, represent it in international relations and deal with issues of all-union significance.

A draft measure designed to extend the economic powers of the republics was published for debate in March 1989.[11] Under its terms, agriculture, consumer industries, environmental protection, local transport, education, health, housing and social services would be transferred to republican control, with the abolition of a number of all-union ministries. Energy, the metallurgical industries, engineering, chemicals, pharmaceuticals and the medical industry, microbiological plants, long-distance transport and the defence industries would remain under all-union management.

It is estimated that over the country as a whole, the implementation of the measure would mean that the proportion of industrial output controlled by the republics would increase from 5 per cent to 36 per cent. In the case of the Baltic republics, where there are few heavy industrial plants, the proportion controlled by local government would increase from 7-9 per cent to 57-72 per cent.

As part of a process of transition to self-management and self-financing, the draft proposes the enhancement of the financial and budgetary powers of the republics. It also proposes that republics should be authorised to hold their own foreign currency reserves, engage in cross-border and coastal trade and set up their own foreign trade bodies – a step already taken by some republics.

Nationalities policy and the issues of republican rights and the division of powers featured prominently at the first meeting of the newly-constituted Congress of People's Deputies in May-June 1989. Mr Gorbachev, elected by the Congress as the Soviet Union's first presidential-style head of state, described how during the Stalin years nationalities policy had been subjected to 'the grossest distortions and deformations'. During the Brezhnev 'years of stagnation' national problems had been ignored or driven underground, where they had continued to fester. At the start of perestroika the need to renovate and re-shape nationalities policy had not been understood; there had been delay in tackling urgent problems. Mr Gorbachev told the Congress that

the federal structure of the state must now be invested with real political and economic content, so that it can fully satisfy the demands and aspirations of the nations and match present-day realities.

In a speech to the Communist Party's Central Committee in February 1988, Mr Gorbachev singled out nationalities policy as 'the most fundamental, vital issue of our society'. He has made clear his view that the Soviet Union needs a 'strong centre' – though Latvian poet Janis Peters reminded him that 'a strong centre cannot be made from weak republics. Weak parts don't make a strong whole'.[12] Mr Gorbachev has condemned the incitement of national and ethnic antagonisms. He has called for a calm and reasoned approach, urging both centre and republics to put aside mutual distrust and suspicion:

Our people of all nationalities, the population of all republics, should have full confidence that the problems that worry them, no matter whether they are related to economic, political, legal or cultural requirements of the present or to uncertainties and 'blank spots' in history – I repeat, all these problems should find a fair solution within the framework of perestroika through methods of democratic discussion and the working out of co-ordinated common position.

The crisis in national relations confronts the Soviet Union with the threat of destabilisation and national conflict,[13] even ultimate disintegration, with incalculable consequences for world peace and stability. But it also offers an opportunity – an opportunity to create a truly socialist association of nations, that 'free union of free nations' first proclaimed more than 70 years ago.

Notes

[1] *Literaturnaya Gazeta*, 28 December 1988.
[2] See Peter Nettl, *Rosa Luxemburg*, Oxford 1969, p 507.
[3] E H Carr, *The Bolshevik Revolution*, Macmillan 1978, vol I, p 258.
[4] *History of the Communist Party of the Soviet Union (Bolsheviks): Short Course*, Moscow 1948, p 322.
[5] The protocol was first published in the Soviet Union by *Rahva Haal*, the newspaper of the Estonian Communist Party (10-11 August 1988). Soviet commentators have said that no original text of the protocol has

been found in Soviet archives (see, for example, Dr Valentin Falin quoted in *Moskovskie Novosti*, 21 August 1988). According to historian Dr Viktor Anfilov, the West German Foreign Ministry, in reply to an enquiry from the Soviet Foreign Ministry, also said it had no original text. 'At the same time, I would hesitate to assert categorically that no such document was ever drawn up, albeit in the form of a draft. I would also not exclude a skilful forgery', he wrote (*Literaturnaya Gazeta*, 22 March 1989).

[6] *Literaturnaya Gazeta*, 28 December 1988.

[7] *Moskovskie Novosti*, 15 January 1989.

[8] *Pravda*, 15 January 1989.

[9] M S Gorbachev, *Perestroika: New Thinking for Our Country and the World*, Collins 1987, pp 118-122.

[10] *Pravda*, 13 January 1989.

[11] See, for example, *Ekonomicheskaya Gazeta*, no 12, March 1989.

[12] *Literaturnaya Gazeta*, 11 January 1989.

[13] The possibility of national conflicts was singled out as the most likely danger confronting Soviet society by 70 per cent of the respondents to a poll conducted by *Literaturnaya Gazeta*. Only 4.6 per cent saw war as a likely eventuality (see *Literaturnaya Gazeta*, 29 March 1989).

Nick Lampert

Democracy and Civil Society

Since the beginning of the current period of reforms, the theme of democracy has dominated Soviet political discourse. In the first two years of the Gorbachev leadership, in 1985-86, attention focussed on glasnost, on the loosening of censorship and the expanding boundaries of public debate. Thereafter, especially after the Central Committee plenum of January 1987, the appeal for a more fundamental change in the political structure came to occupy an increasingly important place in the language of perestroika. That led to the major programme of political change set out at the 19th Party Conference in the summer of 1988, followed closely by constitutional and electoral reforms at the end of the year. All this reflects a sense that the old way of governing, with a high concentration of political initiative in the hands of the party-state apparatus, an emasculation of the elected state bodies at central and local level, and tight controls over public debate, can no longer be sustained.

A number of key ideas and developments have been brought into play. First, there has been a fresh look at the position of the soviets and at the role of the party within Soviet society – a re-examination of the whole question of political accountability. Second, there is a new emphasis on the rights of individuals and groups in relation to the state, summed up in the phrase 'socialist legal state'. Finally, in potentially the most far-reaching development, the years 1987-89 have seen a rapid growth of political activity by 'informal' (non-party) organisations, standing outside the established party-state institutions and pressing a variety of national, environmental and social issues upon them. This embryonic growth of civil society forms the main focus of the present discussion. First, however, I shall briefly review the wider changes, some of which are discussed at greater length elsewhere in this volume.

Glasnost: the first phase

The changes that followed Gorbachev's accession to office in April 1985 were at first felt most strongly in the realm of the printed word and the mass media.[1] The adoption of the glasnost slogan unleashed the media – especially the national press – against those identified as responsible for the intertia, mismanagement and corruption of the Brezhnev years. In 1985-86 the press took on with a vengeance its function as an instrument of central party pressure, criticising and mobilising, justifying the removal of some and giving warning to others. In the future, it was said, there were to be no 'untouchable' officials, organisations and territories. This injunction was unlikely to be taken literally by journalists, but it signalled a state of greatly intensified conflict within the political apparatuses and an attempt by the leadership to mobilise the rank and file against the 'Brezhnevite' cadres. It was another war conducted by the state against itself, but this time without the blood-letting of the 1930s.

Glasnost has thus meant more scope for criticism of the party-state apparatus, from above and from below. It has also removed an increasing number of taboos on the reporting of events and has brought a greater flow of published social-statistical data – a change, in brief, in the approach to bad news. The Chernobyl disaster, which after a lengthy silence was massively covered by the Soviet media, provided a painful lesson in this respect. Unwanted and previously unrecognised phenomena like drug addiction, prostitution and suicide have made new appearances in the press and on television, and information which was 'closed down' under Brezhnev – for example on mortality rates and alcohol consumption – is now emerging into the light of day. Evidently the conclusion has been drawn that awkward facts should no longer be swept under the carpet in the old way, that bad news may be damaging to national prestige but silence is more so. 'We must tell ourselves clearly', said the editor of *Izvestiya* with reference to the inter-ethnic violence

Democracy and Civil Society 205

and mass protests in Azerbaijan and Armenia, that 'if this sort of phenomenon ... delivers a blow to perestroika then an even bigger, or at least not lesser blow is delivered by our silence about these ... events.'[2]

Glasnost in this context is to be understood in the proper sense. It means a greater honesty of reporting, not an end to political supervision of the media. Indeed, said a *Pravda* editorial in 1986, political supervision of the press needs 'constant improvement and deepening in the spirit of the times', in order to establish a 'general party point of view, incompatible with narrow bureaucratic and local interests'.[3] It is with such an object in view that Gorbachev has had regular meetings with people from the mass media in which he has impressed on them the direction in which perestroika is to go.

Yet the expansion in the boundaries of public debate – on economic reform and social policy, political and legal change, on the lessons of the Stalin period – has continued apace, gaining a powerful and surely now unstoppable momentum. In the first two or three years of the Gorbachev leadership the areas that were traditionally immune fom public scrutiny – the leading role of the party, the current political leadership and its policies, the military and security apparatuses – remained immune. But in 1987-88 the boundaries of debate constantly expanded, so that even these key features of the Soviet system no longer appeared unchallengeable.

Glasnost has provided the necessary condition under which the meaning of 'socialism' and 'democracy' could once more become open to discussion. The dominant thread in the thinking of the party leadership is one of guided democratic change, in which intellectual debate is encouraged and political accountability strengthened, while the 'leading and guiding role' of the party is maintained. 'Socialist pluralism' is not then 'political pluralism', but a competition of ideas within the boundaries of the socialist foundations of the system. Yet 'dogmatic' thinking is rejected and a painful exploration of the Stalinist past is under way. In these circumstances the meaning of 'socialist foundations', and the position of the boundaries, can no longer be taken for granted. It is this sense of *openness* to

change which, with all the current difficulties and resistance
to reform, creates the continuing sense of drama and of
future possibilities.

Democracy and legality

The changes associated with glasnost have been of huge
importance, but they could not in themselves create the
changes in political structure that have come to be seen as
vital if reform is to acquire a greater political momentum.
Faced with severe economic difficulties, with the tenacity of
the established political-administrative structure, and with
continuing conflict within the political apparatus, the party
leadership began to call more loudly for 'democratisation'
after the Central Committee plenum in January 1987. The
central importance of political reform was stressed at
subsequent sessions of the Central Committee, and was at
the centre of the concerns of the 19th Party Conference in
June-July 1988. There it was resolved to turn the Supreme
Soviet into a sitting parliament which would play an active
part in the legislative process, to bring in electoral reform
and to introduce major changes in the structure and
functions of the party. The party was no longer to interfere
in the day to day activities of the state apparatus and
management, but to concentrate on overall political strategy,
propaganda, and the selection of people for party posts. The
change would involve a 'deep democratisation' of the party.
The establishment of a joint leadership of party committees
and soviets, which has been widely criticised as incompatible
with the proclaimed emphasis on a separation of powers,
could be presented in this light. It could provide one
mechanism by which party officials might be made
accountable to a wider constituency.

Along with these changes in the political system, discussed
in more detail elsewhere in this book, there has been a
strong emphasis on legality. The key phrase is 'socialist legal
state', a Soviet version of the 'rule of law'. The language of
legality is in part the result of an effort to impose greater
central control over unruly officials, but it also testifies to the
search for some form of constitutionalism that would give
the political system a new type of legitimacy. 'In adding the

concept "legal" to the characterisation of our state,' says one of the theses for the 19th Party Conference,

> it should be emphasised that it is not only citizens who bear responsibility before the state, but also the state which bears responsibility before citizens. The state is obliged to show constant concern for strengthening the guarantees of Soviet people's rights and freedoms.[4]

In line with this project, a number of new laws have been enacted, or are in the pipeline, which are intended to strengthen such rights. Important among these is a law on the mass media which is to lay down rules for the publication or broadcast of critical material, to establish rights of access to information and the obligations of state bodies in that connection. This is a highly contested area, which no doubt explains why the publication of the draft document has taken such a long time coming – much longer than originally predicted. A big package of legal reforms, affecting especially the system of criminal justice, will increase the rights of the individual in relation to law enforcement and other state agencies. Other important pieces of current or forthcoming legislation concern public meetings and demonstrations, and the status of voluntary associations. I shall return to those below.

These legal and constitutional developments testify to a sense of crisis of political authority. The rulers of the Soviet state have traditionally stressed the superiority of Soviet over bourgeois forms of democracy. But the Soviet language of legitimation has other sources, since the 'leading and guiding role of the party' is linked to its position as keeper of a sacrosanct (if changing) body of ideas about society and its needs. The type of authority which was established on this basis now looks increasingly fragile. A critical issue therefore is how far this fundamental pillar of the Soviet system is indeed open to change. The question of the leading role has not yet been confronted head-on, but a number of commentators have suggested that the meaning of 'leadership' and 'guidance' in the official formula needs more careful investigation.[5] This is the beginning of a process in which the established political structures of Soviet socialism – which is not to say its *values* – are coming into fundamental question.

The emergence of civil society?

The changes associated with glasnost, and with legal and constitutional reform, have created the basis for a greater freedom of ideas and for a more accountable political apparatus. Yet a deeper potential challenge to the old system is coming from the informal groups and movements which have multiplied at great speed since 1987, taking advantage of the freer political climate to establish a position outside the party-state apparatus. The year 1988 saw an unprecedented growth of new groups and associations supporting a variety of national, ecological, social and human rights issues. At the beginning of 1989 a prominent reformer could speak of 'tens of thousands' of informal organisations, 'many of which are already taking on a political colouring'.[6]

The development started with the emergence in 1985-86 of youth clubs and associations with mainly cultural interests (rock music was very important in this context), creating a mood reminiscent of the western counter-culture of the 1960s. After a long period under Brezhnev in which the more adventurous cultural activities had been pushed underground, the new climate created an exhilarating sense of cultural freedom. Then during 1987 clubs with environmental and wider political concerns emerged. These included associations with names such as Club for Social Initiatives, Citizen Dignity, Perestroika, Commune, Young Communal Transnationals, Outpost, Federation of Socialist Clubs (established during a big meeting of clubs in Moscow in August 1987), Democratic Union, Democracy and Humanism, Rescue, Council for the Ecology of Culture, Epicentre, Forest People.

The more political groups were concentrated to begin with in the biggest cities, and drew their social support mainly from the intelligentsia. Thereafter there was an expansion of informal activity, especially in connection with growing environmental concerns. This has drawn in broader social strata and given the 'informals' a wider geographical presence. Agitation from Russian cultural and environmental groups had already in 1987 helped to block – though possibly only to postpone – projects to divert the flow of northern rivers to Central Asia; these schemes now have to confront some formidable objections. Leningrad had seen considerable activity arising from concern about ecological threats to Lake Ladoga. In 1988 an increasing number of enterprises, ministries and local authorities were confronted with protests about high levels of environmental pollution. Mass activities (letter-writing campaigns, demonstrations and rallies), along with pressure from the scientific community and from environmental protection bodies, has helped to put the environment on to the agenda in a big way. In some cases popular action has brought a halt to production or speeded the introduction of anti-pollution measures.

In the town of Kirishi near Leningrad, emissions from the Soviet Union's first bio-technology plant have been wreaking havoc with the health of the population (the incidence of bronchial asthma, for example, had increased 35 times in the 12 years since the plant was built). 12,000 people (out of a total population of 60,000) were said to have come out onto the streets in early 1988, and promises of improvement were made by the Minister for Bio-industry. Alarming degrees of air and water pollution (according to Ministry of Health figures, the air in at least 104 Soviet cities is dangerous to breathe, and 50 per cent of the Soviet population is using water that doesn't come up to state standards), unrestrained use of herbicides and chemical fertilisers, and frequent absence of special waste sites, have brought strong popular reactions in many Soviet cities: for example in Nizhnyi Tagil (Sverdlovsk province), Baku and Sumgait (Azerbaijan), Erevan (Armenia), Gorky, Yaroslavl and Kiev. In Ufa in Bashkiriya (an 'autonomous republic' within the Russian republics) the activities of the Social Council For Clean Air And Water were instrumental in getting a new chemical plant transferred beyond the boundaries of a city which already had three oil-refining plants and several chemical factories – after a meeting in which 'thousands' of people gathered outside the local council to call for a change in the existing scheme.[7] The

Ecological Front in Uzbekistan was acknowledged by the
party leader of the republic to have played a vital role in
halting the development of a new plant by the USSR
Ministry of Mineral Fertilisers.[8]

1988 saw further major developments in the shape of mass
support for the Popular Fronts that emerged in Estonia,
Latvia and Lithuania, and the tide of Armenian sentiment in
favour of a transfer of Nagorno-Karabakh to Armenia.
Popular Fronts for Assistance to Perestroika, or organisations with similar names, have been set up in Moscow,
Leningrad, Kiev, Lvov and a number of other cities. The
Memorial association emerged in 1988 to lead a campaign
for full destalinisation, collecting money for the families of
victims of the repressions and for the erection of local
monuments.[9] Proposals have been made to establish a
Popular Front on a national basis, and one prominent
reformer has called for a 'democratic platform of
perestroika' within the framework of the general party
platform.[10]

Environmental and national issues have to some extent
come together. Representatives of some of the non-Russian
republics (Ukraine, Armenia, Georgia, Latvia, Lithuania
and Estonia) met in June 1988 in Lvov to form a Patriotic
Movement of the Peoples of the USSR (separate from the
Popular Fronts) to put forward demands for greater national
autonomy. Among other issues the question of consultation
on the nuclear power programme was put forward.[11]

Russian nationalism has also made a strong appearance
within the political space opened up for the informal
associations. In its milder versions it is preoccupied mainly
with the preservation of Russian cultural and historical
monuments. In the case of the Pamyat organisation,
national sentiment has taken the form of a virulent Russian
chauvinism and anti-semitism. The new political freedom
has thus brought out more clearly than before the various
ideological trends which under Brezhnev had a covert or less
articulated existence. There are different views about the
potential strength of the more extreme Russian nationalist
views, but the emergence of some unsavoury political
currents is evidently part of the price to be paid for greater
political openness.

One consequence of the development of the informal movement has been the emergence of workers' clubs in some Soviet cities, though the numbers involved are thus far small.[12] The difficulties arising from the transition to self-financing have caused many disputes and stoppages. In the event that economic reform takes root, relationships between enterprise management and the workforce will change. If the Brezhnev 'deal' was that workers might get away with low effort while management could get away with very poor work conditions, successful economic reform would require another type of deal. For example, the poor safety record of Soviet industry will surely no longer be tolerated in circumstances where greater demands are being made on the workforce. Up to now Soviet trade unions have had no teeth in this context, and the channels for self-management and election of managerial personnel set up in 1987 seem to have been greeted with scepticism by the majority of the workforce.[13] Under those circumstances informal groups are likely to increase in importance within the working class.

Informal associations: an ambivalent response

All this activity testifies to the emergence of new social forces with a public presence outside the established political structures. None of it was conceivable under the pre-Gorbachev conditions. Still, it is not a surprise to find that the role and status of the informal associations remains a subject of intense dispute and that the official response to such activities has been very ambivalent. The growth of social movements has created a radical challenge to the traditional forms of politics, and the different reactions to the 'informals' within officialdom provides a very sensitive indication of the extent and limits of political change.

The informal movement is a natural consequence of perestroika and has become an important part of the Gorbachev project. Although everyone seems to be in favour of perestroika in principle (it is a strong yes-word, so this is almost a tautology), it is another matter to create a social constituency for concrete reform measures from which there are some winners but also losers. Without the *voluntary* involvement of large groups of people from below, it is hard to see how that constituency can be strengthened and thus how the momentum for reform can be carried through. It is, to be sure, possible to imagine a radical economic reform imposed by political fiat, in which case 'liberalisation' would also mean a 'strong state' in which there would be little space for politically-oriented autonomous groups. But there is no evidence that this is the direction in which things are likely to move.

A representative position of the radical wing of the Soviet establishment on these 'informal groups' can be seen in the views of Tatiana Zaslavskaya, an influential academic reformer whose name has become well-known in the West. Zaslavskaya regrets that 'some groups ... begin to use extreme methods'. But 'this is a new situation for our society' in which the 'striving for independent activity [and] direct participation in social life' is a vital element of perestroika, which must inevitably bring social conflict, not only in the non-Russian republics but also within Russia. Zaslavskaya argues that if these conflicts are to be successfully managed the political leadership will have to learn to cope with a more complex set of tasks, supporting and entering into a genuine dialogue with the independent social organisations. So far only the first steps have been made, but a force has made itself felt which cannot be ignored. It has set an example that could be taken up by a much broader public within the working class, intelligentsia and peasantry. At the same time it will be important to maintain 'control over their activity with the aim of directing it into channels that correspond to the social interest', especially since glasnost and the strengthening of political rights has created an opening for 'chauvinistic, nationalistic and even fascist groups'. There must be a 'reasonable compromise' between further political activity and the maintenance of public order.[14]

Elsewhere, hostile reactions to informal political activity have been gathering over the past year, especially after the experience of the Armenia-Azerbaijan conflict over Nagorno-Karabakh and the explosive development of the Baltic Popular Fronts. To the conservative-minded the informal groups appear dangerously anarchic. However undeveloped their current state, they present a serious potential threat to the time-honoured forms of political control. The task is to prevent a descent into anarchy by limiting their activities or giving control over them to the established political institutions – the party, the communist youth committees, the trade unions.

These conflicting pressures can be seen in arguments over the legal status of voluntary associations. By early 1988 a draft law had been drawn up behind the scenes, which was to determine 'the status of unofficial associations and the principles of their relationship to state institutions and public organisations'. A copy of the draft was obtained by some of the political clubs and subjected to intense criticism because it gave local soviets the authority to decide if a club was worthy of registration and if, therefore, it could be a legal organisation. At a meeting with representatives of the drafting commission it was urged that any groups should be permitted to register as a voluntary society, and that all groups should have access to printing facilities.[15]

A decree on meetings and demonstrations, promulgated without public discussion in July 1988, gives an idea of the shape the new law on voluntary organisations is likely to take. This decree details the right to march and demonstrate which was only vaguely stated in the constitution, but it also allows the local soviets to prohibit meetings whose purpose is deemed to be 'contrary to the USSR Constitution' or is a threat to public order.[16] This gave the Moscow city soviet the legal authority to prohibit, for example, a demonstration by the Democratic Union to commemorate the 20th anniversary of the Soviet invasion of Czechoslovakia – a meeting that went ahead and was broken up by the police. The refusal was given not only on public order grounds but also because the initiators' 'attempt to present the policy of the Soviet government in a clearly distorted form'.[17]

Objections to this decree have been voiced in the press, on the grounds that there is a constitutional right to demonstrate and organisers should not have to ask permission. The local authorities should be able to ban a rally on specific grounds but one should be able to challenge such a ban in the courts.[18] On the other side, an editorial note in *Pravda* in August 1988 commented that the leaders of the Democratic Union 'deliberately go beyond the bounds of a socialist pluralism of views, provoking violation of legal order', and noted that law enforcement agents, 'fearing accusations of excess', had recently weakened their struggle against such violations. Such a policy was 'diametrically opposed to the principles of a legal state'.[19] The rhetoric of the 'legal state' can thus be put to different uses depending on the vantage point of the observer and the political needs of the moment.

The sense of distrust of informal groups came out in a recent interview with G V Kolbin, first secretary of the Kazakhstan party committee. He praised the role of the local Ecological Front in halting the development of a new ferti- liser plant, but gave most of the credit to two regional party secretaries who had sponsored meetings in which 'thousands' in the cities of Dzhambul and Chimkent had been addressed by the USSR Minister of Mineral Fertilisers. In Chimkent the province's party organisation had asked the Front to set up a social committee and cells in enterprises. As a result 'there emerged a well-organised force'. It is apparent that 'well- organised' here means 'monitored and controlled by the party'. Kolbin welcomed social initiatives to help with the building programme or with agricultural development or care for the sick. But one could do without 'salon conversations about democracy [and] freedom of speech' because 'we have enough windbags as it is ... [both] the nightingales of peres- troika among the apparatchiks, and the defenders of the people among the "informals" '. Both types of people discre- dited perestroika. Democracy was a great thing, but 'if one uses it incorrectly one may go very far ... When the party and soviet organs let slip from their hands control over the situation, then apolitical forces may get the upper hand ...'[20]

In the latter part of 1988 more of such sentiments were being publicly expressed than before. A particularly strong statement was made by A Vlasov (Chairman of the Council of Ministers of the RSFSR and candidate member of the Politburo). Various centrifugal tendencies were possibly the 'greatest danger for our society':

> Attempts to undermine the institutions of power, and moods of
> social nihilism must be countered by a policy of strengthening

discipline and order in every way, of strengthening socialist statehood ... We cannot permit a slide into anarchy, aimless meetingism (*mitingovshchina*).[21]

These are the authentic voices of a conservative version of perestroika, the version of which Ligachev has been the most prominent exponent. Social mobilisation is desirable, but strictly on the terms defined by political officialdom itself. The sentiments expressed by Vlasov might well be echoed by the great majority of Soviet officials, especially after the experience of national conflicts over the past year. They would also find a strong resonance among those sections of the wider Soviet population which are likely to equate 'freedom' with 'anarchy'. At a lively public meeting organised by some of the Moscow political clubs in May 1988 (which was watched over amicably by the police), I heard a bystander complain vociferously, before she had a chance to find out what the meeting was about, that it was 'not nice (*ne krasivo*) in our society', it was 'not normal' (*nenormal'no*). In other words, it was OK for 'them' (in the West) to have such meetings, but here it was a sign of unwanted disorder and lack of respect for authority. This perception of things is undoubtedly very widespread, especially among the older generation. However, there is no reason to assume that it is a cultural trait fixed for all time.

Gorbachev himself has adopted an apparently mediating stance. In a major speech to a meeting of the intelligentsia in January 1989, he strongly criticised those whose said that perestroika was bringing chaos and that socialist principles were being abandoned, who were nostalgic for the 'good old days' and calling for a 'strong hand' to sort things out. Discussions and socialist pluralism were vital in order to take into account public opinion and the variety of social interests, and to identify errors in policy. However there was also a danger from those who had decided that 'the framework of socialism is too tight for perestroika'. 'Gradually the idea of political pluralism, of a multi-party system and even private property is being thrown in.' Under the appearance of glasnost attempts were being made to attack the party which had initiated the idea of perestroika and which 'is now leading the work for democratisation'.

The party was exercising its role in the context of an opposition of views, but 'in a period of deep changes we have even more need of a theoretically, ideologically, organisationally strong party'.

There was, then, no cause for panic from the 'right' about a descent into anarchy, but the opposite 'leftist' position was also a threat:

> We consider especially dangerous the adventurist and irresponsible appeals to sharpen the struggle, to inflame passions artificially and to shake up cadres with the use of those same methods that we are trying to move away from through perestroika, through the democratisation of our society.[22]

The uncertain balance of forces is reflected in conflicting reactions to particular events. For example, after the action in Ufa by the Council for Clean Air and Water, which helped to change the siting of a new chemical plant, the local press launched an attack. 'This council, despite its "ecological" name, engages in political activity, thus assuming the role of a political organisation.' One of the organisers was given a dressing down by the local police and KGB, and dismissed from his job in a scientific institute. However, he was later reinstated by a court (though he did not return to his former work), and gained the support of *Izvestiya*.[23]

At present there is an attempt to draw in the reins and to ensure that the process of guided democratisation does not get out of hand. In the new Congress of People's Deputies to be elected in the spring of 1989, 70 seats have been allocated to 'social organisations', but expedients have been found which make informal groups ineligible for representations: organisations must have a central body and be registered in accordance with rules drawn up in 1932. This will help to inhibit the establishment of links between the informal movement and party-state institutions. However, that will not debar informal groups from playing a part in the elections in Spring 1989. The general thrust of things is towards an expansion of the scope of activity of informal groups. That development can be expected to incur a lot of resistance from parts of the apparatus, but the party leadership will not wish to cut itself off from such an important source of social support.

Conclusion

The Soviet Union has embarked on an historic course of change. The obstacles to a democratisation of the political system are formidable. There is the weight of the past on the present. There is the weakness of the present social constituency for economic reform, which so far has brought no tangible results for the great majority of the population. The reform is bound, if deepened, to create losers as well as winners, as a result of greater demands on the workforce, job losses and price increases. The signs of social tension are already there, and this may for a time benefit the more conservative political forces because the difficulties and disruption can be laid at the door of the radical reformers.

The critical question is thus how to win a broader constituency for the radical reform project. This is not made any easier by the vagueness that surrounds the *concept* of radical (or even revolutionary) reform, the idea of perestroika itself. Soviet reformers now draw the distinction between two versions of perestroika: 'radical-democratic' and 'conservative'. The former stands for a 'real' democratisation, the latter represents the old administrative system with soft gloves. But how many Soviet citizens understand the New Order – in whichever version – as a programme to which they can say yes or no? Only a long period of political argument and experimentation could be expected to clarify the nature of the political options. In this setting the role of non-party groups and organisations, standing outside the control of the established political apparatuses, becomes vital. The creation of a bigger political space for the non-party forces (including the 'informals'), if not for an official political opposition, is not a luxury. It is a necessary condition for the development of a strategy of reform and strengthening social support for it.

To judge by his speech to the intelligentsia in January 1989, Gorbachev's stance on this question is open-minded, though how fully his public statements reflect his own views is open to question. On the one hand, he was at pains to

counter those 'left' critics who were saying that the
leadership did not have a clear strategy:

> I think we ought to reject all the speculation that supposedly we
> have no idea where we are heading and what we are doing; we
> ought all of us to become actively involved in the further
> intensification and interpretation of perestroika and in
> constructive work to put the plans mapped out into practice.[24]

He reminded the audience as well that perestroika was to
take place within the boundaries of 'socialist pluralism', and
was not to be sidetracked by the idea of multi-partyism. In
other words, the party remained the source of correct ideas
and programmes and in that sense beyond challenge.
Izvestiya was bold enough to take this on board when it
quoted a letter addressed to Soviet journalists:

> How sincere are your odes to perestroika? Again everyone is in
> favour. So far I have not read a single serious critical article
> about the present policy of the party, yet there are people who
> have another point of view, another conception of develop-
> ment. I do not understand the kind of democracy under which
> one can criticise only after a 'changing of the guard'.[25]

Yet Gorbachev was also at pains to say that 'we are far
from considering that everything is already clear to us now',
and that 'we are coming to know the true seriousness of
many problems only today ... Ever new problems arise for
which there is no easy solution.'[26] The rhetoric of
perestroika makes it look as if the strategy has been worked
out, and it is now just a question of rallying the troops
around the correctly formulated policies. But alongside and
behind this traditional discourse is the recognition that
nothing is any longer certain or sacred. It is therefore quite
conceivable that the Soviet system will find new ways of
accommodating greater spontaneity and a less interventionist role for the party in economy and society. Alternative
scenarios involving new forms of authoritarianism can also
be imagined, especially in the event of economic crisis. But
the direction of political change points towards a new
relationship between the Soviet state and its citizens in

which a more secure civil society could emerge. In this case the 'system' will indeed no longer be the same.

Notes

[1] The argument of this section is more fully developed in 'The dilemmas of *glasnost'*, *Journal of Communist Studies*, December 1988.

[2] *Pravda*, 11 May 1988, at a meeting of mass media representatives with Gorbachev.

[3] *Pravda*, 26 March 1986.

[4] Translated in *Guardian*, 7 June 1988.

[5] L Ionin, *Moscow News*, 1988.

[6] T Zaslavskaya, *Izvestiya*, 24 December 1988.

[7] *Izvestiya*, 4 October 1988.

[8] G Kolbin, *Literaturnaya Gazeta*, 7 December 1988.

[9] M Gorbachev, *Pravda*, 7 January 1989.

[10] *Radio Liberty Research Bulletin*, 466/88; G Popov, *Trud*, 31 December 1988.

[11] *Radio Liberty Research Bulletin*, 465/88.

[12] Information provided by Boris Kagarlitsky, Moscow, June 1988.

[13] This is documented in D Mandel, ' "Revolutionary reform" in Soviet factories', unpublished paper.

[14] T Zaslavskaya, *Izvestiya*, 24 December 1988.

[15] Information provided by Grisha Pelman, Moscow, June 1988.

[16] Decree of 28 July 1988, BBC, *Summary of World Broadcasts*, 2 August 1988.

[17] Comment by G Ovcharenko, *Pravda*, 24 August 1988.

[18] *Sovyetskaya Kultura*, cited in *Radio Liberty Research Bulletin*, 472/88.

[19] *Pravda*, 26 August 1988.

[21] *Pravda*, 26 December 1988.

[22] *Pravda*, 8 January 1989.

[23] *Izvestiya*, 4 October 1988.

[25] *Izvestiya*, 24 December 1988.

[26] *Pravda*, 13 January 1988.

4. The International Context

The Superpowers, Europe and the Third World

Fred Halliday

Superpower Relations in Transition

In June 1988 Fred Halliday analysed the main elements in the shifting terrain of superpower relations.

The Reagan-Gorbachev Moscow summit comes at a moment of great international importance. After six years of the second cold war, commencing in 1979, there has been a substantial thaw in Soviet-US relations since 1985, when Gorbachev came to power in February and the Reagan administration shifted ground on negotiations with the USSR. But so far, image and mood have changed more than substance. The November 1985 Geneva summit yielded nothing, and the Reykjavik meeting in October 1986 produced little more: Gorbachev's attempt to impel the arms control talks forward broke against Reagan's commitment to SDI, itself a reflection of greater US strength in the bargaining process.

The Washington meeting of December 1987 did produce one solid result: the Intermediate Nuclear Forces (INF) agreement. It also occasioned some unpublicised discussions on Third World issues, notably Afghanistan and Angola. But even assuming the INF agreement is ratified, its importance lies above all in the extent to which it too can produce a broader momentum of East-West detente in arms control and the Third World: on its own a 4 per cent reduction in existing arsenals, without any stop on other on-going, 'futuristic' technologies in the strategic and space fields, will amount to little.

The elements of this major period of transition are, in essence, four.

First published in *Marxism Today*, June 1988

Arms negotiations

The first is in the negotiations on arms themselves. Negotiations on nuclear weapons both encourage and reflect broader political and social processes. If the INF agreement reflects some more nebulous willingness of both sides to compromise, it also indicates that Moscow and Washington have run up against substantial internal obstacles in the arms race: the Russians can ill afford a further uninhibited round of strategic competition, the Americans have discovered that even their economic and technological power has its limits, and that the attempt to bankrupt the USSR through an arms race has done not a little to enhance their own budget deficit and weaken their competitiveness *vis-à-vis* Japan and western Europe. The result is the current burst of goodwill in the arms control process.

These political and economic issues aside, the importance of the INF agreement lies not so much in the reduction of European-based missiles as such, as it does in the potential breakthrough which it represents in verification procedures. Both sides are now supposed to provide each other with full details of INF weapons deployment and manufacture, to allow officials from the other side to inspect these sites, to permit sudden visits with only 16 hours warning to suspect positions and to open up for satellite surveillance missile sites which the other side regards as in potential violation of the agreement. Such provisions make surprise attack and mutual suspicion much less likely: the information released by both sides after the December signing of the INF agreement has already surprised experts, in government and in the strategic studies 'community', who now see how wide of the mark many of their earlier authoritative estimates were.

The hope of those promoting the Strategic Arms Reduction Talks – START – is that verification measures such as these can now be carried forward into the current round of talks. But there are several reasons why this may not take place, and there is little expectation that a START treaty can be initialled when Reagan arrives in Moscow in late May. In mid-April George Shultz stated that there were

1200 points in the draft treaty over which the Soviet and US sides were still in disagreement, and there are two overriding problems that divide the INF from the START negotiations: the first is that the INF missiles are not the central pillar of each state's security, whereas the strategeic ones are – (land-based) ICBMs, and (submarine-launched) SLBMs; the second is that it is much easier to verify a *complete* abolition of weapons, as occurred with the INF zero-zero option, than it is to verify that a 50 per cent reduction, the goal of the START talks, has been achieved. Partial reductions allow much more room for doubt, and concealment, than total abolitions.

Many other, more technical, problems remain. The Americans want to cut into the area of Soviet strength, land-based ICBMs, while the Soviet Union wants to place emphasis on US strength, the sea-based SLBMs. The Americans are particularly concerned to reduce or abolish completely mobile ICBMs, where the USSR with its SS-25s has greater strength; the Americans seem to have applied brakes to their own attempts to develop mobile intercontinental missiles, notably through the MX missile which was the subject of much strategic fashion in the early 1980s.

For the Russians the greatest threat comes from sea-launched cruise missiles: these are, in the Soviet view, strategic, since they can hit the Soviet Union's territory, and they could in effect compensate for the loss of the land-based INFs. The Russians are, therefore, intent on blocking US deployment of them. An armada of American ships in the Baltic and Black Seas equipped with such cruise missiles would do much to annul any real significance of the INF agreement.

Beyond these two areas of discussion there lies the even more intractable question of SDI. Reagan has retreated somewhat from the initial position he adopted in 1983, namely that SDI technology could provide a total astrodome shield for the USA as a whole, protecting civilians and military centres alike. But the lure of 'point defense', ie, an SDI system that could protect sufficient US military positions to enable a successful second strike, and so deter a Soviet attack on the USA, remains. Nothing in the US debate on SDI, and in Gorbachev's patient and almost obsequious cajoling at Geneva and Reykjavik, has moved Reagan from this chimera, and insofar as significant amounts of funding have already been allocated to the project in the USA, SDI is already a going concern.

The USSR has retreated from the 1983–6 position of making a ban on SDI a condition for progress on INF and START and has suggested that a degree of laboratory testing would be permitted under the 1972 ABM treaty, where 'laboratory' includes missile firing ranges. The USSR also has its own SDI programme, and has begun developing cheaper antidotes, in the form of missiles that can fly under a US protective screen. But the question of SDI remains, most of all because of the Soviet fear that such a defensive system, however it worked, would provide a shield that would enable a surprise US attack on the USSR.

Gorbachev, like everyone else, must be waiting to see if the new US president will continue SDI: but if he does, then this issue will continue to bedevil US-Soviet relations for a long time, and will lead to an arms race in space. However many commitments to its purely defensive use come from the White House, and however many US experts say it can never work, the Soviet Union can never be sure that SDI will not be used to enable an offensive US strike in some future conflict.

The prospects of future use of nuclear weapons have, if anything, increased in recent years because of the revolution in missile accuracy made possible by technological advance. It is this change that has led to a greater interest in the selective use of nuclear weapons for specific crisis and demonstrative purposes: the Pentagon report on *Discriminate Deterrence* issued in January was precisely designed to promote this idea. Arguing that it was politically incredible for the US to threaten an all-out attack on the USSR, since this would invite massive retaliation against the USA itself, the authors of the Pentagon report called for the discriminate, ie, one-off or selective, use of missiles in future conflicts.

Third World relationships

While this produced considerable alarm in Europe amongst Atlanticist intellectuals, who felt the 'massive retaliation' rug was being pulled out from underneath them, the main import of *Discriminate Deterrence* was with regard to the Third World. This arena, the second area of transition in current US-Soviet relations, has been the main locus of conflict since 1945 and is today the site of over a dozen wars. In the latter part of the 1970s, the balance of forces in Third World conflict moved in the direction of the USSR, when 14 social revolutions weakened the US position, from Vietnam to Nicaragua. Since 1980 there have been no further successful anti-US Third World revolutions, and the balance has shifted in the direction of the USA. In the first place, the USA has put much more effort into counter-insurgency and the diplomatic managing of Third World upheavals. The result has been that in several countries revolutionary movements have been blocked or contained: in El Salvador, Haiti, the Philippines, South Korea, Pakistan. Secondly, the USSR has come to count the diplomatic and economic cost of its Third World commitments, many of them inherited from the triumphs of the 1970s, and has urged caution and conciliation on its Third World allies; most notably is this true in Afghanistan, but it also pertains to Cambodia, Ethiopia, South Yemen, Angola and Nicaragua. Thirdly, the US has taken the offensive in using military force in the Third World. In one case, this enabled Washington directly to roll back a revolution of the 1970s, in Grenada. In another, the USA has been able on two occasions to attack the territory of a Soviet ally with impunity: Libya.

But the most pervasive feature of this US deployment of force has been the 'Reagan Doctrine', the active support for anti-Soviet geurrillas in the Third World, in a tricontinental attempt to get back at the USSR for the guerrilla movements it successfully backed in the 1970s. Washington is supporting such movements in at least four states – Cambodia, Afghanistan, Angola, Nicaragua – and it has dealt in some measure with other anti-communist forces – in Laos, South Yemen, Ethiopia and Surinam. The only one it appears to be clearly opposed to is RENAMO, the South Africa-supported force in Mozambique.

Such support for counter-revolutionaries is justified as a form of Low Intensity Conflict, the doctrine evolved by the Pentagon after the Vietnam war to describe US commitment to military intervention short of a direct role for US combat

troops. It has fed on arms and money channelled in by the
CIA, and whilst there has been some criticism within the US
of the Nicaraguan operation, forcing Oliver North and the
CIA to find money from private sources and diverted
Iranian arms sales, the principle itself commands widespread
support on Capitol Hill.

There has been no congressional criticism of the $2.2
billion supplied to the Afghan mujaheddin, and no press
leaks about the mechanisms of arms supplies or the sites and
forms of training provided in Pakistan. While there is
widespread resistance within the USA to sending US troops
to combat situations, Reagan has successfully relegitimated
covert action and military action in the Third World.

The results of the Reagan policy in the Third World are,
as yet, unclear, and constitute perhaps the greatest question
mark over his presidency. In some areas he would appear to
have failed: the 1982–4 intervention in Lebanon was a
disaster, and Schultz, who tried to undermine the Syrian
position in the Middle East at that time, is now seeking
favour in Damascus for his peace plan. The 1984–6 attempt
to open a secret channel to Iran ended in ignominy and
provoked the greatest congressional and public outcry of
Reagan's administration.

The commitment to overthrowing the Sandinistas in
Nicaragua has proved unrealisable, although enormous
damage has been caused to that country. Pressure on some
Third World allies to change policy has also failed – be this
on Chile or Panama. Perhaps most importantly, the Reagan
administration has failed to consolidate the advances made
by Nixon and Carter in dealing with China, and has so
antagonised Peking that the Chinese leadership is rene-
gotiating its relations with the USSR.

But in other respects the US has been able to use its
military and economic strength in the Third World to
considerable effect. It has used its economic power to
redirect the policies of the multilateral lending agencies, and
to woo such countries as India with the promise of new
technology. It has forced the USSR on to the defensive in
Afghanistan where a combination of Stinger missiles and
Soviet desire to concentrate forces at home has led to the
UN-sponsored agreement under which Soviet forces will

depart. No-one can be certain that the PDPA regime in Kabul can now survive, although it will almost certainly fight. Only if another regional power were to step in to support the Kabul government would its chances of survival be enhanced. The political implications of a PDPA defeat would be considerable – within the Islamic regions of the USSR, in the Soviet army, in eastern Europe and in other Third World Soviet allies.

The negotiations on Afghanistan have been paralleled by other diplomatic initiatives being taken to 'unblock' Third World issues. It is as if the whole agenda of crises inherited from the late 1970s is now coming up for renegotiation. In the Horn of Africa, this has led to progress in normalisation of relations between Ethiopia and Somalia, who were at war in 1977–78: but this progress is offset by the continuation of the war in Eritrea and by the conflict in the southern Sudan. In Cambodia, there have been talks between the Phnom Penh government and Sihanouk, and Moscow has urged Vietnam and China to negotiate directly on this question: Cambodia is not Afghanistan, and the Heng Samrin regime is in a far better position to survive the departure of its Vietnamese allies than is the PDPA to outlast the exit of the 'limited contingent'. In Nicaragua and Angola serious negotiations are also in train to find compromises, in both cases with evident Soviet encouragement.

These negotiations, linked in atmosphere if not substance are, however, only the beginning of a process. It is worth recalling that the Paris talks between Vietnam and the USA lasted from 1968 to 1973, before an agreement was reached, and that fighting continued during, and after, the diplomatic exchanges.

In many cases, Soviet allies in the Third World listen to, and then ignore, Soviet advice. It is evident that in both South Yemen and Ethiopia, two of the leading 'states of socialist orientation', the ruling parties have ignored Soviet urgings to compromise with their opponents. In Cuba, as in some parts of eastern Europe, there is little enthusiasm for the new Soviet economic policies and political opening: Castro celebrated the 20th anniversary of Guevara's death last October with a ringing call to return to Che's idealist economist policies, and a condemnation of what he saw as capitalist and materialist dilutions of socialist economics. His *rectification* is an outright rejection of perestroika.

Above all, of course, the fate of these separate regional negotiations depends on the response from other interested powers, particularly the USA and, in the case of Cambodia, China. Gorbachev and PDPA leader Najibullah spoke in Tashkent in March of the international significance of the agreement on Afghanistan: meaning by this that a degree of political compromise and great power understanding could be helpful in other Third World crises. Washington and its allies understand something very different by this: for them the international significance of the Afghan treaty is that, with sufficient pressure, the USSR can be forced to abandon its allies. As the case of Vietnam showed so well, conflict and negotiation can continue side by side for years: the battle for the Third World is still on. This is true both in areas where there is a clear US-Soviet divide, and in murkier conflicts, such as the Gulf war.

Neither Washington nor Moscow have been able to establish stable relations with Tehran, and, quite apart from its Islamic component which is directed at both East and West, Iranian nationalism is unique in the whole of the Third World as being a response to fresh national memories of both Russian and US intervention. The Iranian revolution is in difficulties at home, since it lacks an answer to many urgent social and economic problems: but it has by no means run out of steam, and it has confounded the attempt by Washington to force it into a corner, using naval presence in the Gulf as a protection for Iraq. Equally, while the July 1987 UN resolution on the Gulf war was a partisan one, explicitly designed to trap Iran in abrupt rejection, Tehran diplomats have successfully stalled and bought time for further discussion.

The Islamic republic has been skilful at throwing crumbs to both Washington and Moscow: it has promised the former collaboration against the USSR in Afghanistan, and early in 1987, well after the Irangate scandal broke, the Pentagon was pleased to receive delivery for the first time of an intact Soviet T-72 tank, a consideration supplied to them by Tehran after it was captured from Iraq. Later in 1987 Tehran agreed to allow the USSR to build a railway through eastern Iran to the Persian Gulf, giving the USSR direct access from Central Asia to the Indian Ocean for the first time: but the mullahs are skilful procrastinators and it remains to be seen if this railway will be built and, if opened, kept running.

Domestic politics in Washington and Moscow

If arms control and the Third World are two areas of great uncertainty, the internal developments of both the USSR and USA place further question marks over the development of East-West relations, and constitute the two other major dimensions of current international change. Gorbachev has to date maintained the momentum of perestroika and the party conference in June will be used to confirm policies and install supportive personnel. The purposes of 'conferences' as distinct from congresses is to signal renovation and discussion of working procedures and the like. However, even if the tenacious conservatives are kept on the defensive, the tasks facing him are enormous. As his speech in Tashkent in late March made clear perestroika has many enemies, not least amongst the non-Russian parts of the Soviet population. With the lifting of complete censorship and political control, all sorts of conflicts separate from the reform-conservative one have emerged, often of an ethnic character: the lesson of the crisis in Nagorno-Karabakh in March, was that ethnic minorities, in this case Armenians and Azerbaijanis, dislike each other even more than they dislike the supposedly dominant Russians. While Gorbachev made concessions to the Armenians in this region of Azerbaijan, including economic programmes, teaching Armenian in schools and the beaming of Armenian tv, he could not accept the demand for the region as a whole to be transferred from Azerbaijan to Armenia because this would have had catastrophic knock-on effects throughout the USSR.

If there are difficulties within the USSR, those in eastern Europe are even greater: as current tensions in Poland and Hungary illustrate, the lifting of economic and political controls there may well threaten the stability of the whole communist party system, and place before Gorbachev dilemmas even more difficult than those of Afghanistan. It is here, above all, that the Nato countries now see a major opportunity. On the one hand, they are encouraging the disaggregation of the Eastern bloc and promoting stronger links between individual eastern European capitals and the West. On the other, they are encouraging a reduction of Soviet military power there, through the conventional arms reduction talks that are acquiring greater prominence in East-West relations.

It is here that the over-arching link between military and political relations becomes most evident: the call for substantial Soviet conventional arms reduction in eastern Europe, as a follow-on from INF and START talks, leads to a political conclusion, that of weakening the USSR. For Gorbachev and his allies in eastern Europe, there are no easy resolutions of this problem.

On the US side, and that of its allies, the situation is not as uncertain, but major question marks remain. There is, first, the question of the US presidential election, and the impact its outcome will have on Reagan's legacy. Bush may turn out to be less consistent with Reagan than he now pretends, Dukakis may yield to the Pentagon and cold war lobbies. In contrast to the 1980 election, there is a much less hostile attitude to the USSR, and many Americans identify Third World foes – terrorists, hostage-takers, narco-traffickers – as more of an enemy than the USSR. Gorbachev's appeal has certainly worked there. Reagan's economics have also taken their toll: the average income of US non-agricultural manual workers has fallen 15 per ent since the early 1970s, and the budget deficit has demonstrated that the US cannot conduct the cold war simply by outspending the USSR on arms. At the same time the Wall Street crash of last October has taken the glitter off Reaganomics. In the presidential campaign itself, there remains one major smoking gun, namely whether the involvement of Bush in the Irangate affair, and of some of the leading operatives in the narcotics trade as a means of financing the contras, will come out. But there may also be other surprises from the White House itself, as Reagan, who knows he has the initiative in the Third World, seeks to throw one more punch at his Third World foes, be these in Tehran or Managua.

Beyond US politics itself, there lies the ambiguous reaction of Nato allies to the new mood in Soviet-US relations: Thatcher, Kohl and their ilk can ill afford to defy Washington, but they would clearly like to see less momentum than is currently in evidence, and they were compelled, against their better instincts, to swallow the INF agreement.

The current direction of the second cold war rests on two other, overarching issues I have discussed. On the one hand, the global initiative has shifted back in favour of the USA: the USSR has given away far more than the USA in the INF agreement, and has conceded a delinking of the SDI question from other arms control negotiations. In the Third World, Moscow has been forced to leave Afghanistan without securing an end to CIA support for the guerrillas, and is on the defensive in Angola and Nicaragua. The economic superiority of the West, in technology and living standards, capitalism's greatest asset, is taking its effect both in the Third World, and in the appeal it exerts in eastern Europe and the USSR itself. On the other hand, the USA under Reagan has over-extended itself, and has neither the military nor the economic strength to pursue the policies Reagan initially espoused. Technological limits may well scupper his fantasy of SDI. The American people themselves, both reassured and chastened by eight years of Reagan, seem much more inclined to find common ground with the USSR. It will only be long after Reagan leaves Moscow on June 2, 1988, and leaves the White House on January 20, 1989, that the overall balance-sheet of the second cold war can be drawn.

Neal Ascherson

Rumblings in the East

These two articles, one published in February 1988 and one in January 1989, chart the effects of perestroika as it percolated through to the Warsaw Pact countries. By the end of 1988 prospects for change seemed stronger; however, there is no guarantee that all the changes will be positive.

The German socialist scholar Ekkehard Krippendorff once wrote that 'foreign policy was internal policy'. He meant by this that it was always illegitimate to regard the external policy of a state in isolation, or to identify 'foreign policy interests' or goals which stopped, so to speak, at the frontiers. Given that the makers of foreign policy can acquire some autonomy, or form a powerful lobby on their own, it remains true – according to Krippendorff – that the decision-making of a state in the external world always relates to the deeper purpose of preserving its internal system or assisting the priorities of that system.

This is a useful way to begin examining the development of Soviet foreign policy in the era of perestroika. How is the Soviet relationship with the outside world, within and without the Soviet 'sphere of influence', affected by the huge drama of 'restructuring' at home, and how – in turn – do events or prospects in the world affect what is taking place or may take place within the USSR?

In some areas, a connection between internal and foreign policy is already identifiable. In the broadest terms, a 'clearing of decks' is taking place. Reform at home requires concentration not only of resources but of attention, and this means that expensive or ticklish commitments must be

First published in *Marxism Today*, February 1988 and January 1989 reviewed and if possible abandoned. The most obvious example is, of course, Mr Gorbachev's headlong drive toward total nuclear disarmament, whose impetus initially so disconcerted the United States – and still disconcerts European Nato members. With this, if it succeeds, will go eventual force reductions on the ground: in Europe, along the Chinese frontier, and by a complete withdrawal from Afghanistan. New efforts, not so far very fruitful, are being made to mend fences with China, which means that Soviet policy in Indochina will have to be reviewed sooner rather than later.

The domestic motives here are primarily to reduce the colossal expenditure of the USSR upon defence, and to release resources for the 'acceleration' of the Soviet economy. 'Summitry' with President Reagan and meetings with other Western leaders serve the same purpose. What is not yet clear is whether this more intense and positive engagement of Soviet diplomacy in the world is a permanent opening, or whether it constitutes a phase designed to remove outstanding problems so that the USSR can, in the longer run, afford to pay *less* attention to the outside world and concentrate on the transformation of Soviet society 'in one country'.

But when the focus swivels from the West or the developing world to Eastern Europe – the states of the Warsaw Pact – the picture is curiously ambiguous. The relationship between the Soviet Union and its client states in Europe has certainly changed over the past three years. But so far these changes have been cautious and piecemeal, and nothing suggests a dramatic transformation to parallel Gorbachev's revolutions in home economic policy or in external arms-reduction policy.

Gorbachev seems to be treating the Pact as a convoy moving at the pace of the slowest ships: encouraging the slow to move faster, but not giving the potentially swifter the green light to surge ahead out of sight.

The early mystery of his attitude to Czechoslovakia has been resolved, to some extent: Gustav Husák, who evidently faced criticism in Moscow, was obliged to resign. That seems to have been the extent of direct Soviet intervention. Miloš Jakeš, Husák's successor as leader of the Czechoslovak Communist Party, does not feel like a Soviet nominee, and probably gained the post as a result of manipulation by Vasil Bílak, the most spectacular hard-liner. The position of Lubomir Strougal, prime minister and the figure most clearly committed to some kind of economic reform, seems actually weaker than before Husák's fall. The whole episode suggests a Soviet policy of trying to initiate change, away from the autarkic stasis of the late Husak years, but of refraining from sustained pressure, leaving subsequent development to the ruling party concerned.

In the GDR, Honecker appears to have resisted any hints that he should alter his internal policies, and acts as if he were confident that he can pursue his developing relationship with the Federal Republic at his own pace and in his own way. Neither does Gorbachev, in spite of evident remonstration, seem to have made much impact upon the increasingly disastrous course of the Ceausescu regime in Romania.

Poland is a particularly fascinating case, for here there has been a limited attempt to extend glasnost beyond the Soviet frontiers. In 1986, *Literaturnaya Gazeta* carried an interview with Cardinal Glemp, but accompanied it with a quite astonishing introduction, disclosing to Soviet readers for the first time the fact of overwhelming Catholic allegiance in the working class and the open tolerance of devout religious faith among its members by the Polish United Workers' Party. The tone of the article was a mild 'all highly peculiar, but that is the way Poland is'.

Soon afterwards, Gorbachev announced that there should be 'no white spaces' in Soviet-Polish history, and a joint commission of historians was appointed to fill them in. One of the Soviet members remarked in a *Polityka* interview that 'Katyn, above all Katyn' should be among the topics covered.

How far this will go remains to be seen. The Polish press, light-years ahead of the Soviet media in its degree of glasnost, published in full details of the Nazi-Soviet pact, including the text of the infamous secret protocol providing for a Nazi-Soviet partition of Poland. But Gorbachev's much-heralded speech on the Stalin years, a few months ago, was strikingly cautious and defensive about the pact.

A visitor to the Soviet Union will be struck by the sharp

limits to what is 'sayable', even in the new climate. One of these limits runs along the relationship, past and present, with the states of Eastern Europe. Many of the most outspoken Soviet journalists, who have burned their boats in commitment to perestroika at home, still justify without hesitation the 1968 intervention in Czechoslovakia, referring in the old manner to 'counter-revolutionary forces' financed by West German intelligence and the CIA.

Rather similar is the rarity of Soviet awareness that the essence of perestroika – the attempt to reform a socialist economy by relaxing central control and introducing market elements – has long been familiar in Eastern Europe, and that all its problems have been thoroughly explored and discussed there. Three such efforts – the ill-fated Czechoslovak reform of 1967–8, the Hungarian new economic model which has been running for 20 years, and the latest phase of the Polish reform programme – go far beyond the present Soviet programme in their radicalism. The lessons, especially the fundamental problem of the transitional period in which the job security and living standards of the working class may fall, have been exhaustively spelled out. Soviet commentators, however, too often write and speak as if the USSR under Gorbachev were breaking entirely new ground.

To sum up, there is so far no sign whatever that the Gorbachev leadership contemplates a basic transformation of the Soviet relationship with the Warsaw Pact regimes. There is plainly a wish to stimulate change in a perestroika direction in the most ossified states, and – less plainly – a readiness to encourage the development of reforms like those in Hungary or Poland. For the moment, Mr Gorbachev appears to want a stable, reasonably prosperous backyard, in which – at the discretion of the ruling parties – some political relaxation may be introduced.

There can be no doubt that, as far as the West is concerned, by far the strongest Soviet credibility card would be a coherent drive to alter this relationship, and to foster the emergence of internally autonomous and pluralistic political systems in Eastern Europe – the 'Finlandisation' dreamed of especially by the Poles. No evidence exists that the Gorbachev leadership contemplates anything of this kind.

Here we return to the notion of external policy as a function of internal policy. Such a transformation might be turbulent and uncontrollable, infecting national groups and perhaps workers within the USSR at a tricky moment, and offering the West levers with which to extort concessions from the Soviet Union in other fields. The recasting of the Soviet economy (and glasnost is, of course, a means to that, not an end in itself) requires a secure international environment, and also continuity in the supply of consumer goods and high-technology products from Eastern Europe.

That said, the huge changes taking place in the USSR have an important impact in Eastern Europe. Societies undertaking reform are given confidence, not least when they feel that they are advancing faster and further than the Soviet Union. Correspondingly, reformers in the more conservative states now enjoy the unexpected pleasure of being able to denounce their opponents for deviating from the Soviet model – a tactic which can be very effective.

With these excitements, however, goes a certain wariness. The Hungarians ask themselves whether a dynamic Soviet Union seeking to pump fresh life into organisations like the Warsaw Pact or Comecon is really in their interests. Their view is that renewed integration in the Soviet bloc could reduce their freedom of action and constrain their trading and financial relationship with the West. The 'period of stagnation' under Leonid Brezhnev was not without its advantages. In Poland, similarly, people have ambiguous feelings about a reform project next door which enhances the leading role of the party, which – as a 'revolution from above' – requires a greater concentration of central coercive power rather than a more open, relaxed and eclectic political system.

So far, then, the picture is of a careful and controlled encouragement of change and reform in Eastern Europe, but of nothing more. The signals in Moscow are that Soviet imagination of the tolerable still stops well before a society in which the Communist Party abandoned the conventional 'leading role', or effectively shared power with a 'non-socialist' force (although I suspect that events in Poland may challenge that imaginative limit again before too long). Alexander Dubček, in his *L'Unità* interview, stated his belief that Gorbachev would never have authorised the 1968

military intervention in his country. For my part, I will wait
and see for a few years before feeling able to agree with him.

At the beginning of 1988, my own question about Eastern
Europe was this. So far, all the rhetoric and all the political
struggles had raged around glasnost, perestroika and
(least-mentioned, but most urgent and perhaps the end to
which the other two are only the means) *uskorenie* –
acceleration. But nothing clear had been said about Eastern
Europe. So what was Gorbachev's intention for that part of
the world?

His aims for the Soviet Union itself had been made clear,
not least in Gorbachev's own writings about 'revolution
from above' and in less authoritative texts from advisers like
Aganbegyan. The aims for international politics had also
become recognisable and impressive: the wish to pull out of
Brezhnev's distant embroilments, in Afghanistan above all
but also in Africa, was more than a rumour and already a
matter of preliminary negotiation. So was improvement of
relations with China, although there were serious doubts
whether the USSR would apply effective pressure upon
Vietnam to evacuate Kampuchea. The aims for disarmament and arms control were already written across the
sky, and the Reagan administration was floundering in a
rising flood of Soviet proposals. Even a year ago, it no
longer looked as if the 'Strategic Defence Initiative' (star
wars) would be allowed to block further arms control
agreements.

It was natural, and correct, for us in the West to ask
whether the internal transformation of the socialist system in
the Soviet Union also implied a similar transformation in
Eastern Europe – or, to put it more cautiously, a
transformation in the relationship between the Soviet Union
and the member states of the Warsaw Pact. But there was
little evidence either way. On the one hand, the Hungarian
reformers were confident that in Moscow their experiments
in market socialism were being closely and admiringly
watched. On the other hand, opinion was divided on what

exactly Gorbachev might think of the state of affairs in Czechoslovakia, where Dr Gustav Husák still ruled a highly repressive and centralised command economy. Some said that he was sick of the neo-stalinists in Prague, and would shortly evict them. Others countered that the undeniable stability of Czechoslovakia, compared to Poland for example, was a source of deep relief and reassurance to the Soviet leader. He had enough problems. The last thing he needed, while he fought for his own political life and that of his programme, was trouble in the 'fraternal countries'.

Evidence for any of these views was scanty, circumstantial. An East-West conference I attended in Budapest in the autumn of 1987 found the Soviet delegates silent on this subject, concerned primarily with relations with the West and the Third World, and with Western failures to understand the historic importance of what was being undertaken in their country. It was suggested to them that far the most convincing and effective demonstration of good faith which the USSR could make to the West, if Western assent was really that important, would be a change in the Soviet power relationship to Eastern Europe which at least pointed in the direction of 'Finlandisation'. But there was no response to this, though some of the Hungarian participants would dearly have liked one. A month or so later, I was in Moscow. The summit was on, admittedly, and many good people were out of town. All the same, the Soviet relationship to Eastern Europe proved to be a closed zone, as far as those I spoke with were concerned. Vivid and heretical as they might be on subjects like corruption or the Stalin legacy, on Eastern Europe they gave the impression that 'we have no instructions in this matter'. In private talk, pressed for a view of the Warsaw Pact intervention in Czechoslovakia in 1968, two people offered me the old version of a plot against that country by the West Germans and the CIA.

The last year has been one of the most exciting and eventful in Eastern and Central Europe since 1956, although – fortunately – infinitely less violent. It can't quite be said that the question has been answered and that we now possess a 24-carat assurance from Gorbachev that Eastern Europe can develop as it pleases. Nobody on the Soviet side in authority has yet tried to make the crucial distinction: between the security interests of the USSR and the internal political structures of Warsaw Pact regimes. Nonetheless, the relationship has changed. Extraordinary things have happened, and have been treated with calm and restraint by the Soviet Union. If there is still a line beyond which ideological heresy becomes a security threat to the USSR, that line would seem to have been moved further away.

In addition, there are a few suggestive, if cloudy, Soviet pronouncements. They seem to mean two things. First, that the revaluation of recent history which has been underway for several years (for example, the joint Soviet-Polish commission of historians) is now beginning to licence a much more rueful view of how the Soviet Union has behaved to the nations of the *glacis* in the last 40 years. The time when unofficial Soviet spokesmen – and there always was such a category – can say that August 1968 was an error is now arriving. Secondly, that the community in Moscow which thinks and advises about policy now recognises that perestroika has released social and political energies abroad, and that rapid and radical changes must be expected within the nations of the Warsaw Pact. The view of these changes seems to be this: 'We will not intervene, but will allow each country to develop in a way that suits it best.'

What, though, if Hungary not only develops a multi-party system but decides by democratic process to end the leading role of the Hungarian Workers Party and consign it to the opposition benches of a freely-elected parliament? There, the answer grows Delphic and misty. 'One must assume that these nations will choose to retain socialism, in a quite new form perhaps ...' Unsatisfactory. But unthinkable mental steps have been taken in the last year, all the same.

My guess is that Gorbachev has now banned the resort to armed intervention in the 'socialist commonwealth', a term which he in fact rejects, except in utterly apocalyptic circumstances (say: a Romanian invasion of Hungary, or a national insurrection in one of the USSR's own republics). He has accepted that some states in the Pact are going to twist 'socialism' out of all recognition, while others will laager themselves in against change for as long as possible. However, he has not yet faced directly the idea that – sooner rather than later – one of these states is going to attempt the non-violent removal of a ruling Communist Party from power. At the beginning of December, I heard his adviser Vadim Zagladin reply to a Western questioner in these words:

> 'You ask if the Soviet system is in flux. I say: the system stays, but the regime changes. You ask, diplomatically but in effect, if the Soviet Union would hinder friends in Eastern Europe from making their own changes. I tell you No! Is that clear?

Even in the insularity of England, the tumult of change in Eastern Europe has been audible for the last 12 months. Change with exceptions, of course. The German Democratic Republic had held to its conservative course without apparent lack of self-confidence. Czechoslovakia went through a puzzling series of face replacements. Dr Husak, who was seen to have lost the confidence of Moscow early in the year, resigned as party leader, but his successor, Miloš Jakeš, attempted no 'opening'. Instead, Lubomir Strougal, for so long associated with a hankering after economic reform, finally lost his job as prime minister: the Prague regime looks superficially harder than it was a year ago.

In Romania, President Ceausescu's isolated dictatorship showed no real signs of internal breakdown. The people remained hungry and wretched, and international loathing of his system grew more intense. Hungarian outrage at Romania's treatment of the Magyar minority increased, and the Budapest regime permitted genuinely spontaneous demonstrations. The West was horrified by 'systematisation', the demolition of villages, and by the monstrous vandalising of Bucharest by the president's building mania. A Gorbachev visit appeared to solve nothing.

In Poland, two waves of strikes brought the situation back to the boil. Solidarity, which was beginning to be dismissed as an effective force, proved to have retained a strong pull on the working class in a crisis, and the ambiguous attempts to get a 'roundtable' discussion going between Lech Walesa, the government and other social forces will probably continue through 1989. The rhetoric on all sides is about pluralism and dialogue, and about how economic reform cannot be made to work without social consensus – or at least, consent. The reality is that the new premier, Mierczyslaw Rakowski, is also fighting a political battle, aimed at discrediting and disabling Solidarity before the impact of the reforms on working-class living standards leads to another explosion.

In Hungary, János Kádár finally left the stage; under his successor as party leader, Károly Grosz, a desperately rapid political liberalisation has been attempted in order – as it seems – to offer deeply discontented sections of society political influence as a substitute for economic security. However, the standard of living went on falling, and will fall further in 1989. There is a nasty feeling among Hungarians that this combination of ineffective civil liberty and disappointed expectations could prove explosive.

This next year may bring about what could be called 'the privatisation of *raison d'état*'. In most East European countries, *raison d'état* means the defence of what qualified independence the state may enjoy. In cruder terms, it's the statement that if we are too heretical, or if there is too much disorder, the Soviet tanks will arrive.

This is an international definition of *raison d'état*. But now nations like Poland and Hungary are approaching the point at which their internal politics and arrangements are genuinely internal, at which they can have what sort of regime they like without fearing Soviet intervention. Perhaps they have already reached that point. Nobody can be sure. What now is defined as 'counter-revolution' in the Soviet Union, and what is the way to treat it? Nobody knows that either. It's prudent to assume that a line will be encountered somewhere at which the Soviet Union finds the situation in an allied state intolerable. But where? It is extraordinarily hard to get used to the conduct of political struggle in which everything is no longer judged against that ultimate fear, but Poles and Hungarians will have to get used to it.

This last year has also shown interesting lines of development in opposition. As mentioned, organised working-class opposition in the form of strikes and banned independent trade unions came back with unexpected vigour in Poland. But even in Poland a trade union is not primarily a political formation. And the question of what 'post-perestroika' politics are going to look like in Eastern Europe remains open. There are, however, some hints.

The prospects for Communist parties in anything like a plural contest by free elections are dim and growing dimmer; especially as the old *raison d'état* argument ('you may hate us, but if you try to get rid of us, they will invade') begins to wane. In Poland, the PZPR is little more than a skelton of apparatchiks and *nomenklatura* patronage. In Hungary, where the idea of power-sharing with genuinely independent non-Communist elements is far newer than in Poland, the HSWP is unpopular: its reforms lag behind the expectations they create. Only in Yugoslavia, racked by conflicts both social and national, have Communist parties discovered a new source of authenticity: as the carriers of regional or national grievances against a supra-national centre. Once, discontent in the component republics of Yugoslavia was expressed by nationalist movements, suppressed by Communist parties in the name of Yugoslav unity under Tito. Today, much more successfully, that discontent is carried by the regional/national Communist parties themselves, whether in Slovenia against Belgrade, in Kosovo against Serbia, or above all by the Serbian Communist League under Slobodan Milošević against the 'federal' Yugoslav League of Communists. Only the USSR itself has a structure like that of Yugoslavia, and it's not a coincidence that the Estonian, Latvian and Lithuanian CPs have been in the leadership of the national movements there.

But the mention of Milošević raises another trend, which seemed to be emerging during 1988. For some 20 years, the West has identified with 'dissidents' in Eastern Europe and the USSR; these dissident groups have been typically composed of individuals with rather internationalist, liberal or social-democratic views, possessing a global rather than a national view of politics, interested above all in human rights and personal freedom. Some have been Christians, but many members of these groups have either been party members or children of Communist parents. Charter 77 in Czechoslovakia, the Committee for Workers' Defence (KOR) in Poland, the Szeta association in Hungary are past or present examples.

My impression is that, in more open conditions for political struggle, the prominence of such groups is ending. They are being replaced – as in Hungary in these crucial months – by much more traditional and nationalist centres of opposition. European intellectuals like Miklos Haraszti or Otilia Szolt carried the torch of opposition through long and dark years. Now, in freer conditions for political initiative, they have become less influential than the so-called *narodnik* movement of old-fashioned Hungarian patriots who claim to be close to the land and who fear the cosmopolitan city asphalt, whose prejudices are populist and not free of racialism.

It may well be that in 1989 *Blut-und-Boden* (blood and soil) nationalism is going to revive in Eastern Europe. Solidarity had essentially social-democratic features, but the strongest purely political formation of 1980–81, growing rapidly by the time that it was suppressed by martial law, was the Confederation for Independent Poland (KPN), a mindlessly right-wing nationalist party whose cult of 'national egoism' recalled the prewar National Democrats. Milošević has contrived to capture Serbian communism for an ideology of this sort. In a way, it all suggests a revival of the old peasant parties which were so powerful in this region of Europe before 1939. But, however it be analysed, I suspect that *Blut-und-Boden* opposition to ruling Communist parties will show a power, an appeal and a capacity to put down roots which the liberal 'dissidents' could never achieve. It's a disquieting outlook.

Jon Bloomfield

From Proletarian Internationalism to Progressive Humanism

The new Soviet foreign policy has hit the world like a whirlwind. From the moment Gorbachev outlined the programme for a nuclear-free world by the year 2000 on 15 January 1986, Soviet foreign policy has been set on a new course. New ideas and specific actions have flowed apace: and the old world of the evil empire, the Cold War and stereotyped confrontation has begun to disintegrate before our eyes. An agreement actually dismantling modern nuclear weapons has been signed; the Geneva accords have led to the withdrawal of Soviet troops in Afghanistan; and Western leaders have queued up eagerly to visit Moscow both to indicate a new spirit of harmony and to sign trade deals and cultural agreements.

Such developments have had a phenomenal impact on Western public opinion. Opinion poll surveys in the major West European countries indicate a remarkable change in public perception since the Brezhnev era with a common acceptance that under Gorbachev the Soviet Union has changed dramatically and a majority believing that it no longer poses a military threat to the West. This view is held most strongly within the Federal Republic of Germany. Even in the United States the ecstatic response to Gorbachev on his two brief visits illustrates the unprecented change of atmosphere.

Western political leaders have been slower to respond, many bound by the habits of a Cold War lifetime. However, the new Soviet thinking has a powerful momentum and appeal. After the visionary *tour de force* delivered by Gorbachev at the United Nations in December 1988 it has become obvious that their traditional orthodoxy can no longer hold.

What are the main features of this new Soviet foreign policy and where and how does it break from the past? How is the overall character of this policy best assessed? What are the main obstacles it faces? And what is its potential for spawning a new era of international relations?

Beneath the dramatic gestures, the media razzmatazz and the personality focus on the Gorbachevs lie three themes of substance which have given coherence and popular appeal to the new strategy. Firstly, it sees militarism as the most pressing issue to be tackled, initially nuclear weapons but increasingly all aspects of military and defence activity. Secondly, it recognises that today's world is interdependent economically, technologically and ecologically, and that the era of autarky is over. Thirdly, it seeks to reaffirm the primacy of politics over force in the conduct of world affairs.

These strands of thought were not presented ready-formed on the waiting world. They have evolved over the period as political dialogue and events both within the Soviet Union and internationally have driven the process forward. Perestroika abroad has gone hand in hand with perestroika at home. The two aspects need and feed each other. International agreements and prestige are crucial to the leadership's domestic political standing and its ability to generate international support and confidence in its domestic reconstruction programme, while disarmament, economic and trade agreements would ease the transformation of the Soviet economy and society. Since 1985 there has been an underlying logic which has given a consistent, strategic direction to Soviet international policy. As with domestic policy the break with neo-Stalinism has had far-reaching consequences. With the quickening pace of perestroika, its content has deepened, radicalised and become more explicit. The primitive model of class confrontation with its heavy emphasis on military might is being replaced by a new model of socialist international relations best described as progressive humanism.

Tackling militarism

During Gorbachev's first few months in office a series of new moves and offers to the West were made. The Soviet government announced a unilateral moratorium on nuclear testing which it then extended; an initial, friendly summit meeting with President Reagan was held in Geneva; and at the end of 1985 the USSR withdrew its previous opposition to on-site inspection of nuclear facilities. The West had always maintained that the Soviet refusal to permit on-site verification was the primary obstacle to a nuclear test ban. This was a prelude to the decisive, public break with the old era which came with Gorbachev's statement on disarmament and foreign policy on 15 January 1986.

This presented the most comprehensive set of disarmament proposals from a Soviet leader since the Khrushchev era. It set out the vision of a world free from nuclear weapons by the end of the century. As important, it outlined a 3-stage process by which this could be achieved. In so doing, the Soviet leadership put the goal of general and complete nuclear disarmament back on the global agenda.

The speech, and the associated proposals of the preceeding months, signified a clear break from the policies of the Brezhnev era. The new policy arose partly because the Gorbachev leadership was fearful of the calamitous consequences of a new arms race in space and of the increased strains it would place on its uncompetitive economy.

However, the speech showed the first signs of the new philosophy that was to become the Gorbachev hallmark. In the absence of an American response, the Soviet Union had good ground for resuming arms testing in January. Gorbachev argued that

> if one were to follow the usual 'logic' of the arms race that, presumably, would have been the thing to do ... that logic has to be resolutely rejected. Otherwise the process of military rivalry will assume gigantic proportions and any control over the course of events would be impossible. To yield to the anarchic force of the nuclear arms race is impermissible ...[1]

Here for the first time were arguments similar to those used by the Western peace movements against the relentless pursuit of military parity in an epoch of nuclear overkill.

Gorbachev continued with a call for 'new and bold approaches, fresh political thinking ...' Implicitly, this was a criticism of the policies of his predecessors, but with Andrei Gromyko, a key architect of those policies, at that time still a prominent political figure, and with his own base not fully consolidated, Gorbachev avoided explicit criticism. Yet the content of the speech was novel. It recognised that the deadlock and escalation of the arms race had to be broken in the political arena. Whatever risks this would hold for the Soviet Union and whatever concessions it would entail, the speech recognised that the best, long-term guarantee for Soviet security lay in the creation of a political momentum for disarmament. The capacity to rival the USA military was stated but given a strictly secondary role.

While the inherent philosophy has evolved and been stated explicitly in subsequent years, it is this speech which marks the decisive turning point in East-West relations. From its premises flow both the subsequent stream of Soviet disarmament initiatives and the West's uncertainty and uneasiness of response. NATO and Western governments have been continually placed on the defensive by Soviet initiatives in this period. A feature article by the *Daily Telegraph*'s diplomatic correspondent shortly after the Gorbachev speech pinpointed exactly why. With striking honesty David Adamson wrote that the Western powers 'believe in nuclear weapons as permanent guarantors against a terminal third world war and that.... will not be an easy case to argue in the court of public opinion'. Despite this, 'the response to Mr Gorbachev should be clear in setting out the West's belief that complete nuclear disarmament is not desirable in the foreseeable future.'[2]

In the following years the Soviet government has determinedly pursued its new course. At the Reykjavik summit it surprised the United States with its sweeping disarmament proposals and provoked shudders of apprehension in right-wing West European political and military leaders. It concluded the INF agreement scrapping medium-range nuclear weapons from the Continent. It opened its military installations to foreign inspection. It pressed ahead with negotiations for a 50 per cent cut in the superpowers' strategic nuclear arsenals, allied to a strict interpretation of the 1972 ABM treaty restricting the development of space weaponry. At the United Nations in

December 1988 Gorbachev announced radical cuts in the numbers and offensive capability of Soviet conventional armed forces. At each stage the predominant Western response has been a mixture of bewilderment and disbelief, with an array of authoritative figures on hand to mutter dark warnings about Gorbachev's political vulnerability. Yet as Weinberger, Perle, Brzezinski, Heseltine and countless other commentators continued to speak of the wolf in sheep's clothing, the new Soviet course has been maintained with an accelerating momentum.

Their leading spokespeople have made it clear that the new policies are underpinned by new thinking on the issues of war and peace, that their actual ideas about military force have changed. As Georgi Arbatov, central committee member and senior adviser on US-USSR relations under both Brezhnev and Gorbachev put it:

> ... today we see much better than before the limited opportunity for using military force and that in our time war cannot be a continuation of politics. We criticise ourselves for our excessive reliance on military power when trying to ensure security.[3]

Here, in two crisp sentences, is a repudiation of the foreign policy of much of the post-war era.

The impetus for this break from the past has arisen from the attempt by the Soviet leadership to draw lessons from its own experiences and wider world developments. The nuclear arms race was showing an alarming capacity to expand without limit and to proliferate to other nations; the intervention in Afghanistan showed the limitations and shortcomings of armed force as well as its economic and human cost; it also underlined the bankruptcy of the reliance on supposedly progressive military regimes which the USSR had been pursuing in the Middle East and the Third World for more than two decades; the military domination of Eastern Europe brought sullen resentment and occasional explosive crises; generally, the Soviet Union's prestige and international standing was on the wane. When these developments were combined with other factors, for example the devastating capacity of contemporary war as shown in the protracted battle between Iran and Iraq, the upsurge and spread of arms exports, the incidence of terrorism and the authoritarian responses it invariably provoked, the need for radical new thinking became clear. Soviet authorities constantly acknowledged the roots of their thinking in Lenin, but increasingly they have sought to justify the policy on its own terms as meeting the conditions of today's world.

In studying that world Soviet leaders have drawn three key lessons. Firstly, that in the nuclear age and with the development of sophisticated conventional technologies the use of military force can no longer have general application to the conduct of international relations. As Gorbachev puts it in his book *Perestroika*, 'Clausewitz's dictum that war is the continuation of politics only by different means, which was classical in his time, has grown hopelessly out of date. It now belongs to the libraries.'[4] Secondly, flowing from this is the belief that security cannot be achieved by military means but can only be meaningful if it is mutual. Here is the concept of common security, first popularised by Olaf Palme. In the nuclear age the security of individual nations or blocs can only be guaranteed in partnership with others, not at their threatened expense, if the world is to overcome its potential for global destruction. Thirdly, given the qualitative, indeed unprecedented, dangers facing the planet then the overriding question is to overcome the threat posed by militarism in all its guises. This assessment distinguishes capitalism from militarism and sees the main priority in overcoming the universal danger presented by the latter.

This new philosophy has both external and internal repercussions. Internationally, it has spurred Soviet diplomacy to use its varying influence to seek political solutions to conflicts in Afghanistan, Angola/Namibia and Kampuchea, while encouraging the Palestine Liberation Organisation to pursue a new course in the Middle East. Domestically, it heralds a change in military philosophy and in the size and shape of the country's armed forces. Accompanying the new thinking on foreign policy has been a lively debate on future military thinking with official indications of support for the concept of 'reasonable defensive sufficiency' and for the move from a mass army to a combination of a much smaller professional army linked in with territorial militia.[5] Gorbachev's UN speech in December 1988, with its announcement both of major troop and tank reductions and the removal of offensive assault equipment from divisions in Eastern Europe indicated that these are no mere academic discussions but an integral component of perestroika affecting both domestic and foreign relations. Indeed it is with the military that the two elements intertwine most closely, since a successful foreign policy strategy would enable Gorbachev to reduce the Soviet army and diminish its weight within Soviet society. This is an essential longer-term component of his project of developing a civilian rather than barrack-room socialism within the Soviet Union.

Recognising interdependence

The explicit acknowledgement of the global danger posed by nuclear war and militarism has been a key element in the second main theme of the new international thinking, namely that the world has become, and is, increasingly ever more interdependent. As well as the escalating military danger, the scientific, technological and computer revolution, the globalisation of manufacturing production and commercial and financial markets, including the draining of finances and resources from the Third World, and the world-wide development of television and satellite communications have been objective factors which have made the nations of the planet more integrated. Despite the tensions and contradictions between blocs and social systems, these trends bind and connect countries and peoples closer together. In today's conditions, with computer, robotic and information technology advancing at such a rapid rate, closed societies seeking to develop apart from the rest of the world are at a marked disadvantage. They will increasingly lag and stagnate. One aspect of glasnost has been the open acknowledgement by Soviet economists and intellectuals that this was precisely what was happening to their own country.

This realisation forced them to look at the world afresh. Most crucially, while fully aware of the urgent problems of economic and social inequality, they discarded their traditional conception of the world as divided into two hostile and opposing camps. This both transferred mechanically the laws of internal social development into the international arena and ignored crucial features of the modern world. These features – economic, scientific, cultural, military and ecological – meant that the world had to be seen as a whole and that the main priorities concerned with the survival and development of human civilisation required the unity of nations and peoples not their division into opposing camps.

As Foreign Minister Eduard Shevardnadze explained to the UN General Assembly in September 1988,

> the Soviet leadership has tried to reinterpret more profoundly the idea, originally inherent in Marxism, of the interrelationship between class and universal human values, according priority to the interests shared by all nations.

This version of peaceful coexistence specifically ruled out the idea that it was 'a special form of the class struggle'. Rather, 'a rigid polarisation of the world ... must give way to its consolidation, which allows the rivalry of two different systems to take on non-confrontational forms'.[6] This view of an interdependent, integral world was first expounded by Gorbachev in his address to the 27th Congress of the CPSU and has been subsequently strengthened. It has not been without its internal criticis. Politburo member Egor Ligachev openly expressed the more traditional view in a speech in August 1988 while Gorbachev was on holiday. Alexander Yakovlev, one of Gorbachev's closest political allies, rebutted the traditionalist arguments in a speech to party activists in Lithuania a few days later, and Ligachev's subsequent demotion in a government reshuffle in September suggested that the new line had been decisively reaffirmed within the top leadership. The economic implications of the new policy are considerable. Henceforth the Soviet Union intends to play a much more active part in the international division of labour. It has already begun to engage in joint ventures and enterprises with companies at the leading edge of new technology. Similarly it has indicated a willingness to approach transnational financial institutions, and possibly in the future the World Bank. In due course it intends to make its own currency convertible on the international market, which will facilitate another key aspect of the policy, the full participation of the USSR in world trade. It is keen to develop international action over the issue of debt. These are all practical indications that the days of autarky, of building socialism in one country or one bloc are over.

This recognition of the changing nature of today's world and its interconnected character has enabled the Soviet leadership to understand and respond to the environmental question in a serious and comprehensive manner. The ecological crisis both accords with, and has influenced, their new approach. As Shevardnadze graphically expressed it, 'the biosphere recognises no division into blocs, alliances or systems. All share the same climatic system and no one is in a position to build his own isolated and independent line of environmental defence'.[7] The realisation of both their own and wider environmental catastrophes has given added impetus to the new thinking and seen a series of Soviet proposals for concerted global action, including an international space laboratory designed exclusively to monitor the environment, and the establishment of a UN centre for emergency environmental assistance.

The primacy of politics

Linking these two aspects together and providing the common thread is a renewed emphasis on the primacy of politics, the need for dialogue with opposing and contending views, the chance for reason, thought and argument to assert themselves and for compromises to be hammered out. This is not just a matter for diplomatic negotiation but also the arena in which public opinion in its broadest forms can be brought into play. The Soviet leadership has publicly acknowledged for example how Western peace movements and the initiatives of the non-aligned countries have helped to inform its own disarmament thinking, while the scientific and cultural forum on a nuclear-free world hosted in Moscow was illustrative of the importance which the Soviet leadership attaches to the world intellectual and artistic communities.[8]

Furthermore, in an era when war and armed conflicts cease to be instruments of rational politics, universal security has to be guaranteed through democratising international relations. The new Soviet thinking increasingly accords a crucial role to the United Nations, as the body through which the interests of all states can be represented and the dangers of great power politics minimised. This elevation of the importance of the United Nations was symbolised by the decision of both Shevardnadze and Gorbachev to deliver keynote addresses on world politics from its podium.

Common to the new thinking is the political emphasis on the primacy of universal human values, in peace as an absolute value and in the priority of humanity's survival. The policy which is clearly differentiated from its more narrowly class-focused predecessor, proletarian internationalism, is best defined as progressive humanism. Not only is the content different but so are the methods for its achievement with the greater priority accorded to consent rather than coercion. What we have here is, effectively, a Gramscian strategy for achieving a progressive hegemony in international affairs, where the primacy of politics and the mobilisation of the broadest range of public pressure seeks to impose restraint on military hawks and permit free choices to nations and peoples. This theme of free choice has gradually become more prominent and was stressed by Gorbachev at the United Nations.

The prospects assessed

Since 1985, in the field of foreign affairs, there has been a massive rupture from the Brezhnevite decades and a repudiation of much of the legacy of great power politics which Soviet international policy acquired under Stalin. Perestroika's impact on international relations has been dramatic and if its progress has been uneven its inner dynamic constantly presses it forward onto a new trajectory. This is even true in an area such as human rights where four years ago it was completely inconceivable that the Soviet

Union could take an initiative. Yet the leadership recognises that the new internationalism has to contain a human rights dimension. In his speech to the UN not only did Gorbachev seek to address some domestic aspects of the issue, but he also proposed that on these matters the jurisdiction of the International Court of Justice at the Hague 'should be binding on all states'. This is a proposal which both the United States and the British governments are likely to treat warily given their respective records in Central America and Northern Ireland. Contesting this arena however, and opening up competition between states on the issue can only enhance the human and civil rights of citizens across the planet.

Perestroika abroad presents us with a genuinely original analysis of present and future global relations. It is a commonplace of conservatives that the Russians have only changed because of the West's policy of peace through strength and that in Sir Geoffrey Howe's words, 'Mr Gorbachev is coming closer to our way of doing things'.[9] This completely fails to recognise the originality of both the analysis being proffered and the solutions being offered. Clearly in many respects this means a rapprochement with the West but the novelty of the approach demands changes from all the participants. Perestroika in the international arena tears up the old rules of forty years standing and shifts the play onto a new pitch requiring all the players to reassess and change. It is not a one-way street. Yet the question remains as to whether this new thinking will transform the conduct and character of international relations. To succeed it has both to overcome a set of formidable obstacles and foster a new internationalism of both thought and action.

One of the policy's most intractable problems lies where the legacy of the past weighs most heavily and directly on the Soviet Union, namely Eastern Europe. When Gorbachev gives the commitment to free choice as a universal value, the question of Eastern Europe is immediately raised, not least in the thoughts of the current leadership of those countries. This has been a subject which Soviet politicians and commentators have tended to side-step or to refer to obliquely. While there have been a series of statements ruling out the use of force in resolving disputes between socialist states, and Gorbachev openly stated in Yugoslavia the right of each Communist Party to choose its own model of socialism, the specific discussion of the Eastern European experience has tended to remain a taboo subject. This arises partly from a wish not to offend the susceptibilities of the existing leaderships, and partly from a political calculation that it is better to establish the credentials of the new thinking on easier terrain before tackling the hardest problems.

This situation cannot persist for much longer. It is simply not credible to characterise the domestic politics of the Brezhnev decades as an era of stagnation and yet try to evade discussion of its most crucial foreign policy decisions in Eastern Europe. This is especially so in the case of Czechoslovakia where the military suppression of the Prague Spring was the key event in the consolidation of the Brezhnev leadership on a conservative course.

Furthermore, there are already signs of explosive turmoil and volatility in Eastern Europe. In Yugoslavia there is resurgent nationalism. Widespread hostility exists between Hungary and Romania over the latter's plans to demolish many villages populated largely by ethnic Magyars and Germans in Northern Romania. Hungary and Poland have both entered unknown territory with their dramatic and far-reaching proposals for structural reforms. Both the GDR and Czechoslovak leaderships refuse to engage with the new thinking but there are growing signs of restlessness among the population, with sporadic demonstrations and civil unrest.

In the Soviet Union's search for a more positive, less domineering relationship with its Eastern European neighbours an early requirement is to address the region's post-war history with realism and honesty. On this basis it should be possible to reach out to a range of political trends and voices within the region for dialogue and rapprochement. Reasons of national sentiment and history make it certain that the region's future political leadership will not be contained solely within the framework of existing Communist Parties. However, one of the Soviet leadership's sharpest and most important tests will be their ability to speak to like-minded reform Communists in these countries who are currently either barred from influence or party membership. It is obvious, for example, that the leaders of the Prague Spring have rather more to offer on the future of both Czechoslovakia and Eastern European socialism than the present Jakeš leadership, a point emphasised by Dubček's measured interview with *L'Unità* in winter 1988. A Soviet display of open-handedness here would be an acknowledgement of past error but, more importantly, a key asset to the new relationship which they are seeking to promote. It is reform-minded Communists who are likely to offer the main avenue for coherent, strategic reform in the region. Without that type of political leadership the combination of ancient ethnic antagonisms, economic hardship and a historical absence of a democratic civil society could trigger a series of messy upheavals. While the Gorbachev leadership has resolutely stressed that there will be no resort to military intervention in any circumstances, it is precisely the scenario of endless turmoil in Eastern Europe which would strengthen the hand of his domestic opponents and wreak damage on the broader international goals of the policy. Yet if its far-reaching goals and high principles are to stand up, the whole issue of the Soviet relationship with Eastern Europe has to be tackled. This will require more courage and sagacity than has so far been displayed and a willingness to make the kind of bold political moves which have characterised the new policy in other spheres.

The second and probably decisive arena for the outcome of the new policy lies in the political response of the West. Already a diversity of responses are evident both between and within political parties and nations. The German foreign minister Genscher, a Liberal, displays more enthusiasm for the new policy than the socialists responsible for French policy. Ex-Cabinet Defence minister Michael Heseltine strenuously urges a continuation of a hawkish 'peace through strength' policy, while his former Cabinet colleagues Leon Brittan and John Biffen issue calls for major changes in Britain's defence posture. In the Federal Republic right-wing politicians call for negotiations on the removal of short-range nuclear weapons, while the US and British governments demand their swift modernisation. At the end of the 1980s there is widespread uncertainty within the West about how to respond to the new Soviet policy, with no one position yet gaining dominance. The outcome of this dispute will determine the fate of perestroika in the international sphere. It will be a major test of the primary emphasis placed on politics by the new thinking.

There are real grounds for optimism. Firstly, the new policy has begun to shift the terrain on which the issue is fought out. It is no longer primarily an ideological issue but rather one of human survival, in which common interests outweigh those of class. In Western domestic politics this has the potential to shift the argument from 'defending the Western way of life' to how to proceed through mutual disarmament to a safer world. In the British context it may yet permit a break from the simplistic unilateralist/ multilateralist argument to a broader discussion around the choice of disarmament or rearmament.

The implications of this are only just becoming apparent. Potentially it lifts the defence and foreign policy questions out of the Left/Right arena and permits Centre/Right parties to adopt a positive stance towards the Gorbachev proposals. There are already strong indications that right-wing politicians within the Federal Republic see in perestroika a unique opportunity to switch resources and expenditure from the East-West confrontation into the development of trade, markets, modern investment in new technologies and the social infrastructure.

This process of rethinking on the Right is likely to extend because of the second factor that gives grounds for optimism, the tremendous shift in popular attitudes across Western Europe towards the Soviet Union. This phenom-enon has occurred largely independently of political parties, since socialist parties have often displayed Cold War attitudes similar to their conservative opponents. Yet even the most hawkish elements in the West recognise the sea change, with constant complaints about the success of Soviet public relations and Gorbachev's 'propaganda coups'. If this qualitative shift is maintained, then parties throughout the continent will be compelled to alter their policies.

A further factor likely to influence the outcome is the economic position of the United States. While the political conditions there are not as favourable as in Western Europe, with a much more powerful and crudely anti-communist New Right, nevertheless the profligacy of the Reagan era cannot continue regardless. The pressures of the mammoth balance of trade and budget deficits will place an unaccustomed squeeze on the country's defence expenditure. With the USSR making significant unilateral reductions in its own armed forces and anxious for far-reaching cuts in nuclear arsenals, the political balance may well shift within the Republican administration.

However, the political outcome to this struggle remains very much an open question. Cold War thinking dominates in the ranks of NATO and among the leaders of most Western governments. For example, while Mrs Thatcher praises much of Mr Gorbachev's glasnost and perestroika, she resolutely refuses to countenance his non-nuclear thinking and remains firmly committed to a policy of new nuclear weapons for both Britain and NATO. Her government sticks firmly to Cold War stereotypes. It is unable to recognise that the post-war international settlement is dead and that Gorbachev's perestroika demands conceptual shifts by Western governments rather than the repetition of Sir Geoffrey Howe's stale cliches.

It will take a formidable political movement to disrupt Western orthodoxy on these matters and it is a process which is likely to take several years. Those on the Left and in the peace movements concerned to further this process will have to conceive of their activities on a much broader basis than previously, seeking dialogue with centrist and conservative forces and reaching into military and business circles. There will have to be more thought given to the future shape of the European continent and its relation to the two superpowers. The Gorbachev conception of a common European home remains to be fleshed out, while the orthodox Left will have to address the limitations of a simple anti-Americanism. Above all there will need to be engagement and argument with the hawkish Right. A particular effort is needed to challenge their assessment of the current military balance. By presenting a distorted picture, minimising the role, capability and superior strike power of Western air forces, they hope to turn public opinion away from its positive stance towards the new Soviet policy. The swift implementation of the reductions announced by Gorbachev at the United Nations, the scrapping rather than just the removal of both tanks and offensive, river-crossing assault equipment and further moves by both Soviet and Eastern European governments to reduce their land forces would sustain public confidence and trust in the sincerity of the Soviet policy and increase the pressure on NATO and Western governments to reciprocate. By the early 1990s it should be clear which trend has gained the upper hand in the West or whether the issue is deadlocked. Currently, an outright victory for the hawkish tendency appears most unlikely.

A third factor influencing the outcome of the new foreign policy will be the capacity of the existing and proposed global institutions to fulfill the substantial tasks which are being asked of them. The new policy places major responsibilities on the United Nations and seeks to revive existing UN bodies and create new ones to oversee environmental issues and developments in space. At the same time the Soviet Union is seeking to participate in transnational financial and commercial institutions and in the process to alter the political character of their judgements.

There is understandable scepticism about the prospects for this policy, especially in regard to the World Bank and the International Monetary Fund. Similar doubts also apply to the UN, despite its crucial role in bringing a conclusion to several major conflicts during 1988. The bungling of the Namibian settlement is a salutary warning in this regard. Its future impact will require a concerted political drive by several major powers or regional groupings *pour encourager les autres*. This will have to be backed by finance and resources in specific areas. The Soviet Union has itself begun to do this, acknowledging in the process that its own past positions and attitudes had been shameful.[10] This may be one area where the developing, positive relationship with China will find expression. Clearly, a successful global politics requires effective global institutions but the task of transforming a historically weak, bureaucratic institution will not be easy.

Fourthly, the value and success of the new policy will be gauged by its impact in resolving international conflicts and promoting a more favourable political framework for the non-aligned and Third World countries. The withdrawal from Afghanistan, despite the intransigence of the mujaheddin and the continued armed support from the US and Pakistani governments, illustrates the Soviet Union's determination to abandon the path of military adventurism. Furthermore, the Soviet leadership hopes that its policy will influence others to follow suit. The shift of PLO strategy in the Middle East, with the unarmed popular uprising combined with the historic compromise of the two-state solution involving the acceptance of a separate state of Israel, has to be seen in this context. Soviet officials lobbied strongly in favour of this development. In Southern Africa, there has been similar lobbying in favour of a negotiated settlement on Namibia and Angola, while the indications are that the new thinking is encouraging a reassessment by the African National Congress of its strategy for dismantling the apartheid state. The discussions with the official rugby authorities, following those with white businessmen were the first signs of an attempt to disrupt the system from within, to build islands of multi-racialism in a racist society. They suggest a shift in strategy from full frontal assault to a long haul. On these two crucial conflicts, it remains uncertain whether a new strategy laying primary emphasis on politics, with mass internal struggle combined with mounting international pressure, will suffice to compel two powerfully-armed, reactionary governments to back down. The outcome will influence the credibility of the new internationalism, just as the non-aligned countries will be keen to see whether the fine words about debt, famine and ecology will be translated into concerted international action.

Finally, there is the question as to whether the theory underpinning the new internationalism is flawed. In traditional parlance, is it really feasible to tame capitalism? Didn't Lenin argue that imperialism always led to war? There is no doubt that the present analysis is novel and breaks from many traditional Marxist positions. It is impossible to gauge the extent of support for Ligachev but there are indications that his views have support within the CPSU and amongst sections of the wider public. Should the present policies stall, a revival of these more orthodox positions is possible. Rumblings of unease have been expressed by the French and Portuguese Communist Parties. The Socialist Unity Party in the GDR has been publically circumspect but privately the Honecker leadership has made its distaste for the new course clear. Within the British Left some voices have been raised expressing disquiet at the USSR's retreat 'from class positions' and its lack of solidarity with the Third World.

Both theoretical and political issues are at stake here, which it is important to clarify. Theoretically, there are elements which pick up from earlier strands of Soviet thinking developed during the common struggle against Nazism, and in the case for peaceful co-existence presented by Khrushchev in the 1950s. Yet the main elements are new. Their most important and distinctive quality is that they arise from a careful materialist analysis of the world as it presently exists. Grasping the Marxist maxim that the only absolute is change, the new thinking tackles the key contradictions of today's world and suggests the new course needed to tackle them. Undoubtedly, novel theories have rough edges, while some of the protagonists, suddenly freed from the dead hand of dogma display a dangerous naivety about some of their adversaries. Questions about the precise relationship of class to universal values, of the military industrial complex to capitalist production, remain to be thought through. However, the new policy remains partisan. It still takes sides. It wants to change the world but it is more open-ended and flexible about its goals, recognising both the limitations of existing socialism and its grasp of the future. The strategy strives for progressive outcomes to international affairs through a primary, though not exclusive, emphasis on politics rather than military force. It recognises the limits of Soviet military power; the need for compromises; the urgent global imperatives; the necessity of alliances with a diversity of political forces. This breaks from the old policy and practice of according a pre-eminent role in advance to Communist Parties and also signals a heightened rapprochement with socialist and other democratic parties.

Some Communist Parties have found this shift in particular too much to take.

Although considerable study and discussion on these questions remains to be undertaken, the main theoretical pillars of the new course are in place. Compared to both its predecessor, and to any other socialist position currently on offer, its political impact is undeniable. Gorbachev's vision has tremendous attractive power precisely because it has grasped the key features of the modern world and proposes a new way to conduct international affairs. It has turned a Communist leader into the voice of humanity's future. The vision challenges the exponents of generations of great power and Cold War politics within both blocs. It forces some of the most traditionalist parts of the Left to face up to today's world and challenges the stereotypes and formulas endlessly repeated by scores of conservative Western politicians. As Shevardnadze has declared, the basic challenge it lays down is the replacement of 'peace through strength' by 'peace through reason'. The former represents 'the faded commandments of the past', but the latter 'is a commandment of the future'. While 'the past has great power over us ... the future has an even greater gravitational force.'[11] Can that aspiration be turned into reality?

Notes

[1] M Gorbachev, *For A Nuclear Free World*, Speech, 15 January 1986.
[2] *Ibid*.
[3] G Arbatov, *Moscow News*, No 39, 1988.
[4] M Gorbachev, *Perestroika*, Collir s 1987, p 141.
[5] See Lt Col A Savinkin, 'What Kind of Armed Forces Do We Need', *Moscow News*, No 45, 1988.
[6] E Shevardnadze, *Pravda*, 28 September 1988.
[7] Ibid.
[8] On this point see Gorbachev, *op cit*, pp 153-54.
[9] Sir Geoffrey Howe, Sir Cyril Foster lecture, Oxford 27, October 1988.
[10] E Shevardnadze, *Moscow News*, No 52, 1988.
[11] Conclusion of Shevardnadze's address to the UN, *Pravda, op cit*.

Glossary of Soviet Names

Abel Aganbegyan A long-standing economic reformer who has played a central role in advising the Gorbachev leadership on economic matters.

Nina Andreeva A Leningrad chemistry lecturer whose open letter to *Sovyetskaya Rossiya* in March 1988 entitled 'I can't forego my principles' was seen as the political platform of the conservative forces hostile to perestroika. The article was firmly rebutted in a *Pravda* editorial three weeks later. She has continued to be seen as the symbol of conservatism.

Yuri Andropov General Secretary of CPSU 1982–1984. Rule marred by illness but saw the first signs of a break from the Brezhnev era.

Georgi Arbatov Head of USA and Canada Institute at the Academy of Sciences. CC member. Adviser to Brezhnev and Gorbachev on superpower relations and disarmament.

Leonid Brezhnev General Secretary of CPSU 1964–1982.

Alexandra Biryukova Member of the Secretariat of the CPSU Central committee. Elevated to the Politburo in 1988, its first woman member for nearly thirty years.

Fedor Burlatsky Prominent reformer, journalist and political columnist on *Literaturnaya Gazeta*.

Viktor Chebrikov Former head of the KGB. Currently Politburo member responsible for legal affairs.

Konstantin Chernenko General Secretary of CPSU 1983–1985. The last gasp of the Brezhnev era. His Selected Works unlikely to become a best seller.

Mikhail Gorbachev General Secretary of CPSU from April 1985.

Andrei Gromyko Soviet Foreign Secretary from 1957.

Elevated to President of USSR under Gorbachev before his retirement in September 1988.

Nikita Khrushchev General Secretary of CPSU from 1953 to 1964. Introduced first attempt at de-stalinisation with famous secret speech at 20th Congress of CPSU. His erratic and commandist drive for reforms in early 1960s allowed a coalition of disaffected forces to remove him from office in 1964.

G V Kolbin First Secretary of the Kazakhstan Communist Party.

Boris Kurashvili Prominent intellectual reformer and jurist.

Alexandra Kollontai The most prominent advocate amongst the Bolsheviks of feminism and sexual liberation.

Larisa Kuznetsova A journalist and activist on women's issues.

V I Lenin Leader of Bolshevik Revolution.

Egor Ligachev Currently member of Politburo responsible for agriculture. A main exponent of the more conservative brand of perestroika.

Vadim Medvedev Promoted to Politburo in September 1988. Responsibility for ideological affairs, as Chair of Central Committee's Ideology Commission.

Gavrili Popov Editor of the main journal of economic theory *Voprosy Ekonomiki*. A powerful supporter of economic reform.

Zoya Pukhova Chair of the Soviet Women's Committee.

Nikolai Ryzhkov Promoted under Andropov. Politburo member and Chairman of the Council of Ministers of the USSR.

Andrei Sakharov Top Soviet nuclear scientist. Forceful critic of the system in the Brezhnev era, when suffered persecution and internal exile. Rehabilitated under Gorbachev and elected to the Congress of People's Deputies in Spring 1989. Member of the Academy of Sciences and active advocate of perestroika from an independent position.

Vladimir Shcherbitsky Party leader in the Ukraine. The last Politburo survivor of the Brezhnev era.

Eduard Shevardnadze Soviet Foreign Secretary. Closely

identified with the Gorbachev leadership.

J V Stalin   General Secretary of CPSU, 1922–1953.

Valentina Tereshkova   First woman in space. Until 1987 chair of Soviet Women's Committee.

A Vlasov   Chairman of the Council of Ministers of RSFSR.

Alexander Yakovlev   A key Gorbachev supporter, brought back to the Politburo from the Brezhnevite wilderness of Ambassador to Canada, initially to head up propaganda and information. Currently responsible for the party's international relations.

Boris Yeltsin   Supporter of perestroika. Appointed as Moscow party leader after Gorbachev's accession to office but subsequently sacked after a bitter Politburo row in October, 1987. Won a resounding majority in elections to Congress of People's Deputies in March 1989.

Lev Zaikov   Politburo member, head of the party in Moscow.

Tatiana Zaslavskaya   Prominent sociologist and academic.

Select Chronology

1953 Death of Joseph Stalin.

1956 Khrushchev's secret speech at the 20th Congress of the CPSU condemns Stalin's 'cult of personality'.

1961 Stalin's body removed from the Kremlin mausoleum.

October 1964 Fall of Khrushchev. Brezhnev succeeds as General Secretary.

August 1968 Warsaw Pact troops invade Czechoslovakia and bring an end to the Prague Spring and the movement for 'socialism with a human face'.

Christmas 1979 Soviet troops intervene in Afghanistan.

December 1981 The Brezhnev leadership supports the imposition of martial law in Poland and the outlawing of the Solidarity trade union.

1982 Brezhnev dies. Andropov succeeds as general secretary.

1984 After long illness Andropov dies. Replaced by Chernenko.

March 1985 Chernenko dies. Replaced by Gorbachev.

April In report to CPSU central committee Gorbachev reveals 'unfavourable trends' in the economy.

May Campaigns initiated against alcoholism and corruption. Series of major personnel changes in government and party leadership begin.

October Draft of more realistic Communist Party programme issued for nationwide discussion prior to party congress.

November Friendly first summit with Reagan at Geneva.

January 1986 Major speech outlining a programme for a nuclear-free world by the year 2000. Signals crucial changes in the philosophy and outlook of Soviet foreign and defence policy.

January/February Glasnost takes hold with many critical contributions to the pre-congress discussion. Privileges of top party and state officials attacked in letters published by *Pravda*.

February/March 27th Congress of CPSU. Gorbachev's report stresses need for 'radical reform' of the economy and indicates new international thinking. Significant turnover in composition of new central committee. For the first time since early 1960s a woman, Biryukova, promoted to a top party post.

April Chernobyl nuclear disaster. Initial 'old-style' Soviet reaction, subsequently replaced by extensive media investigation.

June Government plan for diverting Siberian rivers attacked as ecologically unsound at Soviet writer's congress.

August Government drops Siberian river diversion plan.

Summer and autumn On visits to Soviet regions Gorbachev makes increasingly hard-hitting speeches stressing the need for democratisation.

October Second summit meeting at Reykjavik breaks down on Reagan's commitment to Star Wars but both leaders talk of the desirability of a nuclear-free world. Mrs Thatcher is not amused.

November Supreme Soviet adopts law extending scope for private enterprise in service sector.

December Andrei Sakharov allowed unconditionally to return to Moscow from internal exile in Gorky. Some other 'dissidents' freed from prisons and labour camps.

For the first time *Pravda* openly criticises the Brezhnev leadership.

Nationalist disturbances in Kazakhstan after corrupt party leadership replaced.

Major legal conference envisages a reform of the legal system to protect citizens' rights.

January 1987 Crucial Central Committee plenum drives democratisation process forward as Gorbachev acknowledges that 'the problems that have accumulated in society are more deep-seated than we first thought'. Meeting agrees to convene a special party conference in June 1988.

June CC meeting strengthens Gorbachev's position on the Politbureau with promotion of three supporters of perestroika including Yakovlev.

August First nation-wide conference of informal organisations. 300 representatives from 47 organisations meet in Moscow. A number of groups join to form a federation of Socialist Clubs.

October/November First major setback for Gorbachev with row in Politbureau as Yeltsin accuses Ligachev of blocking reforms. Yeltsin sacked from Politbureau and as Moscow party chief without his accusations being published.

November At 70th anniversary of Russian Revolution Gorbachev makes fullest acknowledgment to date of crimes of the Stalin era. Sets in motion rehabilitation of murdered Bolsheviks.

At a gathering of communist, socialist and social-democratic parties the pluralist and interdependent character of the new international thinking more clearly revealed.

December At summit meeting in Washington US and USSR reach an Intermediate Nuclear Forces agreement. The medium-range, land-based nuclear weapons of both sides to be removed, the zero-zero option.

January 1988 New law on state enterprises comes into operation designed to promote greater economic efficiency and self-reliance through 'complete self-financing' and cost-accounting, as well as greater democracy at the work-place with the election of the works director by the workforce. However, the central ministries and state orders continue to exert a dominant influence over individual enterprises.

February/March Ethnic crisis explodes in Nagorno-Karabakh, an Armenian enclave within the republic of Azerbaijan. Extensive strikes in Armenia in support of the region's transfer to Armenian jurisdiction. Bloody reprisals in Azerbaijan including a pogrom of Armenians in Sumgait. Official death toll of 32.

March A conservative offensive against perestroika

launched with the publication of a lengthy article in
Sovetskaya Rossiya entitled 'I Can't Forego my Principles'
by Nina Andreyeva. Reproduced in forty other journals
throughout the country.

April After three weeks delay the official response to
Andreyeva's article comes with a powerful editorial in
Pravda arguing the case for perestroika.

Spring The pace of reform quickens with the publication of
The Theses for the party conference and the subsequent
discussion. The dismantling of all aspects of Stalin's
'command-administrative' system now on the agenda.

May Reagan-Gorbachev summit held in Moscow. End of
the era of 'the evil empire'.

June-July Special Party Conference sees open debate and
disagreement in top party forum for first time in more
than 50 years. A significant package of political and legal
reforms agreed involving contested elections for both the
Soviets and party posts. A two-term time limit placed on
holding major office.

Summer 1.2 million copies sold of Anatoly Rybakov's
novel about life in Stalin's Russia, *The Children of the
Arbat*. Reprinting ordered.

All the defendants in the two big political trials of 1934
and 1937 rehabilitated.

August While Gorbachev on holiday Ligachev seeks to
reaffirm more traditional positions on economic and
international questions. Swiftly countered by Yakovlev.

September Gorbachev reshuffles Politbureau and conso-
lidates both his personal position and that of those most
committed to perestroika. Gromyko is retired and
Ligachev moved away from ideological affairs to the 'hot
potato' of Agriculture.

Shervardnadze makes a major speech at the UN calling
for international co-operation on the key global issues of
disarmament, development and the environment.

November The Memorial Society and the radical weekly
Ogonyok organise a Week of Conscience to commemorate the victims of Stalinism and to raise money for a
memorial complex to them in Moscow.

December In a universally acclaimed speech at the United
Nations Gorbachev outlines in the clearest way to date

the nature of the new international thinking. Accompanies this with the announcement of substantial unilateral reductions in Soviet troops in Eastern Europe.

Devastating earthquake in Armenia. In contrast to Chernobyl fully and swiftly reported in Soviet media and offers of international help welcomed immediately.

January 1989 Nagorno-Karabakh put under Special Administrtive Rule, its governing body directly accountable to Moscow.

February Shevardnadze visits China. An end to the Sino-Soviet split heralded by agreement that Gorbachev and Deng to meet in May.

Last Soviet troops leave Afghanistan.

March/April Central Committee plenum agrees to an extensive reform of agriculture, encouraging farmers to be able to lease the land they cultivate on long-term contracts. Sharp criticisms made of history and experience of collectivisation.

Same meeting decides to defer price reform of food subsidies.

First elections held to the new Soviet parliament, the Congress of Deputies. Despite conservative resistance majority of seats contested; many lively meetings held throughout the country; and a decisive blow struck against the legacy of fear. A number of party and government officials defeated and a clutch of prominent advocates of far-reaching reform elected, including Boris Yeltsin, Roy Medvedev and Andrei Sakharov. Publication of Krushchev's secret speech.

Notes on Contributors

Roy Medvedev Soviet marxist historican and political analyst, ostracised during the Brezhnev period but elected to the Congress of People's Deputies in spring 1989. Author of a monumental work on Stalinism, *Let History Judge*. The essay reprinted here appeared in *Marxism Today* in September 1982 and is remarkably perceptive in its assessments. The interview with Monty Johnstone appeared in the August 1988 edition of *Marxism Today*.

Julian Cooper Lecturer in Soviet technology and industry at the Centre for Russian and East European Studies, University of Birmingham. The positive assessment of Andropov and the recognition of his significant changes in leading personnel appeared in *Marxism Today* in April 1984.

Monty Johnstone Member of the Executive Committee of the Communist Party of Great Britain and of the *Marxism Today* Editorial Board and an extensive writer on Soviet politics. His review appeared in *Marxism Today* in 1985.

Archie Brown A Fellow of St Anthony's College, Oxford and co-author of *Political Culture and Communist Studies*. This article, initially written for The Political Quarterly, was printed in Marxism Today in June 1987 and has an updated addendum for this volume.

Martin Walker, Moscow correspondent of the *Guardian* until summer 1988 and author of *The Waking Giant: The Soviet Union under Gorbachev*. This article was written for *Marxism Today* in June 1988.

Fedor Burlatsky A prominent journalist and Gorbachev aide. This article translated from '*Literaturnaya Gazeta*' appeared in *Marxism Today* in July 1988.

Stephen White Reader in Politics and Member, Institute of Soviet and East European Studies, University of Glasgow.

Author of *The Origins of Detente* and *The Bolshevik Poster*.

Mary Buckley Lecturer in the Department of Politics, University of Edinburgh and author of *Soviet Social Scientists Talking: An Official Debate About Women*.

Dennis Ogden Former Moscow correspondent for the *Daily Worker*. Lecturer in Soviet politics at the Polytechnic of Central London.

Nick Lampert Member of the Editorial Board of *Detente*. Lecturer at the Centre for Russian and East European Studies, University of Birmingham.

Fred Halliday Professor of International Relations at the London School of Economics and author of *The Making of the Second Cold War*. The article reprinted here comes from *Marxism Today*, June 1988.

Neal Ascherson Political columnist for the *Observer* and a specialist for many years on East European affairs. These pieces were written for *Marxism Today*, February 1988 and January 1989.

Jon Bloomfield Member of the Editorial Board of Marxism Today and author of *The Passive Revolution: Politics and the Czechoslovak Working Class*.

Index

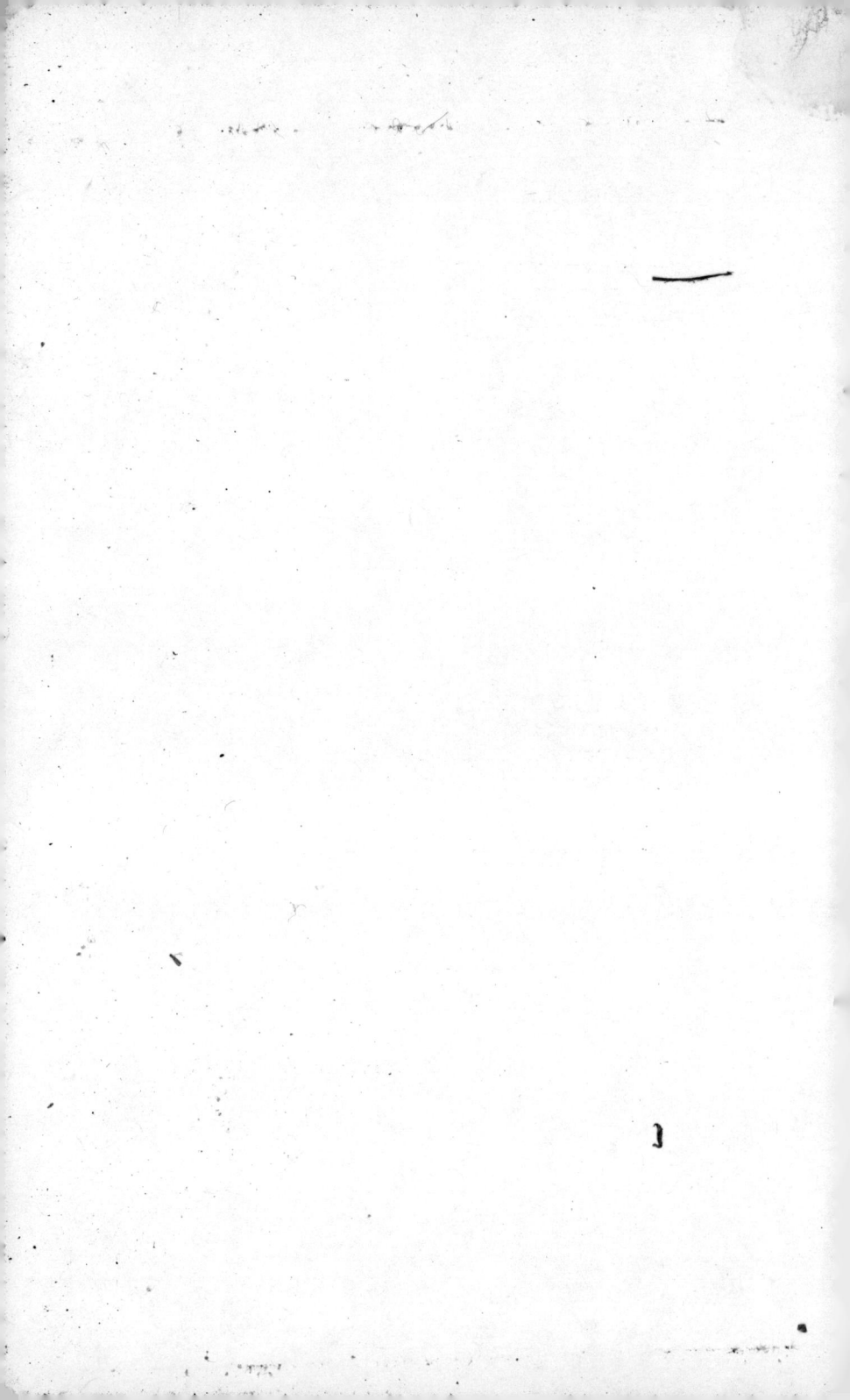